MW01035375

THE
EUCHARIST

*Bodies, Bread,
& Resurrection*

Andrea Bieler
Luise Schottroff

Fortress Press
MINNEAPOLIS

THE EUCHARIST
Bodies, Bread, and Resurrection

Cover image © Per-Anders Pettersson / Getty Images
Cover design: Ann Delgehausen, Beth Wright / Trio Design Works
Book design: Douglas Schmitz

Library of Congress Cataloging-in-Publication Data
Bieler, Andrea, 1963–
[Abendmahl. English]
The Eucharist : bodies, bread, and resurrection / Andrea Bieler, Luise Schottroff.
    p. cm.
Includes bibliographical references (p.   ) and index.
ISBN 978–0–8006–3867–2 (alk. paper)
1. Lord's Supper. I. Schottroff, Luise. II. Title.
BV825.3.B5413 2007
234'.163—dc22
                    2007032612

The paper used in this publication meets the minimum requirements of American National Standard for Information Sciences — Permanence of Paper for Printed Library Materials, ANSI Z329.48-1984.

Manufactured in the U.S.A.

11   10   09   08   07   1   2   3   4   5   6   7   8   9   10

CONTENTS

ACKNOWLEDGMENTS

THIS BOOK IS THE PRODUCT of an intense dialogue that has developed between the two of us, Luise Schottroff and Andrea Bieler. Over the course of several years we have been co-teaching a class called "Eucharist as Holy Eating" at Pacific School of Religion and at the Graduate Theological Union in Berkeley. In these classes we have met students from Korea, Taiwan, Uganda, Kenya, and the United States who have shared tremendous insights about the question of how to life a Eucharistic life and celebrate Holy Communion in a church and in a world painfully torn apart in so many hidden and tangible ways. Many of these students are serious searchers and academics, compassionate people of faith, and activists, in their churches and beyond. We are most grateful for the ecumenical exchange we have had the privilege to witness in the classroom. The insights, questions, and struggles these students are engaged in have accompanied us as we went about writing together.

We are particularly grateful for Richetta and Ra Amen, Bruce Saunkeah, D. Mark Wilson, and Colette Jackson, who gave us permission to publish their texts. Our research assistants Jennifer W. Davidson, Sharon Fennema, Katherine Kunz, Alicia Dean, as well as Ute Ochtendung, offered invaluable support. Their comments, thorough proofreading, and technical expertise enhanced the manuscript tremendously. We thank Marion Grau, Professor of Theology at the Church Divinity School of the Pacific, for her helpful comments on chapter 3. Claudia Janssen, University of Marburg, enriched our discussion through her innovative biblical interpretations and her enthusiasm. Heartfelt thanks go to Aeri Lee, Music Director at Pacific School of Religion, with whom we discussed the musical examples. Doug Adams, Professor of Religion and the Arts at Pacific School of Religion, broadened and illuminated our perspective on art works depicting scenes of holy eating. The Liturgy and Postmodern Questions Seminar of the North American Academy of Liturgy read a draft of the final chapter.

We are grateful for the Pacific School of Religion, who granted Andrea Bieler one semester of research leave to finish the work on this book. Special thanks to Dean emeritus Delwin Brown and Dean Mary Donovan

Turner, who have supported this endeavor. We thank the GrenzgängerIn-Verein for financial support.

We extend our word of gratitude to Fortress Press, to Michael West, and especially to Neil Elliott and Tim Larson, who with a passionate and keen spirit helped us express what we really wanted to say. We are also indebted to the Gütersloher Verlagshaus, and here especially to Diedrich Steen, who published this book in German.

We thank our translator, Linda Maloney, for her splendid work.

After this long journey, we, Luise and Andrea, are still friends who work, eat, and laugh together. We are grateful for all the meals and all the friends and strangers who share table fellowship with us. Among the many: Ines Pohl, Lynn Rhodes, Mai-Anh Le Tran, Hoang-Anh Le Tran, Odette Lockwood-Stewart, and Jim Lockwood.

INTRODUCTION

*At the heart of all Christian prayer and worship
is the cry for God's will
and covenant promises in Jesus Christ
to be made real.*[1]

A Eucharist in Advent

IN THE GRAY DAWN, PEOPLE are entering the gloomy sanctuary, one by one, some in pairs. They enter silently; some lower their voices, whispering. The woman next to me looks incredibly tired; two rows in front of us, a young student is crying. All of a sudden it feels like all words have disappeared; a silence emerges between us. For some this is comforting, for some this is frightening, and others are just tired. This is how we sit for minutes. Then the organist begins to intone, very slowly, "O Come, O Come, Emmanuel." A pause. A woman processes alone through the middle aisle of the church. She holds a lit candle in her hand. Sometimes she raises her left hand as if she is trying to protect the flickering light. The congregation rises. The people of God join in unison:

> O come, O come, Emmanuel,
> and ransom captive Israel,
> that mourns in lonely exile here
> until the Son of God appear.
> Rejoice! Rejoice! Emmanuel
> shall come to you, O Israel.
>
> O come, O Branch of Jesse, free
> your own from Satan's tyranny;
> from depths of hell your people save,
> and give them vict'ry o'er the grave.
> Rejoice! Rejoice! Emmanuel
> shall come to you, O Israel.[2]

One of the liturgists gets up and greets the congregation: "This is the day that God has made." And the assembly responds: "Let us rejoice and be glad in it." The liturgist continues: "Last night the state of California executed Stanley Tookie Williams at 12:35 A.M. by means of lethal injection."[3] Again, another prisoner has been punished with the death penalty at San Quentin. It is Advent. We are awaiting the coming of God in the midst of this. This morning, we pray stammering, but with eager longing:

> O come, O Key of David, come,
> and open wide our heav'nly home.
> make safe the way that leads on high,
> and close the path to misery.
> Rejoice! Rejoice! Emmanuel
> shall come to you, O Israel.
>
> O come, O Dayspring, come and cheer;
> O Sun of justice, now draw near.
> Disperse the gloomy clouds of night,
> and death's dark shadow put to flight.
> Rejoice! Rejoice! Emmanuel
> shall come to you, O Israel.
>
> O come, O King of nations, come,
> O Cornerstone that binds in one:
> refresh the hearts that long for you;
> restore the broken, make us new.
> Rejoice! Rejoice! Emmanuel
> shall come to you, O Israel.[4]

The woman lights the first candle of the Advent wreath, and then the second. It is the second week of Advent. It is the morning after Tookie Williams was executed. Later in this worship service the assembly will gather around the table, sharing a meal together.

This book is about people who pray stammering but fiercely for the end of tyranny; it is about people who from time to time face death's dark shadows, and by doing so are confronted with their own helplessness and despair. In the midst of this turmoil they await the coming of God. It is about people who share a meal together in which the Dayspring comes and cheers the spirits, disperses the gloomy clouds of night, and puts death's dark shadows to flight. It is about people who juxtapose in odd, sharp, and sometimes painful ways the texts of reality with the living traditions of the Christian faith that embody resurrection hope. In the abyss this juxtaposition creates, between death penalty and the words and sounds of "O Come, O Come Emmanuel," they yearn for the encounter with the Risen One.

This book is about the Eucharist as resurrection meal.[5] In the Eucharist we remember Jesus, a victim tortured and killed by state terror. And Christians say at the same time: In the Eucharist we participate in the body of the risen Christ, seeking redemption for our own bodies, our communities, and the global body of the planet Earth. Participating in this resurrection experience in fragmentary ways leads us not beyond this world in which bodies are subjugated to violence through systemic terror, malnutrition, and hunger. Rather, the opposite is the case: body realities and food politics move to the center.

We seek to develop a theology of the Eucharist that holds together the materiality of bodies and ordinary things as they are lifted up and shared in liturgical practice *and* the eschatological horizon of the holy meal in which we celebrate the Eucharist as resurrection meal and await with eager longing God's coming. The material world is lifted up in God's promise to be present in the very ordinary things of bread and wine and in the bodies of ordinary people. In ritual actions such as food processions we celebrate the creator as the giver of all these precious gifts. The created world in its ordinary physicality is cherished in the breaking and sharing of bread, in bodies eating and drinking, chewing and swallowing. Or, as Teresa Berger puts it: "The real of lived life, after all, is co-constitutive of liturgical meaning. Without attention to this real of lived life, God's transforming and healing presence cannot be said to be truly real in a broken world."[6]

At the same time, Eucharistic liturgies from the beginning have been grounded in an eschatological perspective, in which the death of the *Kyrios* is proclaimed until he comes (1 Cor. 11:26). This yearning for the coming of the *Kyrios* opens up a space of imagination that is filled with hope. We claim that this eschatological hope as it is expressed in our Eucharistic liturgies today needs to be grounded in people's everyday life experiences with food. By focusing on bodies, bread, and resurrection, we seek to draw connections between the real bodies that gather around the Christian holy meal, eating and drinking actual bread and wine, as an active participation in, expression of, and hope for God's reign. We thus situate our project among those efforts that shift the discourse in Eucharistic theology from ontological reflection about the presence of Christ in "the elements" of bread and wine to the eschatological imagination that emerges from the celebrating communities into the world.[7] In that sense, we stress with many sacramental theologians that sacraments are not things we possess; rather, they are relational events and personal encounters among people and God. These encounters are always embodied. It is the human body in its physical, social, and contextual specificity that is the ground for sacramental encounter.[8]

The Eucharistic Life

On the basis of the convictions expressed above, our project extends into the arena of liturgy and life by sketching out the *Eucharistic life*—a way of living with regard to food, body politics, economic exchange, and memory practices that flows out of liturgical practice. The Eucharistic life is embedded in micro- and macro-structures that shape individual bodies as much as they shape the global economy. Both dimensions are equally important and must be examined side by side. Both contain ambiguous experiences between pleasure and despair. From our early childhood on, being fed and receiving satisfying nourishment is a foundational experience that builds up basic trust in relationship. And, conversely, global issues around food, hunger, and body politics produce severe distress in the lives of individual women, children, and men and for the ecosystem of the planet Earth.

The notion of Eucharistic life touches on the general question of how we see the connection between liturgy and life. We proceed from the assumption that Eucharistic celebrations might deepen our religious affections, our basic attitudes toward life.[9] Our habits might be affected and potentially reshaped. We, however, do not see that this has to be the case in all circumstances. Another aspect of this connection points to the eschatological imagination that liturgical practice might bring forth: that we envision, taste, and see what is not yet realized in our personal lives, our communities, or on the global scale. The relationship between liturgy and life can also be the reverse: conflicts that our personal, social, and political contexts hold might disrupt and question the familiar flow of liturgical practice. We gave an example of this at the beginning: Sometimes you have to stop after the second stanza of a very familiar advent carol. There needs to be a place for Stanley Tookie Williams in the liturgy.

Besides the Eucharistic life, we introduce two related aspects that serve as hermeneutical lenses: *sacramental permeability* and *eschatological imagination*.

Sacramental Permeability

We ask how a constructive liturgical theology of the Eucharist might look if it focuses on the notion of sacramental permeability and thus takes seriously the realities of human bodies as a central part of Eucharistic practice and life. Sacramental worship embraces a permeability in which the bread we consume at our kitchen tables, the bread we steal from the poor, and the bread that is consecrated and consumed during Holy Communion are related. Sacramental permeability means that physical matters and actions such as eating and drinking can become vehicles that make transparent the Holy One who gives birth to the Eucharistic life. Virtually everything has the potential to reveal the sacramentality of life, yet we need the ability to see it. Thus, sacraments like the Eucharist can be understood as gifts that make God's love and self-giving visible to us. We emphasize potentiality instead of realization because the physical life is also the place where alienation and violence are revealed.[10] That means: The sacrament of Holy Communion points to the presence of God among us and in the world. And yet it simultaneously lifts up the hiddenness of God inasmuch as people experience the absence of God in the body politics related to food, from hunger to eating disorders.

Fig. 1. An early fresco depicts seven people seated at a common table. Is it a Eucharist, or an ordinary meal? "Sacramental permeability" refers to this ambiguity. 3rd century CE Catacomb of St. Callisto, Rome. Photo: Scala / Art Resource, N.Y.

Those experiences are in many contexts highly conflicted. By exploring the theological dimensions of how bodies are subjugated to global starvation, to the obsessions of "dieting America," and to eating disorders, we seek to understand what it means to talk about the Eucharist as the eschatological feast in which, through communion with the living Christ, we are immersed into the mystery of the redemption of our bodies. Sketching out a Eucharistic theology that lifts up the conflicts as they are related to real bodies and real bread, we intend to retrieve eschatological insight about the Eucharist as a resurrection meal. By focusing on the notion of sacramental permeability, we want to emphasize that the Eucharistic life, with its celebration of the sacraments is a place full of conflict; it creates presence and absence, love and alienation, hunger and abundant life.

When we concentrate on sacramental permeability, we are interested in the underlying implications of certain phenomena and how they might correspond to liturgical practice. We explore, for instance, how we can bring the economic exchange that happens in Eucharistic actions into conversation with the economic theory of the *Homo oeconomicus* that assumes market exchange as its basis. Or we are interested in the biblical and liturgical notion of remembrance (anamnesis) and, at the same time, in the neurophysiological and social phenomenon of memory when we spell out our Eucharistic theology with regard to the dominical command, "Do this in remembrance of me."

Eschatological Imagination

With regard to eschatological imagination, we understand the holy meal practices of the followers of Jesus and of the early churches as celebrations in which experiences of resurrection were shared as a foretaste while social conflicts related to poverty, slavery, and privilege—experiences of the powers of death—were not suppressed. Those who took part in the meal were infused into the body of Christ with their actual bodies. Those meal practices express faith as a relational act of trusting in God's future with God's people. Those who followed Jesus participated in resurrection in a fragmentary way.

Also today, eschatological imagination is about the real stuff of life in all its pleasure, pain, and alienation. Bodies in pain are and will be transformed into resurrected bodies at the table—bodies that are indeed the temple of the Holy Spirit (1 Cor. 3:16) abundantly filled with divine life. Bread that is stolen from the poor in a globalized economy, bread that contains the marks of death, is transformed into bread of life, into bread that gives eternal life. This is what we yearn for when we come to the table and when we dare to hope that our sins are forgiven. Eschatological imagination is at the heart of the Jewish-Christian tradition. It provides the hermeneutical power to connect the storytelling that gives witness to the overwhelming violence that human beings act out against each other with the yearning for the solidarity and community (*koinōnia*) in which the resurrected Christ reveals his body.

We are convinced that the eschatological perspective on Eucharistic theology and practice might save us from tearing apart corporeality and eschatology. These two belong together. The apostle Paul expresses this beautifully in Rom. 8:22-23 when he speaks about the whole creation that has been groaning in labor pains until now, awaiting adoption and bodily redemption. When we come together at the table, we engage in the work of lifting up the groaning of creation and the labor pains of the people to God. We remind God of the suffering of concrete bodies; we give voice to those who are not heard in the public square. We remember the death of the martyrs, who witnessed to the *basileia*, to God's just world, as they went before us. We engage in this work not because we believe that suffering in itself is redemptive or because we are attracted to the pain of others in a necrophilic way. We engage in this work of liturgical empathy because when we appreciate Christ's ministry and his death, we cannot stop ourselves from telling the story of the resurrection of our bodies at the same time. The Eucharistic narrative contains God's profound no to the forces of evil and destruction that surround and drive us. Eschatology is for people who dare to hope that resurrection happens and will happen in a world that is driven by adoration of the forces of death. A celebration of the holy meal that plumbs its eschatological depth will be an initiation into the Eucharistic life as a protest against the powers of death.

Eschatological imagination occurs in flashes, here and there, in history and in contemporary contexts, in biblical stories, in liturgies, in visual art, and in narratives of people. It cannot be kept in static concepts and systems. This is why we offer our interpretation of examples throughout the centuries and from diverse voices that emerge from very different places: from Chile, El Salvador, and Argentina, from the United States and Germany, from Sweden, and from a trip to Ghana. We do this in the spirit of Jesus, who called the disciples to "Gather up the fragments left over, so that nothing may be lost" (John 6:12). Referencing this passage, Teresa Berger remarks:

> No wonder early Christians wove the language of gathering and of fragments into their own eucharistic reflections. . . . The verb "to gather" comes to speak of those assembling for the breaking of the bread and "the fragments" name the bread which is broken. Here, then, is both the reality of brokenness and a hope of wholeness, all in one.[11]

This is exactly what the eschatological imagination holds: the reality of brokenness and a hope of wholeness. For sure it is available to us in fragmentary ways in practices of eschatological imagination.

The Eucharist in the New Testament

In this book we regularly consider New Testament meal traditions. On the one hand, they are the basis for the later history of the Eucharist. On the other hand, they prove to be a source of inspiration for a deeper consideration of what happens at the Eucharist today. We begin with an overview of these meal traditions; later we examine individual aspects more thoroughly as they occur within the systematic treatment.

The most important New Testaments sources are: 1 Cor. 11:17-34; 10:16-17; Mark 14:12-26; Matt. 26:17-30; Luke 22:7-38; Acts 2:42-47; John 6:52-58; 13. In 1 Cor. 11:17-34, Paul reports a Eucharistic conflict in the Corinthian community that shows how he and others understood the connection between economic justice and Eucharist (see especially pp. 118-22). In 1 Cor. 10:16-17, Paul refers to the way in which communion with Christ is established through the meal (see, e.g., pp. 137–41). The narratives in Mark 14:12-26 and Matt 26:17-30 contain the events from the Jesus community's preparation for the Passover supper until the end of the meal. These accounts of Jesus' last meal are cultic legends that tell of Jesus' institution of the later meal practice before his death. Luke's account of Jesus' last meal differs from those in Matthew and Mark; it presents a different sequence for the meal and a longer speech by Jesus to his disciples. The summary account of the first community in Jerusalem found in Acts shows how fundamental the meal is for the community praxis of such a congregation. Four of these accounts contain Eucharistic words from Jesus. We read these sources as coherent literary texts, each for itself. We do not consider it very promising to try to reconstruct an oldest version of the so-called words of institution from these texts. Rather, in parallel form they show that at that time—roughly from the middle to the end of the first century—there was not yet a unified Eucharistic practice, nor do the texts reveal any interest in producing such a unified practice. All these sources presuppose that the readers are familiar with Jewish meal practices and know Jewish meal prayers. The so-called words of institution are additions to traditional Jewish prayers at meals. The words over the bread, which speak of Jesus' body, are added to the benediction to God for the gift of bread. Jesus' words over the wine are appended to the great table prayer at the end of a Jewish meal[12] or to the short blessing over the wine. Jewish meal practices at that time, likewise, were not unified and fixed; their differences were still the subject of discussion. The term *words of institution* is problematic, since there was also early Christian Eucharistic practice that did without them, as the *Didache* shows (see pp. 65–68). "Words of institution" also presupposes a degree of institutionalization of Christianity that began to develop, at the earliest, around the middle of the second century.

It is impossible to say whether Jesus' last meal was really a Passover meal, as the three Synoptic Gospels portray it.[13] The Gospel of John interprets Jesus' death with reference to the Paschal lamb. For John, the Last Supper is not a Passover meal (John 13). Jesus' Eucharistic words in the Fourth Gospel (John 6:52-58) are very different from the other versions of those words. John also appears not to have the idea that there are words of institution that must be spoken at the Eucharist. The early Christian sources reveal a lively and living praxis that was continually being reshaped. Even the sources that do not see Jesus' Last Supper as a Passover meal do, in common with the Paschal tradition, refer to Israel's departure from Egypt, for example by interpreting Jesus as the Paschal lamb (Gospel of John; 1 Cor. 5:7). Israel's liberation through that departure, the exodus, is part of the meal tradition in early Christianity and in Judaism. In the great Jewish table prayer at the end of the meal, God is thanked for the gift of the land (the second benediction). We do not know whether that prayer already existed in the first century in its present form, but that or a similar prayer was certainly spoken at table.

The Sequence of the Meal

Paul in 1 Cor. 11:23-25 and the Gospels of Mark and Matthew present the following picture: The meal begins with the Jewish blessing of the bread (see pp. 118–22). Jesus says the blessing, breaks the bread, and gives it to those present. He speaks a word of interpretation over the bread. It is clear from Paul and Luke (1 Cor. 11:25; Luke 22:20) that this is the beginning of the meal proper. The blessing of bread includes, as was customary, all the other food. After the meal, Jesus takes the cup and prays. To this prayer he adds words of interpretation about the significance of the wine, or the cup. The accounts in Mark and Matthew do not say anything about the communal meal. It is simply taken for granted. Whether Jesus speaks a short blessing over the wine or intones the long Jewish thanksgiving prayer[14] at the end of the meal is not entirely clear. Luke mentions a cup of wine before the bread and after the bread. This could mean that he intends to clarify the character of the meal as a Passover supper. The reference to the Passover meal is likewise evident in the sequence of the meal in Mark (14:26) and Matthew (26:30): As they leave the supper room, the community of disciples sings the second part[15] of the *Hallel* (Pss. 115:1–118:29).

What is in dispute is primarily whether the Last Supper was a normal meal or—as in later Christianity—a cultic "meal event" in which only bread and wine were received, so that eating was only symbolic. A decision on this question cannot be derived from the wording of the sources. Likewise, the question whether, in the second century, there was an *agapē* in addition to the Eucharist[16] cannot be decided on the basis of the texts. When a separate *agapē* meal is posited, it is usually viewed as a meal for the poor. In any case, the texts permit two interpretations: The Eucharist was a common meal in cultic form, or it was a cultic "meal" that did not serve to satisfy hunger. *Agapē* can refer to the Eucharist itself, which included all the poor, or it can mean a separate, charitable meal or a community meal separate from the cultic meal. The solution depends on the presuppositions with which the sources are read. Since we understand the history of the early Christian communities as a part of the history of Judaism, we presume that the meal, as in Judaism, was, as a matter of course, a meal taken in common. A Eucharist separated from the meal also presupposes a dualistic anthropology that is foreign to the early Christian sources.

In these sources the table prayers are distinguished by two Greek verbs: *eulogein* (bless) and *eucharistein* (thank). They cannot be unequivocally categorized in terms of Jewish prayers. Moreover, the sources occasionally treat these two verbs as equivalents. The blessing over the bread in 1 Cor. 11:24 uses *eucharistein*, and in Mark 14:22 and Matt 26:26 it is *eulogein*. Nevertheless, as we have shown, certain assumptions about the embedding of the Eucharist in Jewish prayer practices at the Passover meal, or some other common meal, seem highly probable.

The Community at Table

Because the later church tradition emphatically reduced the community with Jesus at table to the twelve apostles, the New Testament sources were read the same way—until recently. As a result, the church lost sight of the eschatological character of the meal, in which the Twelve represented the twelve tribes of Israel (see pp. 53–56). The company at table clearly included the whole community (see pp. 118–22), which naturally also contained women,[17] children, and men who were not members of the community leadership. The community at table presupposes the reconciliation of all peoples. The common life of the community was of central importance to the community and its meal. We must suppose that the community meal was the normal main meal of the community members, most of whom were poor and hardworking people. Acts 2:46 speaks of their "breaking bread" together every day. Justin (mid-second century) seems to know only of a weekly community meal on Sunday. In the meal tradition Jesus is the host, and women or men who preside at the meal assume his duties.

How was the community meal prepared, and in particular, who did the necessary work? First Corinthians 11 shows us a meal whose elements were brought from people's homes. But it is also entirely possible that there were common preparations, since for the most part private dwellings, "house" communities, were the places of assembly. In these house congregations, women assumed crucial duties on behalf of the community. The communities claimed to be making fundamental changes in the power relationships within the patriarchal household. Therefore we should suppose that men also took part in the housework—though not without conflict. The clash depicted in Acts 6:1-6 shows that there were men who fended off these duties with the argument that doing housework caused them to neglect the "service of the word" (Acts 6:2). This conflict also shows that there were women, the "widows" in the Greek-speaking part of the original Jerusalem community, who refused to be "supervised" at the daily meal. In this context, that can mean that there were men who considered it demeaning to serve women at table. In any case, the work of preparing and serving the meal was not performed according to the gender-hierarchical division of labor that was customary in society.

Jesus' Interpretive Words

Jesus' interpretive words are addressed to the company at table who represent and give a foretaste of the longed-for eschatological community of peoples. They interpret the meal's significance for its participants. These are incorporated into the body (*sōma*) and life (*haima*) of Jesus Christ (see pp. 134–41). That is what the so-called words of institution say. Jesus is taking his leave, and his death is the beginning of the new life—unlike what the wielders of power intend (see pp. 56–58). Jesus' interpretive words transform death into life, and violence into love. The transformation of the food—here not yet the "elements" of the later Eucharistic sacrament—happens through the blessing at the beginning. The food becomes God's property, in which the community shares (see pp. 118–22).

This Book

Biblical as well as liturgical traditions and current practices are crucial for our attempt to reflect on the Eucharist as a resurrection meal by focusing on Eucharistic life, sacramental permeability, and eschatological imagination. From here we proceed as follows: Chapter 1 introduces the concept of eschatological imagination. We suggest understanding eschatological and apocalyptic imagery in biblical and liturgical traditions as poetic and mythic language with which people express their hope for God's justice to come in life-transforming ways.[18] Eschatological imagination is not so much prognostic as it is relational; it is an expression of faith in God's nearness. We introduce eschatological imagination as embodied practice that creates windows that disrupt common sense about the course of history. We look at some major eschatological threads that the New Testament spins in their relevance for the Eucharist: for instance, we revisit the motifs of the new covenant and the coming of God. In this chapter we also talk about the captivity of eschatological thinking and its abuse for imperial ambition.

In chapter 2, we focus on the Eucharist as eschatological meal by identifying four eschatological dimensions that have been crucial in liturgical and biblical texts. Reclaiming those traditions for current Eucharistic practice seems pivotal to us. These four dimensions are the hope for the scattered people of God to be united, the proclamation of the crucified Messiah and his coming, the understanding of "the new covenant in my blood," and the holy meal as the celebration of resurrection. We look at biblical and liturgical traditions that see the Eucharist in an eschatological light. A special focus will be given to the *Didache*.

Chapter 3 is titled "The Bread of Life in Two Economies." We ask how the Eucharist embodies God's economy while we are deeply immersed in the market exchange economy at the same time. We begin with the bread of death, with global and individual eating disorders that destroy the connection between holiness and food consumption. We look at biblical examples that reflect the brutalizing effects hunger has on human relationships with each other, with God, and with the environment. We introduce bread stories from the New Testament that present the excruciating experience of starvation and poverty, as well as eschatological hope. We take a look at Jesus' hunger and the temptation to live in a "by-bread-alone economy." The story that tells us about the multiplication of bread is read in the context of eschatological imagination.

There is no doubt that questions of economic justice are intimately interwoven with holy meals then and now. By exploring the imagination of the *Homo oeconomicus* in antiquity as well as in modern economic theories, we ask what occurs when the *Homo oeconomicus* partakes in the holy meal. We affirm that the economy of grace expressed in the various ritual actions of the Eucharist has the potential not to follow the logic of market exchange, but rather to generate a gift economy. However, we acknowledge that there have been many circumstances over the course of history in which the symbolic order of gift exchange was destroyed or corrupted. We analyze how that order is embedded in particular ritual actions such as prayers of thanksgiving, the returning of gifts to the table, money and food collections, and prayers of intercession. By taking into consideration major issues in eco-feminist economic theory, we lift up the ambiguity of gift giving, as well as the problematic rhetoric of abundant life.

Chapter 4 focuses on body politics and holy eating. We ask what it means to speak metaphorically about the body of Christ in relation to the Eucharist in such a way that actual "body realities" do not disappear. We unfold the multitude of body realities as they are present in the meal. We seek to reflect on the complexity of our own bodily experiences as we gather around the table. We suggest an interpretation of *sōma* in Paul's writings that shifts between metaphorical and literal meaning. We describe the holy meal as a ritual in which the redemption of our bodies is celebrated. Reading Paul's body theology in a non-dualistic way, we come to the conclusion that the early communities celebrated the resurrection of the body in the midst of the reality of the empire.

In chapter 4 we also have to speak about the *body given for you*. We reflect on the problem of how to reclaim this language without idealizing violence that is acted out against concrete bodies. We will claim the Eucharist as a counter-liturgy to violent state politics that deny the dignity of the human body. We will offer a biblical interpretation of Jesus' words that derives from the context of Jewish martyrdom theology.

This leads to our final chapter, "Eschatological Remembrance (Anamnesis)." We seek to remember the passion of Christ in a life-giving way in the horizon of the resurrection narrative. We want to explore the fine line between anamnesis, that is, the work of remembrance, and the idolization of violence. How can we understand anamnesis as a practice that initiates dangerous memory? We begin answering these questions by looking into liturgical practices and into the biblical concept of remembering and how it is related to the holy meal. We ask: *what* do we actually remember in Eucharistic liturgies and *how* do we remember? We introduce anamnesis as a reciprocal and embodied activity and reflect on the depth and the limits of empathy in the process of remembering. Again, the perspectives of sacramental permeability and Eucharistic life are crucial. We want to know what happens to bodies when they remember and how acts of memory give shape to collective identity. If remembering in the context of the Eucharist is a crucial practice in order to encounter the resurrected Christ, we want to discern how this practice might be an everyday life practice that sustains, disrupts, and reshapes our sense of who we are and how we perceive others, our social environment, our history, and God. Particularly when we consider the intercultural dynamics within our communities, the question of empathy is radicalized: how do we remember stories of violence, racism, sexism, and other forms of dominance that separate us and scar our relationships? The microcosm of our actual bodies as containers of memory and the abyss of collective memories emerging from the depths of forgetfulness to the surface make the conflicted body of Christ visible.

Our body memory is connected with collective memory, in its specific performances and in the ways in which collective memory shapes our collective identity. Collective memory is ambiguous. It can foster conflict as well as reconciliation; it can lead to collective forgetfulness as well as to truth-telling. Body memory and collective memory are grounded in place memory. Particular places hold, in intense ways, energies of bodies in pain and bodies moving in the realm of the reign of God. Place memory grounds and externalizes body memories.

The practice of eschatological anamnesis can make room for the articulation of memory in all these dimensions. Eschatological anamnesis extends beyond actual liturgical practice. In this final chapter, we hear different examples of "anamnetic sites" that offer glimpses of resurrection experiences as they are related to bodies, cultures, and places. All these anamnetic sites can be fertile ground for the Eucharistic life.

Chapter 1
ESCHATOLOGICAL
IMAGINATION

A Procession to the Table[1]

INTO THE SILENCE, A SOLO accordion gently intones the *estribillo* (refrain), F-A-F-G in a four-four rhythm; it swings back and forth playfully in a searching mode until it finds the melody so that a guitar is able to connect with the swing. One after the other joins with handheld rhythm instruments, claves, wooden sticks hitting against each other, the dark and sandy sound of cabanassas, then a tambourine followed by strings. The swing-rhythm grows more vigorous; a forcefully forward-moving energy evolves until the church is filled with carnivalesque sounds. The choir sings the *estribillo*:

> Vamos todos al banquete,
> a la mesa de la creación;
> cada cual con su taburete
> tiene un puesto y una misión.

> Let us go now to the banquet,
> to the feast of the universe.
> The table's set and a place is waiting;
> come everyone, with your gifts to share.[2]

This is the call to join the fiesta. Then, on the opposite side of the room, two women throw the doors of the sanctuary wide open. People in the congregation turn their heads, witnessing the procession of people from all over the globe entering through the middle aisle: People from Uganda and Nigeria, from the Philippines and Korea, from Japan and Samoa, from Vietnam and Ireland, from the United States and Germany join in a common song while processing in.

Hoy me levanto muy temprano;
ya me espera la comunidad;
voy subiendo alegre la cuesta,
voy en busca de tu amistad.

I will rise in the early morning;
the community's waiting for me.
With a spring in my step I'm walking
with my friends and my family.[3]

Some come in jeans and T-shirts, others in festive and colorful native clothing. A woman from Thailand wears a blouse with a *chakri* collar, a tubelike skirt pleated in the front, and a cloth (*kaprong*). A man who grew up in South Vietnam is clothed in an *ao dai,* slacks worn under a tunic. Another Vietnamese-American woman who has spent most of her childhood and adulthood in the United States cannot identify with these clothes; she comes in her usual Western business outfit. A woman from Nigeria wears her traditional *onyonyo.* People in the procession carry an abundant variety of food and drink: food that some would use in their motherlands for communion, food that is precious, simple, and delicious, food that is a gift of God, fruits of creation.

Venimos desde Soyapango
San Antonio y de la Zacamil,
Mejicanos, Ciudad Delgado,
Santa Tecla y de la Bernal.

We are coming from Soyapango,
San Antonio, and Zacamil,
Mejucanos, Cuidad Delgado,
Santa Tecla, and La Bernal.[4]

They move forward to the table in procession, some with steady and moderate steps; others, catching the swing, begin to dance, some lift up the food in front of their bodies, one woman carries a basket filled with fruit on her head. A wave of excitement moves through the congregation. People jump out of their pews, start clapping, join in the song. All sing in Spanish. For many this is not the mother tongue; people make their way through the lyrics, stumbling. But this is the time when we put words and sounds in our mouth that are unfamiliar. Some of the Latinos and Latinas in the congregation smile—maybe because of the funny pronunciation that surrounds them or because this is finally a chance to sing in Spanish.

> Dios invita a todos los pobres
> a esta mesa común por la fe,
> donde no hay acaparadores
> y a nadie le fata el conqué.

> God invites all the poor and hungry
> to the banquet of justice and good
> where the harvest will not be hoarded
> so that no one will lack for food.[5]

The procession gathers in a semicircle, the altar in front of them. The accordion and rhythm instruments are still carrying forth the rhythm when the Vietnamese-American woman on the outer left side of the circle moves toward the center of the table, lifts up what she has brought, and presents it in a horizontal gesture to the congregation: *Đây là bánh của sự sống.* And then in English: "This is the bread of life." A man from Korea follows: *Egotun sangmyunge bbang emnida:* "This is the bread of life." A woman from the Philippines offers the bread in Tagalog: *Ito ang tinapay ng buhay.* The Nigerian woman at the outer end of the circle presents the bread she brought to the table: *Sese udia uwem:* "This is the bread of life."

Preparing for the Great Thanksgiving, another woman from Malaysia moves forward to the altar and greets the congregation, "The Lord be with you!" And the congregation responds, "And also with you." She continues with the *sursum corda*, "Lift up your hearts!" And the people of God say, "We lift them up to the Lord. . . ." Later, flashes of whispering and laughter emerge between the people of God as we share bread and rice, juice, water, and wine. All seems real. There is Real Presence.

The beauty of diverse colors, body shapes, languages, food, as well as the various senses of rhythm and flow, sound and movement, open a window into the splendor of Christ's global body. This procession to the table reveals to us the beauty that lies in the embodiment of connection without negating difference. *Vamos todos. . . ,* "Let us go together." Now. Let us join in the banquet God has provided for us. Christ is among us. Right here and now.

What prevents this Eucharistic celebration from becoming a superficial display of exotic otherness in which Northern Europeans and Anglo-Americans can indulge? How does this event gain ecumenical depth by bodying forth a fragment of the church catholic, the church universal? We suggest this is so because this procession in the context of the whole worship service embodies a sense of eschatological imagination and sacramental permeability for us. The processional song *Vamos todos al banquete* itself embraces the tension between the hope for God's fiesta to occur and the memory of the suffering of the El Salvadoran people. It is "the 'entrance song' of the *Misa Popular Salvadoreña* (Salvadoran Popular Mass) written by the composer Guillermo Cuéllar at the request of Archbishop Oscar Romero. The text for this song comes from homilies preached by Rutilio Grande, the first priest to be martyred in El Salvador during the repression of the 1970s. Father Rutilio's proclamation of a 'table large enough for everyone,' his example in organizing peasants of Aguilares, and the horror of his assassination had a profound effect on his friend, the young Archbishop Oscar Romero, who was in turn martyred in 1980."[6] It is this history of the song, its lyrics, and the joyful performance that holds a sense of sacramental permeability and eschatological imagination for us. It is through the proclamation of these martyrs that we get a sense of the resurrection meal.

Another important juxtaposition needs to be mentioned as well. Before the congregation joined together at the table, we heard testimonies of Christians all over the globe that reflected how global food politics, the creation of hunger and malnutrition, the obsessions of dieting America, and the despair that comes with eating disorders damage table fellowship, reveal injustice, and challenge life in the body of Christ. The text of reality that shines through these testimonies was juxtaposed with the invitation to come together to the banquet.

With this liturgy a window is opened through which people from different continents engage in their expression of self, hope, and faith without forgetting the stories of colonized and marginalized people. This is the realm in which the Eucharist is celebrated as eschatological experience. This kind of embodied imagination is important to us because it is at the heart of ritual practice and of biblical stories about the reign of God. Celebrating the Eucharist in the horizon of eschatological hope is an imaginative act. We enter into a world of colors, body shapes, languages, food; we are wrapped into various senses of rhythm and flow, sound and movement that make the tension of the "already" and "not yet" alive—this specific realm of in-betweenness in which our hearts are lifted up to the Holy One. Theologians have tried to capture this realm with the notion of eschatology. In what follows, we invite our readers into a deeper reflection of eschatological imagination.

Expectation: Waiting with Eager Longing

> *The hope for some of the disenfranchised women*
> *may be a place to dry their fish on the beach,*
> *enough seeds for next spring,*
> *or money enough to send their children to school.*
> *The future is not a grand finale, a classless society,*
> *or even a kingdom of God,*
> *but more immediate, concrete and touchable.*[7]

We begin with the notion of eschatology.[8] We can distinguish at least two strands of interpretation in eschatological theology. *Eschatology* first appears in the final section of Abraham Calov's *Systema Locorum Theologicorum* from 1677.[9] From the seventeenth century onward, Lutheran theologians made the topic *De Novissimis* (About the End) the concluding chapter in their dogmatics. Eschatology is developed here as the doctrine of the *eschata*, the last things. Those *eschata* include topics like death, the end of the world, resurrection and new creation, and God's judgment as salvation toward eternal life or condemnation to eternal ruin. Eternal life is here mainly understood from the perspective of life after death.

In the second understanding, eschatology deals explicitly with the idea of future as a mode of expectation and addresses the prospects of Christian faith in the world. This second approach is interested in the future as God's coming and how it affects Christian life and faith in the present. Major questions are: What dare we hope? How does God, who is in Christ and who moves from the future into our lives, shape our present and our future? In which sense does Christian eschatology break open a linear understanding of time? Eschatology is here interpreted as a radical critique of the understanding of time as continual progress.

From this approach flows an understanding of eschatology as the basis of theology, its radical grounding and not only the last chapter tacked onto formulations of Christian dogmatics.[10] Eschatology has to be the starting point and the hermeneutical perspective through which the whole task of theological inquiry is to be articulated. Here the focus is not so much on the *eschata* but on the *eschaton*. In twentieth-century European and North American theology, we can see the discussions about eschatology shifting from the *eschata* to the *eschaton* as the "ultimate in every sense which confronts the reality of history and time."[11] *Eschaton*, however, remains an opaque concept. For Tillich it is "the ultimate of history which points beyond history, it is the transcending meaning of historical events . . . which is equally close to every moment in history and relates every moment in history to its ultimate goal."[12] Or, as Karl Barth puts it, the *eschaton* is the "eternal confronting everything temporal as its ultimate crisis and as an indication that redemption must come from a dimension which is wholly other than everything temporal."[13] Another interpretation is offered by Rudolf Bultmann's existential approach, which interprets the *eschaton* as the "ultimate of my existence as it confronts me in the call to decide for or against authentic existence."[14] This approach to eschatology has a christological focus. It was John A. T. Robinson who reminded us of the personal character of the ultimate. He observes that the neuter construction *to eschaton* does not exist in the language of the New Testament, and we find instead *ho eschatos*, which refers to Christ and not to an abstract concept of time.[15]

In the 1960s, Jürgen Moltmann saw the topic of hope and future-oriented expectation as the heart of Christian eschatology. Hope is to be found in Christ's life, death, and resurrection. It is from these events that the Christian praxis of transformation will emerge. Eschatology is mainly about God's future, which is more than just future time. Time past, time present, and time to come are qualified by the messianic time, which has already begun with the coming of Jesus.[16] With the messianic time the kingdom comes and justice exerts its power over the present, freeing the present from the death-bringing powers of the past. Christians practice their faith by expecting God's advent in this world filled with violence. Living into the anticipation that the future of God's reign will turn this planet into the dwelling place of God's glory leads to a practice in communities of faith that shows something of the newness that Christ will complete on his Day. With the focus on the advent of God, Moltmann reintegrated the ethical approach and the quest for liberating praxis into the eschatological enterprise. Moltmann's theology of hope was adapted, criticized, and further developed in various contextual theologies.

It is within womanist theologies, which focus not so much on liberation as on survival, that we find a new interest in eschatology and apocalyptic imagery. Joan M. Martin describes prophetic eschatology as the capacity to look at the world with different eyes. In the socioeconomic situation that denies so many African American people the possibility of improving their quality of life, eschatological imagination is a perception of the world in which Jesus' ministry to the poor, the deaf, the lame (Matt. 11:5) has not yet come to an end.[17] The sources for fostering apocalyptic sensibilities and eschatological hope are the Bible, the historical context of slavery and racial discrimination in the Americas and, finally, the liturgical sources and spaces of empowerment. Spirituals such as "Lord, What a Mo(u)rnin'" or "Oh, He's Going to Wake up the Dead"[18] express an eschatological expectation that finds hope in the midst of deadly powers that depress those who are marginalized, and reclaims the resurrection of the body.[19] In her book *In a Blaze of Glory: Womanist Spirituality as Social Witness*, Emily Townes writes:

> The prayer to live and to believe in justice stares down the suffering with an apocalyptic vision. This is not an apocalypse of gloom and doom. It does not exhort a kind of fascination with utter destruction that simply begets passivity of inaction and worth indifference. It does not appeal to a wrathful God who is sending the four horsemen even as millions of us kill millions of us through starvation, war and greed. The apocalyptic vision that demands a cold, hard Womanist stare at suffering rejects its inevitability and chooses life over extinction. The passionate apocalyptic vision of a Womanist ethic poses the question much as Micah posed the question: "is it not for [us] to know justice?" (3:1).[20]

The apocalyptic vision and the eschatological hope that womanist theologians strive for is inextricably interwoven with their struggle against white supremacy, economic exploitation, and gender violence. This theology fosters apocalyptic sensibilities that soberly analyze the structural and personal implications of social evils. In the midst of oppression, womanist eschatology recognizes the blaze of God's glory "in the lives and commitments of children, men and women of faith who seek to live their spirituality as social witness."[21]

We are aware that in the framework of postmodern thinking it is suspect to speak about hope and future. All these narratives of eschatology are challenged and shown to display a totalitarian approach to reality. What people hope for and what they fear cannot be compressed under the roof of one monolithic unifying vision. These hopes and fears are so diverse that it almost looks as if we are not able to speak about a common future. In the face of nuclear threat and ecological disaster it seems more appropriate to speak about the fact that we are running out of time, or at least that our time is limited. The spirit of eternal revision as the signum of modernity has radicalized its face in our days: "Whereas for modernity the principal good was cumulative achievement along the upward sloping line of time, for postmodernity the principal good is accumulating experiences, continually plunging into the discontinuous moment, in search not of eternity but of ecstatic momentariness. For life as progress read life as tourism."[22]

In our understanding of eschatology, we read biblical and liturgical texts that talk about the coming of God, about the risen Christ, about the messianic meal and about the end-times as poetic and mythic language with which people express their hope for God's justice to come in life-transforming ways. The dimension of future is not to be understood in prognostic but rather in relational and qualitative terms. The question is not: *when* is Christ coming "again"? But *how* is God's nearness experienced and embodied in every day life practices? From a biblical and liturgical perspective, eschatological utterances do not offer a timetable for future events, nor are they statements about expectations related to the future. They express a relational quality:

> The experience of God's nearness in space and time is not separable from the people who have that experience and share it with one another. Their eschatological hopes interpret and alter their present and their future. Their experience of time is one of fear and trembling, as well as one of joy over God's nearness; it is the experience of a time of waiting and of hoping for a future that God grants. Those who wait on God in the present live eschatologically: their present is fulfilled and they are full of yearning for the future of God.[23]

Apocalyptic imagery and eschatological imagination are the language of those who are in the midst of struggles for survival, marginalized people who find in the apocalyptic images of God, the angels, and the community of saints agents of life. Understood in this manner, the talk about the end of time intends to restrict the time of oppression. It is the poetics of people who yearn for the end of time. They await with eager longing the disempowerment of those imperial forces that bring death and violence to people.[24]

Catherine Keller refers to Karl Barth's understanding of eschatological hope as a constructive move against totalizing and essentialist understandings of the future.[25] Barth understands hope as taking the next step; hope is an activity that, at least for Christians, has its place within the activities of a community: "The Christian does not think or act as a private individual [but rather] hopes in and with the community, and in and for the world, that there will not be lacking to the world, even in all its needs and perplexities, provisional lights, concrete aids and deliverances and preservations and advancements, but also salutary crises."[26]

Additionally, we want to emphasize that eschatological hope is deeply intertwined with the needs of the physical body. Eschatological hope does not transcend the body in a disembodied spiritual realm. It does not deny the neediness and the desire of bodies; it rather lifts them up to God. When we are called to the table with the words, "Come, see and taste how friendly our God is," we are invited with our senses to participate in the mystery of Christ's presence. We move our bodies when we gather around the altar. We turn to our neighbors and touch hands and backs when we pass the peace. We lift our hands. We open our mouths, smell the food, chew and swallow bread and wine. We have the taste on our tongues. We close our eyes when we pray or we pray with our eyes open. We listen to words and into silence. Our whole bodily existence is involved in the holy meal. An embodied theology of the Eucharist examines these very ritual activities as its foundation.[27] This kind of understanding refocuses the debate about divine presence in the meal not concentrating exclusively on the "elements," but on the bodies of people.[28] Hermeneutically, it is important to us that there be no divide between the material and the spiritual world. It is by the material means of eating and drinking that community is created among the participants in the meal and with God.

Imagination: Come, See, and Taste

Practicing eschatological hope is an act of imagination. We define imagination as a sensual, embodied activity and a sociopolitical practice. Imagination makes accessible to our minds an idea, a concept, an image, or a symbol as well as body knowledge, and a felt sense of something that would otherwise not be available to us.[29] It can either refer to something that is real but physically absent, or to something that is imaginary. There are two major modes of absence: the temporal and the spatial.[30] Both are highly significant for ritual actions as well as for religious imagination in general. Temporal absence can refer to past as well as future realities. In terms of past realities, imagination is crucial for the anamnetic work that takes place in Eucharistic prayers. The recalling of God's saving history with God's people and the anticipation of the reign pictured in the heavenly banquet as well as in the coming of Christ offer images that nurture the religious imagination of worship participants. Imagination helps make these past realities accessible to us.

Spatial absence describes the distance between us and the other. It embraces the otherness of God and of human beings. We imagine the holy city, the reign of God, the place of refuge, the womb of God. Imagination transforms spatial or temporal absence into presence. In this sense the anamnetic activity in the Eucharistic liturgy can be seen as an act of imagination that breaks open spatial distances as well as the common paradigm of linear time.

Theologically speaking, human imagination can be conceived as the *point of contact* between divine revelation and human experience. In the interest of overcoming the classic theological dilemma of natural theology versus the positivism of revelation, it is helpful to understand imagination not in a foundational sense as a prerequisite for divine self-disclosure. Imagination as point of contact should rather be understood as a place where this encounter happens.[31] Imagination can be understood as the place where God's word becomes effective in human life by means of perceiving, symbolizing, and conceptualizing. "Nothing about the imagination *per se*, properly conceived, implies the possibility of revelation; nor does anything in the *concept* of imagination prohibit someone from interpreting all religious imagination as imaginary, rooted in the illusory projection of human experience."[32]

At the heart of the paradigmatic imagination is the ability to see one thing as another. Seeing one thing as another implies the heuristic awareness of a variety of perceptual possibilities. Seeing the world as God's creation or as dominated by a master race or by the stock market will evoke different ways of imagining one's self in the world. Paul Ricoeur states that imagination is a *seeing as*.[33] This *seeing as* refers to making connections between things, images, thoughts, and concepts that are different in order to perceive dissimilarities as well as emerging congruencies. Through the acknowledgment of difference one is enabled to overcome literal meanings by bringing two previously unconnected elements together. The new insights afforded by this connecting are immersed into a realm of meaning that evolves in the space between those two elements. In addition, "the images of our imagination are not representations of something (a substitute and weakened sensorial impression for something absent or unreal); rather imagination displays relations so that a new intended connection is grasped as what the icon describes or depicts."[34] It is the contention of many postmodern thinkers that there is no original that is represented in the imagination. A last reference does not exist; rather, there is only the self-referential play of images.[35]

We follow Green's thesis that imagination is crucial for ritual practice as well as for theological reflection: "*Revelation* is the technical term for describing the inspiration of the original witnesses' imaginations. The doctrine of *scripture* goes on to describe the inspiration of the texts in which those witnesses recorded what had been revealed to them. *Theology*, finally, is the technical term for the critical interpretation of revelation by means of the interpretation of scripture."[36] With regard to this movement from revelation through scripture to theology, the scriptures serve as a lens through which we refocus the patterns that shape our imagination.

What is missing in this model is the concrete sociopolitical context of tangible bodies that already bring to the table concrete images of what the Eucharist is about. Those images and affections are shaped by many aspects derived from consciousness, as well as from the realm of the unconscious. Experiences of hunger or of abundant access to food shape our imagination, as does the knowledge that we consume poisoned food and food that produces hunger in the Two-Thirds World. Eating disorders expressed as invisible and visible conflicts about control over one's eating habits shape the imagination of those who participate in rituals of holy eating.[37] Paradigms of interpretation that are transformed into moods that affect what we expect or how we behave at the table shape our imagination. From the perspective of liturgical theology it is critical to study this encounter of real, tangible bodies in the movement from revelation, through scriptures, to theology in order to value the question of *how* people imagine as much as the question of *what* people imagine.

We want to stress that imagination is an embodied practice that has a profoundly relational quality. It is the encounter of real bodies with texts, symbols, concepts, sounds, smells, and the interaction of bodies with each other in ritual activity that produces the imagination. The network of relationships we live in influences our imaginative processes and the affective connotations that are attached to particular images.[38] Thus we locate eschatological imagination in the embodied practices that are immersed in the hope for the coming of God's reign.

The Fabric of Eschatological Imagination

We conclude our inquiry into eschatological imagination by asking pragmatically what eschatological imagination *does*. The following characteristics are inspired by our interpretation of liturgical events as well as of biblical texts. They are derived also from worshiping communities that embody glimpses of these insights. They will serve as hermeneutical lenses for our further investigations:

- Eschatological imagination creates *windows* through which we receive glimpses of what the reign of God is about.

- We see through those windows by means of *analogy*.
- What we see works disruptively with regard to commonly held world-views; eschatological imagination creates *disruptions*.
- Eschatological imagination introduces us to a *critical otherworldliness*, for instance, by means of reversal and thickening of experience.

These characteristics are not to be understood as a closed system. Rather, they are like a fabric, like threads woven together. As we have mentioned before, eschatological imagination neither presents an advance report about humanity's moral and technological progress, as classic modern enlightened theology has put it, nor does it offer a super-theory about the course of history in the sense of a universal salvation history (*Heilsgeschichte*) or of history as encompassing reality in its totality. We do not develop theoretical knowledge or prognoses about the world to come when we pray "thy kingdom come" or when we sing "vamos todos a la banquete," eagerly longing to participate in the banquet. It is within a wide range of liturgical activities that this kind of imaginative trust is built up in communities of faith. When we join in the words of the Nicene Creed, "We look for the resurrection of the dead and the life of the world to come," we do not produce prognostic statements. Rather, we express our *hope* that the power of resurrection may transform our lives, which are dominated by the powers of death. Not prognosis, but hope, is at the heart of eschatological imagination; in this sense, eschatology has a deeply relational perspective.

We understand biblical stories and songs such as the multiplication of the bread (Mark 6:30-44)[39] or the Magnificat (Luke 1:46-55) as imaginations that disrupt the dominant perception of the course of history and of power relations. These stories do not put forward complete and coherent concepts for an alternative vision of the world; they are more like *windows* that show a potential for life's flourishing that is not yet realized.

This understanding of eschatological imagination as window, which enables the disruption of our common sense of reality, is also appropriate for the interpretation of Eucharistic prayers. Although the prayers seem to follow a linear progression that portrays God's story with creation, with Israel, and in Jesus Christ, we propose to understand the eschatologically based passages in particular as a cry of those who are praying that the time of oppression will come to an end.

What we see through these windows can only be understood in *analogical terms*. We imagine the world to come, the coming of Christ, and the reign of God by analogy to something that is familiar to us, either in our actual experience or as unfulfilled yearning. People in Palestine who became familiar with the bread stories of the New Testament might have been nurtured in their desire to be filled physically. The heavenly banquet, a motif that has its origins in Jewish apocalypticism, might have served as a window that confronted the daily experience of hunger;

> the analogical nature of eschatological visions means that the imagery of temporal future functions metaphorically to represent eternity. At least since Augustine, it has generally been acknowledged by theologians that God does not create *in time* but rather creates time as an aspect of his creation of the world *ex nihilo*.[40]

When we pray "from eternity to eternity," we embrace the confidence that God's time, which we call eternity, creates a qualitative leap that generates a discontinuity in the alienation we experience in time. Eschatological imagination that envisions another world works by means of analogy. What is not present yet can only be grasped by referring to something familiar.

> For Christians, because their paradigm is Jesus Christ, the likenesses are necessarily historical. Christians envision the world to come by analogy with the past—a very specific past contained in Holy Scripture. We imagine the future by imagining its likeness to this past: as new creation, heavenly Jerusalem, the return of Jesus Christ.[41]

Celebrating the Eucharistic prayers adduces a similar phenomenon. The remembrance, that happens in the act of praying breaks open the pattern of linear time. Eternity is evoked as God's time while we remember God's solidarity with God's people as it is revealed in the story of Israel and in Jesus Christ. In this act of remembrance, God's presence here and now is experienced. As the disciples shared their (last) meal with Jesus, so do we partake in a meal, yearning for the transforming presence of God in our lives. Analogously, we are also a community of traitors and fearful human beings. Like them, we are invited into community with Christ in order to experience the friendliness and goodness of God: "Come, all things are ready. See and taste how friendly our God is." This invitation to come to the table is a call to eschatological imagining of God's eternity with all our senses. Seeing and tasting are the vehicles for the analogy that grounds the eschatological imagination.

In calling this imagination disruptive, we are inspired by the Roman Catholic theologian Johann Baptist Metz, who calls disruption the briefest definition for religion.[42] It is especially Jewish and Christian apocalypticism that disrupts an understanding of time as the graceless continuity of an evolutionary logic that confirms the dominance of death as the major force in history. The Jewish and Christian traditions are filled with dangerous memory that lifts up the experiences of destruction and damaged life. The *memoria passionis* of the Gospel contains the dangerous memory of Jesus Christ as the victim of totalitarian oppression whom God saved from death and resurrected into new life. The refusal to tell only the successful story of realized possibilities disrupts the modern narrative of progress. In remembrance of the victims of history, theological reflection and liturgical practice that seek to be truthful *imitatio Christi* move toward a practice of missing what is lost. When we remember Christ's life, death, and resurrection along with the suffering of victims of violence in history and in our time, we enter into the realm of eschatological imagination, which anticipates the promised future for the oppressed and hopeless.

> The story of what God has done in the death and resurrection of Jesus is a shocking interruption, a (negative) critique, to any teleological argument justifying economic profit or technological efficiency or ideological power, as well as a (positive) hope which sustains efforts to combat the forces of oppression that arise therefrom.[43]

Apocalyptic and eschatological imagination, with its power to disrupt the overpowering experience of violence, has the potential to offer a language of hope for those who are voiceless. [44]

Eschatological imagination introduces a *critical otherworldliness* by means of radical reversal and thickening of experience. *Otherworldliness* is a loaded term; the modern masters of suspicion often equated it with escapism, the desire to flee from real conflicts in this world into a world of illusion by means of ritual practices or fantastic views of eternal life. We can see this suspicion of otherworldliness in Freud's early writings on religion as well as in classical Marxist critique of religion. Green rightly states that it is not only those modern masters of suspicion but also many Christians for whom otherworldliness is a troubling issue:

> Christians in the pews have sought to play down or even to eliminate entirely the otherworldliness of Christian faith and doctrine, which has meant the elimination or the radical reinterpretation of eschatology. They have felt an apologetic pressure to declare their loyalty to *this* world while eschewing the claims that another world might make upon us, including the 'otherworldly' aspects of Christian tradition.[45]

There are, however, other critical scholars who reclaim the notion of otherworldliness in a constructive way that can inform our interpretation of eschatological imagination. With regard to liturgical practice, we proceed on the assumption that there are diverse ways, depending on the specific context, in which critical otherworldliness can be embodied. From a general functional perspective, one can identify a variety of intentions that rituals fulfill: from coping with existential *angst* in daily life or in extreme situations to social integration through the portrayal of moral or cosmic systems. Within this spectrum of possibilities, rituals can also function as performances of otherworldliness that help to create a stance of protest against the injustices we see.[46] These intentions that rituals fulfill might exercise mutual influence; they can also describe the grounding intentionality of liturgical practice. Indeed, there are both prophetic and consoling aspects to the performance of otherworldliness. At least those who do not profit from the business of "this world," who are not the winners in history, might be consoled by eschatological prayers that yearn for a different world to come. Eschatological imagination articulates a distinction from this world in order to regain a new and critical point of reference. Utterances about a hereafter only make sense when the reference to this world is explicated.

> Christian otherworldliness is an otherworldliness of the imagination which remains necessarily always in tension with our immediate experience of this world. Such anticipation cannot constitute a metanarrative because *this* narrative is not yet at an end (not even "proleptically"). Strictly speaking, it is more nearly "fiction" than "fact," because it describes events that are not yet real. And this is precisely why those events can be mediated to us only by way of our imagination, and the imaginations of the biblical witnesses.[47]

Otherworldliness can be embodied in a variety of ways, for instance, by means of *reversal* and thickening of experience. In the Magnificat, Mary sings about this reversal: God has scattered the proud in the thoughts of their hearts. God has brought down the powerful from their thrones and lifted up the lowly. God has filled the hungry with good things and sent the rich away empty (Luke 1:51-53). The reversal is directed toward the proud, those in power, and the rich. It contains the promise that their time of dominance has been restricted; it will come to an end. At the heart of the eschatological imagination, the body appears again: empty stomachs are filled. They are filled with bread and wine, olives and fish, milk and honey, good things that are a pleasure to enjoy.

Critical otherworldliness is also practiced in the thickening of experience. We suggest interpreting stories such as the multiplication of the bread as a dense way of showing the struggles of the people. In the midst of these struggles, God's economy of grace emerges as people begin to share their small resources and leave the logics of scarcity behind.[48]

The New Testament is filled with stories that are nourished by the fabric of eschatological imagination. In the following, we show how in the New Testament windows are opened to give us glimpses of God's reign. We will concentrate on four major aspects: the understanding of messianic time in relational and qualitative terms, the notion of the new covenant that is liberated from dualistic and anti-Jewish interpretations, the arrival of the Son of Man, and the coming of God. Following our reflections about Eucharistic life and sacramental permeability, we begin with a wider circle of reflections that take into account not only liturgical practice, but everyday life and its struggles, and how the hope for God's coming is expressed in it. It is about the special hope of ordinary people.

Making Sense of New Testament Eschatology

"Today"

There is a rabbinic legend from the Babylonian Talmud that gives us access to New Testament eschatology. It is some centuries later than the New Testament texts, but it belongs within the history of Jewish discourse about God, which includes New Testament eschatology. Rabbi Joshua ben Levi asks the prophet Elijah:

> "When will the Messiah come?" He replied: "Go, ask him yourself."—"Where is he?"—"At the gates of Rome."—"How can I recognize him?"—"He is sitting between poor people laden with diseases; all the rest are unbinding all [their wounds] at the same time and binding them up again, but he is unbinding them one at a time and rebinding them, because he thinks: Perhaps I will be needed, and there must be no delay." At this he [Rabbi Joshua] went to him and said: "Peace be with you, Lord and Master!" He replied: "Peace be with you, Son of Levi!" He asked: "When will the Master come?" and the other answered: "Today."
>
> Then he returned to Elijah, who asked him: "What did he tell you?" He replied: "Peace be with you, Son of Levi!" Then he said: "He has promised to you and your father the world to come." But he responded: "He lied to me, because he said he would come today, and he did not

come." Elijah replied: "This is what he meant: If today you would listen to his voice (Ps. 95:7)."[49]

In this legend, the Messiah and the prophet Elijah interpret time quite differently from Rabbi Joshua ben Levi. The latter, in the first place, embodies a lack of understanding of the eschatological language of hope. He asks "when?"—meaning what day and hour. He misunderstands "today"[50] in the Messiah's answer. He does not comprehend that "today" demands something of him, that "today" is when the voice of God is heard—and deeds must follow hearing. We could also say that "today" is when people listen to Scripture, "to Moses and the prophets of God" (Luke 16:31). "Today" changes lives; a life "today" is a life in relationship with God. The legend does not say whether Rabbi Joshua changed, but it was retold by people who likewise asked his critical questions and shared his longing for a life in relation to God. The legend teaches us to seek its continuation in ourselves. There is also a slightly mocking nuance: Religious scholars are sometimes slow to grasp what is important.

The Messiah and the prophet Elijah interpret time solely in terms of relationship to God. The Messiah is seated before the gates of Rome, among poor, sick people. It is as if he had seated hiimself next to poor Lazarus, whose story is told in Luke 16:19-31. Lazarus sat before the gates of a rich man's house, suffered from hunger, and was helpless to fend off the dogs who licked his sores. Both stories—the Talmud legend and Luke 16:19-31—describe typical real situations in the life of the Roman Empire.

The city of Rome and the sumptuous life of the rich man (Luke 16:19-31) represent the tiny elite of the Roman Empire, who lived at the expense of the majority of the population. Sick people like Lazarus who had a severe skin disease (whether it was leprosy in the modern sense is uncertain) were the poorest of the poor. The great many people who lived as day laborers feared such a fate. The Messiah shares their life, as did Jesus and those with him. Therefore, we can call their life messianic, and the Jesus movement a messianic movement.[51]

The Messiah only removes one bandage from his sores so as to let in air, but does not take off all the bandages at the same time. He has to be ready to leave at a moment's notice; his hour, God's summons, can make it necessary at any time. The New Testament uses a variety of images to describe this alertness and readiness, and not only for a single messianic figure; they apply to all those who live messianically: "Keep awake . . . for you know neither the day nor the hour" (Matt. 25:13). "It is now the moment for you to wake from sleep . . . the night is far gone, the day is near" (Rom. 13:11, 12). If people can anticipate during the night when the thief will break in, they can keep it from happening (Matt. 24:43). So they have to be watchful at all times. These are New Testament images that can be set alongside the Talmudic legends. It is not a question of reading this imagery in allegorical fashion: Is the coming of the Messiah being compared to a thief's intrusion? It is about watchfulness; the ability to hear what God's voice is saying and the readiness to set out on a transformed life of messianic solidarity. The Messiah in the Talmudic legend embodies this messianic solidarity. The prophet Elijah plays the same part as Abraham in Luke 16:19-31. He reminds us of life's basis: You have Moses and the prophetic writings; listen to them.

This messianic or eschatological understanding of time is expressed in the New Testament in some key sayings about time: "*Today* salvation has come to this house" (Luke 19:9): When the chief tax collector Zacchaeus changed his life and shared his ill-gotten wealth with the poor. "Now" God's righteousness has become visible "apart from law . . . attested by the law and the prophets" (Rom. 3:21). This is the "*now*" when people begin to trust Jesus Messiah. This is the "*moment* . . . to wake from sleep" (Rom. 13:11). It is the *kairos*, the time that has been fulfilled because God's reign,[52] God's just world, is near at hand (Mark 1:15). This interpretation of time is not the result of philosophical reflection; it comes from a life-praxis of relationship with the God of Israel. All the time-concepts in New Testament eschatology are words that express relationship. They are misunderstood when they are read as referring in any way to linear time. That was Rabbi Joshua's mistake in his conversation with Elijah, and that was the misunderstanding of all the people in Jesus' company[53] who were so often warned that they knew neither the day nor the hour. If we read Paul's letters as continuous text, it becomes clear that the statements about the eschatological "now," like the short exclamations of praise and thanksgiving, serve to interrupt his thoughts. The experience of the joy of God's nearness had set him in motion from the time when Christ revealed himself to him. The presence of the crucified Messiah as the Risen One changed his life and made him a prophet. This joyful experience continually breaks through in his life. It is the basis for everything he says, writes, and does during his long journeys. It draws the new messianic communities together. The common meal is the place where many people long for and experience this joy.

In the Gospels, these experiences of joy are often expressed in the so-called Beatitudes. Already, in a daily life in which hunger and poverty oppress people, they experience in the messianic community that God has set a rich table for all. The sisters and brothers, all of whom know hunger, share their food as if there were bread in abundance. They act like profligates. Thus already, in their giving and receiving, they are healed by joy.

A nineteenth-century liberal theology still influential today, which worked with the notion of a "delay of the parousia" and hence with a linear concept of time, misconceived early Christian hope.[54] In this interpretation, Jesus' and Paul's expectations were mistaken. They had anticipated the coming of God's just world, the reign of God, in the near future, within a few years. It did not happen. Therefore, according to this theory, the early church had to deal with the delay of the parousia very soon after the death of the first generation and establish itself in the world, something neither Jesus nor Paul had desired. This delay of the parousia was then the time of the church, now two thousand years long, the time of an institution, the time of compromises and "love patriarchalism."[55] This theory entails a depoliticization of early Christian eschatology. According to this elitist notion, the Sermon on the Mount and Jesus' radical preaching derived from a small, radical minority that proposed this ethic for itself. Such an ethic was not, however, proposed as something to be lived by "normal" people who dwell in families and have to conduct business and statecraft. Jesus' way is said to be one of consistent nonviolence, renunciation of family and possessions. But a "normal" Christian life in church and state cannot be lived in such a way. This depoliticization of Jesus' message goes well with a hierarchical church and society. "Let each of you remain in the condition in which you were called" (1 Cor. 7:20). This (false) translation of 1 Cor. 7:20 was for centuries a kind of Christian maxim expressing and giving biblical legitimacy to a conservative concept of society.[56] These theories of New Testament eschatology do not do justice to the hope of the people who made up the communities of earliest Christianity.

The New Covenant
In 1 Cor. 11:25 and Luke 22:20, the interpretive words over the cup read: "This cup is the new covenant in my blood." The God of Israel makes a new covenant with the people that had not kept the exodus covenant (Jer. 31:31, 32). "This is the covenant that I will make with the house of Israel after those days. . . : I will put my law within them, and I will write it on their hearts; and I will be their God, and they shall be my people" (Jer. 31:33). Now, in the hour of the common meal, this voice of God can be heard speaking God's healing promise that the people are under God's protection (cf. also Zech. 9:11).

How has this divine promise in the words over the cup been read? The "ecclesiological" interpretation has had serious consequences. According to this reading, the Christian church is God's partner in the new covenant, in contrast to the old covenant with Israel. The contrast between church and Israel was thus understood as part of salvation history and it became the basis for much of the anti-Jewish model of theological interpretation. This "ecclesiology" is set in quotation marks here because it is triumphalistic and can only be called a misinterpretation—though a common one—of ecclesiology. In this version, church is seen as the one, true, and final embodiment of the new covenant, which was and will be victorious. Other cultures and religions are, by contrast, of lesser worth; here "Judaism" is always named first as an old religion, inferior to "Christianity" and necessarily inferior from a theological standpoint.[57] The "New Testament" is so named for this reason: New Testament/New Covenant in contrast to "Old Testament," the old covenant. This designation for the collection of apostolic writings appeared in the second century and was one consequence of the "ecclesiological" triumphalistic interpretation of the new covenant in Jesus' words at the supper.

An eschatological interpretation of the "new covenant" returns to the roots of the phrase in the Torah and the prophets. It is God's saving promise to Israel and, beyond Israel, to all the people of God. This promise lives where it is heard, and it means the beginning of a journey into God's just world. God's promise is powerless when it is misused in a triumphalistic way. In New Testament times, just uttering the words "new covenant" was enough to make the voice of God audible. Its content is the keeping of the Torah and being sheltered under God's protection. Thus Jesus' words at the supper, when repeated in present time, become an eschatological moment: We, the participants, hear the voice of hope *now*. We are invited to be people of God. This tradition of a new covenant is bound up with the vision of healed humanity in which all peoples will have their place, no matter how different they are.[58]

The "ecclesiological" interpretation is a hermeneutical model that has overgrown and smothered the perception of New Testament traditions. Thus the traditions were read with the concept that "we" are on the right side, God's side, even though we are sinners. We are the wise virgins (Matt. 25:1-13), and the bridegroom shuts the heavenly door against the "others," the "wicked." We and the others, the good and the evil, are in opposition. In the political rhetoric of the U.S. government's "war against terror" since September 2001, the theological legitimation of war according to the model of "ecclesiological" theology is omnipresent: The "evildoers" are contrasted to the people who are bringing freedom to the whole world. And yet only these people's own dead are counted, not the "others," in this case the Iraqis.

An eschatological interpretation can be described on paper, but above all it must be fought for, over and over, against the power of the "ecclesiological" interpretation: at the community table, in listening to God's promise, and in a life that puts an end to violence. In the next chapter we will return to the meaning of the content of the new covenant.

The Arrival of the Son of Man

In the evangelists' eschatology, the Son of Man is a central figure; he will judge humanity. He is the end-time judge. The fact that he is called Son of Man means that he is a human figure endowed by God with power over all nations. Daniel 7:13-14 says of the end-time judgment God will hold: "As I watched in the night visions, I saw one like a human being coming with the clouds of heaven. And he came to the Ancient One and was presented before him. To him was given dominion and glory and kingship, that all peoples, nations, and languages should serve him. His dominion is an everlasting dominion that shall not pass away, and his kingship is one that shall never be destroyed." The dominion of the Son of Man, the Human One, is identical with the kingship and dominion that "shall be given to the people of the holy ones of the Most High" (Dan. 7:27). This dominion of the Son of Man and of the people of the Most High is the utopia of the just world that puts an end to the unjust rule of the world empires, especially that of the "fourth beast." The fourth beast will be more horrible than all those before it, "it shall devour the whole earth, and trample it down, and break it to pieces" (Dan. 7:23). So the Son of Man represents the human world that will finally be liberated by God unto worldwide justice. He is a mythical figure, and yet quite clearly is not a divine being; he is a human being among other human beings, at last in a just human world.

In the Gospels, this mythic figure is always clearly tied to the vision in Daniel. Here, too, it comes on the clouds of heaven. Here the Son of Man himself exercises divine judgment (Matt. 24:30; 25:31; Mark 13:26; Luke 21:27; Mark 15:61, and frequently elsewhere). Daniel 7 was also read in the first century CE as referring to a political utopia with explosive power. Josephus,[59] after he had become a faithful servant of Roman rule, applied it to the future emperor Vespasian, seeking thereby to avert anti-Roman interpretations. The high priest in the story of Jesus' Passion regards Jesus' proclamation of the Son of Man as blasphemy (Mark 15:61), not because the Son of Man is a divine figure and Jesus claims to be identical with him, but because Jesus, by proclaiming the coming of the Son of Man, announces God's judgment on the power of the high priests, which was approved and supported by Rome. The friends of Rome feared the power of

Daniel's prophecy, as is clear from Josephus and from the Passion accounts in the Gospels.

In the time of Jesus, as in that of the Gospels, the Roman Empire was experienced by subjugated peoples just as Daniel had prophesied: as the beast that "will devour the whole earth, and trample it down, and break it to pieces." This imperial power, which harshly controlled the tiny Jewish state on its eastern border and ruled it with particular severity, contrasts with Daniel's prophetic utopia. Jesus never said directly, "I am that Son of Man,"[60] but he continually proclaimed the coming of the Son of Man—a judgment on the nations is coming, a judgment on Rome and its vassals, that will bring about the universal reign of God's righteousness. It appears that in later Christian generations Jesus was identified with this Son of Man (e.g., Matt. 25:31-46). But a "Son of Man Christology" is a dogmatic construction in the service of a Christology from above, a Christology of exaltation, that is foreign to the New Testament. At that time, "Son of Man" was not a christological "title." On the contrary, the Son of Man embodies the nation of the saints, a simple human being among others, and precisely *not* the figure of a ruler like other rulers.

Let us look more closely here at one of these prophecies of the coming of the heavenly human figure in order to illuminate New Testament eschatology in its historical context and in our own time. The passage is Matt. 24:37-42 (cf. Luke 17:26-37):

37 For as the days of Noah were, so will be the coming of the Human One.

38 For as in those days before the flood they were eating and drinking, marrying and giving in marriage, until the day Noah entered the ark,

39 and they knew nothing until the flood came and swept them all away, so too will be the coming of the Human One.[61]

40 Then two will be in the field; one will be taken and one will be left.

41 Two women will be grinding meal together; one will be taken and one will be left.

42 Keep awake therefore, for you do not know on what day your God is coming.

We have already said that eschatological thought and discourse sets God in relationship with "today." This judgment saying from Jesus, which is present in Luke's tradition also, describes human life in its present form:

people eat and drink, marry and give in marriage. This is a typical patriarchal household in which the father makes all the decisions and the "family" is the social and economic "kernel" of the state.[62] The verbs that describe life in a patriarchal household are in the imperfect tense, which in Greek indicates continuous action. What is being described is a typical and ongoing way of life. No one is supposed to change it; it is eternal. But this life is not innocent; it rests on injustice. Not everyone can live this way: free-born women, female and male slaves, and other dependents have to deliver unpaid labor to make this way of life possible. They are beaten, because that was regarded as normal among those who ruled over others. The text makes it clear that this life only appears innocent to those involved because they do not want to know the truth: "and they knew nothing until the flood came and swept them all away" (Matt. 24:39). They lived like Noah's generation, the last before the flood. According to Genesis 6:5, "But when God saw that the wickedness of humankind was great in the earth, and that every inclination of the thoughts of their hearts was only evil continually," God wanted to "blot out" humanity from the earth. In Jewish tradition, Noah's generation was a "type," the image of a humanity that does not want to know God and God's justice, and that moves toward its destruction in apparent ignorance.

The Babylonian Talmud (*b. Sanh.* 108a, b) says that Noah wanted to awaken the people, but they only laughed at him.

> Raba said: It is written (Job 12:5): *a despised flame before the thoughts of the assured, prepared to make the foot stumble*; this teaches that the pious Noah corrected them and spoke words to them that were as urgent as flame, but they ridiculed him by saying to him: Old man, what is this Ark for? He answered them: The Holy One, blessed be He, will bring a flood upon you. They said: What kind of flood? If it is a flood of fire, we have something [to use against it], namely Alitha, and if it is a flood of water, if it should come out of the earth we have iron plates to cover the earth, and if it is from heaven, we also have something [to use against it], namely Aqab.[63]

In our own time, it seems, we no longer talk about the generation before the flood; our "type," our symbol of people who don't want to know, are the oblivious people on the sinking Titanic. These are the kind of people who didn't know anything "about it"—nothing about the Holocaust when it was happening, nothing about the bloody injustice of the Iraq War, nothing about the endemic racism that emerged in the months after Hurricane

Katrina, nothing about the destruction of the basis of life for future generations, nothing about the destruction of the earth's waters. They believe the propaganda that justifies violence. In a breath, the "today" of God's voice can awaken this generation of human beings. God's justice can no longer be ignored. When the Human One comes, God's judgment will not be bribed. It brings the justice that can no longer be lied about. It separates the just from the unjust, the two men in the field and the two women at the mill (Matt. 24:40, 41). This separation of those who are saved from those who are lost and will be lost before God is altogether God's doing. No human can say: You, I, we are on the right side. "They have Moses and the prophets; they should listen to them." Now is the time to wake up.

The typologizing of the generation of the flood produces a conscious memory of history. This remembering changes life and opens up the future, for those who hear this word of judgment can stand up, wake up, stay awake, share the poverty of the lepers, and thus spread healing. In this sense, rememberings the history of the ancestors is the sister of hope. That is why, in Judaism and (early) Christianity, memory is at the center of religious culture.

The Coming of God

The parable of the fig tree (Mark 13:28-29) tells of the experience of God's nearness and God's coming. "From the fig tree learn a parable: as soon as its branch becomes tender and puts forth its leaves, you know that summer is near. So also, when you see these things taking place, you know that God is near, at the very gates."

In the final clause we translate "that *God* is near." The Greek text provides no subject for the clause, and some translations insert "he," referring the clause to the Son of Man (see 13:26) or to God. Others choose "it" or "the end." It is typical of Jewish language about God that the name of God is often paraphrased or indicated only indirectly (for example, by a *passivum divinum*). We insert "God," because the context in Mark 13 suggests it. In the history of Christian interpretation this text, like many others, has been read as a statement about the "return" or "second coming" of Christ, but it is important to reject that kind of reading.

New Testament eschatology speaks of "the end" (e.g., Mark 13:7, 8, 13) and the reign of God. It also refers—just as frequently—to the coming of the Son of Man for judgment. But the two should not be identified. In 1 Cor. 15:23-28 it is clear why the two are not identical, and why the judgment of the Son of Man should not take the place of the "end." The Messiah's reign brings victory over all the destructive powers of the world: "every ruler and every authority and power." The last enemy to be destroyed is human-created death. Then the Messiah hands over the kingship to God. The end means that "God will be all in all" (v. 28). The reign of God is described in a minimum of words. Nothing is elaborated. Sometimes we encounter images, such as the festive meal, but the final judgment of all people and all nations is more fully described, the judgment that precedes the longed-for "end" (Mark 13:7, 13). There are panoplies of judgment, such as the "great judgment of the world" in Matt. 25:31-46 or the words about Christ's victory over the powers of destruction in 1 Cor. 15:23-28. Thus is all-encompassing justice awaited: finally, the destructive powers and human-caused death will be destroyed. But what God's reign and God's future mean is something that can only be expressed in mystical language or in sketches. What cannot be blotted out are the words about what this hope for God's future means today. It means sitting among the sick at the gates of Rome and participating in the festivals of the poor. This eschatology transforms life, the lives and bodies of human beings. That is why meal traditions, the Last Supper and the many meals shared by Jesus with his people, are central to New Testament eschatology. The concept of the *basileia tou theou*, the reign of God, is an expression for God, for God's action in the present and future. It encompasses space and time. It can scarcely be translated; at best we might say "God's world" or "God's just world."

When Jesus read the "gospel of the poor" from Isaiah 61 in the synagogue at Capernaum, he proclaimed, "Today this scripture has been fulfilled in your hearing" (Luke 4:16-21). The dinner scene at the "toll collectors' banquet" in Luke's Gospel (Luke 5:27-32) illustrates the consequences of hearing the scripture "today." Jesus participates in a great banquet with male and female toll collectors,[64] male and female sinners. All these people violate the Torah because they earn their living by work that allows, or even compels them to do so. The women and men who collect tolls are not the rich tax collectors who have leased the collection rights from the state. These are people who can find no better occupation than this one that makes them an object of hatred in the eyes of other people and forces them to cheat and to divert part of what they collect for themselves. Even escaped slaves appear to have taken up this obviously poorly paid work. The other notorious violators of Torah may have been prostitutes who were married, or people who out of necessity broke other commandments of the Torah, for example, the Sabbath law. They may have worked for the Roman army, which did not recognize the Sabbath. There were enough economic compulsions to force violations of Torah. Consequently the groups of the sinners, the poor, and the sick with whom Jesus and his friends lived are difficult to distinguish. Jesus invites the poor and sinners into the reign of God. For them, too, there is a way to change their lives. It may be that, from an economic point of view, they could not change their way of life, but they have the opportunity nevertheless to follow the more difficult commands of Torah (Matt. 23:23): justice, mercy, and trust.

If we not only read Jesus' eschatology today as a teaching or a hope, but recognize its rootedness in a renewed way of life, the little parable of the fig tree in the springtime reveals its genuine content. The people who follow Jesus understand the tiny messages of happiness; the signs of spring on the fig tree awaken joyful anticipation of summer's fruit. Jesus' table communities give a hint of how it could be, how it will be, when God comes. The coming of God is something longed for. "When, finally," "when will the end of suffering come?" The word *end* (Greek: *telos*) is a word of hope in an eschatological context. It can be translated "end" or "fulfillment." Now, already, those who hope can discern the future and work on the signs of that future.

In Western biblical interpretation, God's future is usually read through the lens of a concept of linear time: Jesus imagined God's future as the end of history, a great catastrophe that will bring the human world to an end. Most scholarly reconstructions of New Testament eschatology work with this notion of the end and a corresponding interpretation of "apocalypse." Therefore, some say that Jesus was mistaken; that end never came and will never come. Others found this idea of the end so inhuman that they attempted to reconstruct a "non-eschatological" Jesus.[65] Even the proposals that offer a description similar to ours of both aspects of New Testament eschatology—its orientation to the present and its hope for the future— remain, as regards their idea of the future, within the framework of a dualistic concept that retains the notion of linear time. Accordingly, the reign of God is extra-worldly, an end-time event, beyond the human body and human history. But in the New Testament, a concept of the future in terms of linear time is not associated with the expectation of God's coming.

Likewise, the notion of the "return" of Christ or the "second coming" has no basis in the New Testament. What is awaited there is the arrival (*parousia*) of Christ or the Son of Man. It is *not* called a return. The notion of a return does not appear until the second century.[66] This meant adopting the perspective of a theological view of Christ's coming. The result was that his arrival, his *parousia*, must necessarily be his second coming. This reflection is not yet found in the New Testament, nor is there the projection of a linear path of time. In the New Testament we see only the perspective of those who wait with longing: for Christ's coming, for his arrival, and for the coming of God (e.g., Matt. 3:11 par.). The appeal "Our Lord, come!" (*maranatha*) was part of the early Christian eucharistic liturgy[67] and expressed this longing for the coming of the Messiah and the coming of God. To speak of God is to speak eschatologically—of God's presence and of the future that will be when God is all in all. God's memory is greater than human memory. God forgets no suffering, no unfulfilled life, and none of our tears, not even those we do not shed. The Eucharist celebrates the nearness of God and allows us to experience with our senses the taste of the real life that God wills.

The Captivity of Eschatological Imagination
Colonial Desire

On our journey into the world of eschatological imagination we have found powerful images, stories, songs, and prayers that embody the yearning for God's coming as a language of sober hope for God in the midst of the vulnerability of life. It is a language of desire that revolves around images of God's coming. Eschatological imagination is a practice of hope that encompasses a deep listening to the vulnerable voices that confront poverty and the destruction of life-sustaining resources. Eschatological images retrieved in songs, stories, and prayers foster a sense of being awake and acting responsibly in a world full of possibilities: from total annihilation through nuclear and ecological warfare to the opportunity to nourish everyone on the planet.

On our journey we have also found that it is tremendously difficult, especially in the United States, to reclaim these traditions as people of faith. Thus we want to conclude our inquiry into eschatological imagination by talking about the captivity of that imagination. We recognize that North American Christians in particular, when they seek to find alternatives to fundamentalist teachings about God's judgment, the "second coming of Christ," or the "rapture," often shy away from eschatological imagination by concentrating exclusively on the "historical" Jesus as an example of moral behavior.[68] There are good reasons for this reaction. Eschatological and apocalyptic imagery has been used in the context of American civil religion to legitimate all sorts of conquest and imperial ambition. It is deeply engrained in the (sub)consciousness of the majority of the American people. It is part of foreign policy and of popular culture. It is stunning to realize that Tim LaHaye and Jerry Jenkins' *Left Behind* books are overwhelmingly successful bestsellers,[69] with more than 50 million copies sold.[70] *Left Behind* pictures the end-times and therein the fate of a small group of people who are fighting evil. It talks about the lucky ones who are raptured by Christ into heaven and thus are saved while the countdown toward total annihilation of the globe ticks mercilessly on.[71] The majority of the earth's population will, however, be left behind. The plot begins with the airline pilot Rayford Steele, who has to come to terms with his wife's being raptured into heaven while he was flying an airplane.

It is sad that so many American readers would subscribe to the worldview of these novels: that we are living in the end-times and that all sorts of "catastrophes," from September 11 to Hurricane Katrina and the East Asian tsunami, prove that the end is near. These things *must happen* so that a few can be snatched away by Christ and rescued. Wars and famine are not seen as events produced by human actions, but as steps in God's final plan. The apocalyptic and eschatological imagery activated here pictures global destruction, while salvation is being rescued from the final catastrophe, a privilege reserved for a tiny group. The eschatological imagination as it is spelled out in *Left Behind* is cruel: it is life-denying and elitist. It fosters a kind of salvation egoism: Will *I* be left behind? Or will *I* belong to the chosen ones who are rescued in the rapture?

Unfortunately, the kind of thinking that justifies wars, violence, and colonization as a means of bringing about Christ's reign has deep historical roots. Apocalyptic and eschatological texts were and are used in various processes of colonization, fostering the colonial desire to occupy territory and space as a means to bring about divine salvation. As we can see in the example of Columbus (and we could add numerous other examples), apocalypticism from the perspective of dominance inscribes itself into the topography of the "New World." Christopher Columbus wrote in 1500: "God made me the messenger of the new heaven and the new earth of which he spoke in the apocalypse of St. John after having spoken of it through the mouth of Isaiah, and he showed me the spot where to find it."[72] This statement shows how descriptions of divine calling go hand-in-hand with conquest and occupation of space. Columbus's perception of himself as God's messenger gives him authority and is justified with a reference to the apocalypse of John and the prophet Isaiah.

A similar pattern can be recognized in the missionary consciousness of the Puritans. They saw themselves as the chosen people elected by God to bring to a perfect close the imperfect European Reformation in the "New World." They interpreted the occupation of North American territory as an exodus into the Promised Land and understood themselves as the rebirth of Israel, charged by God to build the New Jerusalem. John Winthrop, the first governor of the Massachusetts Bay Colony, was recognized as the new Moses.[73]

Many religious movements and leaders in seventeenth-century America had similar apocalyptic and eschatological convictions. One of the most poignant examples was Cotton Mather, who thought that the Western hemisphere was the predestined location for the final eschatological events of history. In his *Magnalia Christi Americana* he announced:

> I WRITE the *Wonders* of the CHRISTIAN RELIGION, flying from the Deprivations of *Europe*, to the *American Strand:* And, assisted by the Holy Author of that *Religion,* I do, with all Conscience of *Truth,* required therein by Him, who is the *Truth* it self, Report the *Wonderful Displays* of His Infinite Power, Wisdom, Goodness, and Faithfulness, wherewith His Divine Providence hath *Irradiated* an Indian Wilderness.[74]

We could probably go on endlessly listing examples in which apocalyptic and eschatological motifs are spelled out in an imperial framework. Catherine Keller draws our attention to the gender connotations of these ambitions:

> Those who invade what they believe they have discovered enter from the raw outside of the given space; they do not know themselves as being grown in delicate reciprocity with the relations constituting a place. The new place is called "paradise" and then "wilderness" and "wasteland"—it throbs with mystery, resources, sex, and threat. In short—again—with femininity. Or, then again, it bifurcates into that wild place of "natural" femininity to be colonized and that already domesticated femininity awaiting the hero upon his return.[75]

It was but a small step from imagining the occupied land as a female body to the exploitation of actual bodies. Kwok Pui-lan describes in a similar vein the so-called "discovery of the New World" and the colonization of indigenous people as jammed with sexual overtones: "In 1492, Columbus wrote home from the Caribbean saying that the earth was not round but shaped like a woman's breast, with a protuberance on its summit in the unmistakable shape of a nipple."[76]

As Keller and others have shown, the history of imperialism, especially in the Americas, can only be understood if we recognize as one of its foundations the *Wirkungsgeschichte* of apocalyptic texts. A reading from the perspective of dominance turns the texts upside down. We proceed on the assumption that the dominant theological interpretation that legitimates colonial ambition, the conquest of the "New World" and the enslavement of Native Americans and slaves from Africa is still at work. It is the imperial approach to a God-talk that places God and the future on the side of one's own interest in domination. It coincides with a tradition of proof-texting with biblical texts, using the Bible as a tool to legitimate one's position of power and privilege. This history holds our eschatological imagination captive. It imprisons our Eucharistic celebrations and their eschatological dimension.

Reclaiming eschatological and apocalyptic imagination needs to go hand in hand with the criticism of its captivity. Another aspect of this captivity besides the occupation of land and bodies is the understanding of the future as a controllable terrain in which mostly male and white agents can strive toward perfection. Here the notions of future and progress are inextricably interwoven. The ways in which theologians developed their thoughts in the field of eschatology can only be understood against the background of the Enlightenment's understanding of time and progress. It was the Enlightenment that produced an antitraditionalist energy that legitimated a continually accelerating change in public consciousness as well as in the aesthetic theory of the avant-garde in the nineteenth century.[77] The Enlightenment trait of criticizing traditions and rejecting the past as the exclusive basis of collective identity formation evoked an interest in the future.

> The future becomes the space of open possibilities for human self-fulfillment. The idea of human perfectibility, so abundantly present in Enlightenment thought, presupposes that the future is an open future, offering an unrestricted scope for the development of the hitherto restricted human potentialities.[78]

The European Enlightenment produced a "spirit of eternal revision." It implied a sense of time that does not simply give attention to the present alone, but that, as a category of movement, describes what drives the present beyond itself into the future. This way of thinking about time arose out of the context of a present that was perceived as passing away so rapidly that it always appeared to be a time of transition, a past for a present that is coming out of the future. In Europe, the experience of the constant acceleration of social and cultural life since about 1830 led to the conclusion that every new expression of modernity is designed to surpass itself. In this sense, we can speak of a perception of the present as an extension of transition that is mainly oriented toward the future.[79] The understanding of past, present, and future produced by the Enlightenment goes hand in hand with the concept of linear time, envisioned as a dynamic that rapidly strives toward the future.

We have suggested, however, that eschatological imagery read against the background of the concept of linear time can become a repressive tool. The framework of rapture, the powerful end-times discourse with its careless attitude toward the future of the planet, turns our proposed understanding of eschatological imagination upside down.

Dualistic Thinking

We have already mentioned the second captivity of eschatological and apocalyptic thinking. It is a dualistic framework of interpretation that promotes a monolithic theology of disembodiment. This dualism consists of binary oppositions that privilege one of the poles over the other; for example, the spiritual, the linear, the new, and the individual over the material, the circular, the old, and the communal. We have shown how a dualistic framework has affected the understanding of the "new" covenant that is crucial for Eucharistic theology.

Various feminist theologians see a dualism at work especially in sacramental theologies that devalue the material world and thus also devalue crucial activities that are in many cases associated with women's lives. For instance, Debra Dean Murphy states that some of the ritual activities acknowledged as sacraments in various Christian traditions relate to the everyday activities of women:[80] baptism is related to giving birth, the Eucharist to the preparation and serving of meals, the anointing of the sick to women's care for the ill and the dying.[81] These activities, which in the social construction of female identities are designated as best fitting presumptively female nature, are devalued in the human realm, since they are judged as being less important, less powerful, and less effective in comparison. By devaluing these activities, a male priesthood could emerge from the ritualization, and consequent elevation, of "female activity" in public Christian worship. This devaluation serves a dualistic way of thinking that suggests that the spiritual (sacraments) is of higher significance than the material and/or natural world, that Sunday is more sacred than the other days of the week, and that consecrated bread is holier than "ordinary" bread. Instead of arguing for a holistic integration of the spiritual and the material world in which sacraments become an inbreaking and participation in the reign of God, this strategy substantiates a hierarchical dualism that privileges one side over another. This kind of understanding also supports the dualism that asserts that the sphere of public Christian sacramental worship is more significant than Jewish prayers connected to common and special meals consumed in the "private" sphere of the home.[82]

Dualistic thinking is present in many theologies of the Eucharist; it also pervades eschatology. Theologians like Rosemary Radford Ruether and Debra Dean Murphy[83] show that feminist theology has had little use for eschatology because its typical focus on the final consummation, the spiritual nature of heavenly existence, and the resurrection of the soul seemed to devalue life in *this* world. Eternal life has been envisioned as life without bodies and life without end. In this sense, the critique of a disembodied theology is directed toward Eucharistic as well as eschatological theologies.

Facing the *Wirkungsgeschichte* of eschatological thinking, Catherine Keller insists passionately on the integration of our material living conditions into eschatological reflections. She suggests that a counter-apocalyptic theology begin with the recognition that we stand

> in some particular fragility of place and time, with one's fragments of community and materialities of gender, and to love life: that is perhaps the only real basis of action against the end of the world. ... To theorize a counter-apocalyptic theology of relations is simply one among many possible strategies for stabilizing the unsentimental conditions of life lived in the mutuality difference affords, a way of conceiving a sustainable, just and lovable future by living it *already*. There is no way *there* but *here* and *now*. At the latest "end" of a history that crowds, consumes, and closes the present, the opening of the present as the only site of memory and hope grounds—without founding—the political work of disclosure.[84]

Another outcome of dualistic thinking with regard to eschatology is the binary opposition of the existential situation of the individual and the social dimension of the kingdom of God, which accentuates that we live in a web of interconnectedness within our communities. To highlight only one of these dimensions is to diminish the meaning of hope in the context of Christian faith. "The central images of hope stress in different ways that God's eschatological action relates to our whole relational being in all its dimensions and not only to one of them. The social metaphor of the Kingdom of God and the bodily metaphor of the resurrection make that abundantly clear."[85] Thus an eschatological theology of the Eucharist that overcomes this polarization will focus on the material and spiritual existence of the individual as well as on the body of Christ as the community of faith.

Colonized Imagination

The various forms of distorted eschatological imagination have a definite influence on how worshipers experience Eucharistic liturgies. Worship services are not protected spaces. What is at stake here is not only the interpretation and the reclamation of texts and tradition, but the ability to live into the fullness of Eucharistic life in our liturgical celebrations and in our everyday practices. Thus we need to ask what colonized imagination *does* to people.

June Goudey stresses the fact that our Eucharistic celebration can produce both a liberated and a colonized imagination. In general, she appreciates imagination as the faculty of seeing the physical world sacramentally, that is, as a place that has the potential to reveal divine mystery. However, she is also interested in the ways in which the imaginative processes that happen in ritual practices, such as the Eucharist, harm people.

> Strong forces within and without conspire against us. Because our unconscious minds fail to distinguish between image and reality, all images are treated as real, as are their consequences. Negative images limit our active engagement in the world by limiting our capacity to love. They also undermine our immune system and distort our relationships with others; in essence they restrict our ability to build well-being.[86]

In other words, imaginative processes fostered by ritual practice can also create a colonized imagination. The formal features[87] of a colonized imagination can be described as follows: it is fear-based, it constrains people's ability to enact what we have described as *seeing as*, and it restricts the ability to see the world and God from a variety of perspectives. It produces separation and isolation among people instead of connection and solidarity. It generates devaluing images of the self as well as low self-esteem. Colonized imagination produces the fear of falling out of the realm of orthodoxy and of the resultant rejection by those who are in power. In colonized imagination, God becomes

> the enemy within: the one who demands the destruction of the relational self in order to maintain the privileged position of dominance through fear. Psychic suffering occurs when our imagination becomes so damaged by fear that hopelessness rules, for it is then that the possibilities of God become subject to the *im*-possibilities of our personal deities.[88]

Colonized imagination can be developed and nurtured by individuals and their communities in a gradual process over many years. It can also be forcefully imposed from the outside through particular practices of church or state. Goudey refers to the experience of torture as one of the most drastic examples for colonized imagination.[88] How particular biblical images function in relation to psychic and communal well-being can only be answered by looking at the effects those imaginative practices have on particular individuals and communities. We assume, however, that fundamentalist teachings about the end-times produce colonized imagination par excellence. We see it as our task, as scholars and people of faith, to offer interpretations of biblical texts and liturgical traditions that might liberate imagination that is held captive, and that might inspire renewed practices. This is what we continue to do in the following chapters.

Chapter 2
THE EUCHARIST AS
ESCHATOLOGICAL MEAL

THE PRECEDING CHAPTER WAS DEVOTED to the task of presenting our approach to eschatology. Next we consider four dimensions of the Eucharist as eschatological meal. The first of these rests on the Jewish tradition of hope for God's gathering of those who are scattered. Against this background the Eucharist anticipates the feast of the renewed peaceful community of all nations. The second dimension includes the proclamation of the death of Jesus Messiah. Thus the act of eating together anticipates the end of all violence and oppression. The third dimension arises as the eschatological new covenant is made present in the Eucharist: we are bound to God's Torah. The fourth dimension comes from the event of the resurrection of the dead in the Eucharist. These four dimensions were all present in the Eucharistic celebrations of the early Christians, and they were continued in the history of Christian prayers and church rituals, sometimes in fragmentary form. We begin with a glance at this late Christian tradition and then return to review the New Testament material.

Christ Has Died, Christ Is Risen, Christ Will Come Again

Let grace come and this world pass away.[1]

Discovering the Eucharist as eschatological meal is not easy.[2] It is not only fundamentalist teaching and our response to it that holds our eschatological imagination captive. It is also the controversies the Reformation era brought forth. The reformers and their adversaries focused almost exclusively on how to speak about the presence of Christ in the Eucharist and how to interpret the sacrificial nature of Christ's death as it is remembered in Holy

Communion. Their debates left little room for eschatological dimensions of Eucharistic theology and liturgy.[3] Those debates have shaped our liturgical "felt sense" until today.[4]

In this chapter, we want to focus on the Eucharist as messianic meal. Messianic hope as a form of eschatological imagination is articulated in various ways. Eucharistic liturgies have been—from an early time—grounded in an eschatological perspective, in which the death of the *Kyrios* is proclaimed until he comes (1 Cor. 11:26).[5] The *Anaphorae of St. James,* the *Apostolic Constitutions,* the *Alexandrian St. Mark*—to name only a few—lift up the eschatological perspective: "until I come." The Aramaic acclamation *maranatha,* "LORD, come," already voiced in 1 Corinthians 16, makes its way into the *Didache.* In *Did.* 10:6 we find this intriguing dialogue between the president and the congregants:

> *President:* Let grace come and this world pass away.
> *People:*　　Hosanna to the son of David.
> *President:* If anyone is holy let him come. If anyone is not, let him
> 　　　　　　repent. Maranatha!⁶

As we have already suggested, the desire to see that this world might come to an end might be interpreted as a word of hope that longs for the end of suffering. The request "Let grace come and this world pass away" characterizes the Eucharist as it is depicted in the *Didache* as an eschatological meal. This longing is messianic hope that has the son of David as its center.

Over time the *maranatha* disappeared from Eucharistic liturgies. In Western and also in some Eastern anaphorae we find instead the *Benedictus qui venit,* with which the assembly blesses the One who comes in the name of the *Kyrios.*[7] The *Benedictus* references Matt. 21:9 in the context of Jesus' triumphal entry into Jerusalem. It is the cry of the people who greet Jesus as the Messiah: this man on a donkey who is going to be tortured and crucified. It is the cry of the people in the streets who desperately await him to come and rescue them.[8]

Another eschatological aspect is the hope for the gathering of those who are scattered. For instance, in the *Didache:*

> As this broken bread was scattered over the hillsides, and when brought together became one, so let your church be brought together from the ends of the earth into your kingdom.[9]

Many modern Eucharistic prayers also draw on this motif. For instance, in *The United Methodist Book of Worship* we find the following prayer:

> As the grains and grapes, once dispersed in the fields, are now united on this table in bread and wine, so may we and all your people be gathered from every time and place into the unity of your eternal household and feast at your table for ever.[10]

The desire for eschatological unity, that God might gather those who have been dispersed, is a classic motif.[11]

Many Eucharistic prayers express eager longing, restless anticipation of God's coming. They do so in an attitude that is not life-denying, not an escape from the material world of bodies and bread. In the *Anaphora of the Twelve Apostles,* for instance, we can hear the prayer that the consecrated gifts may

> be to all who partake of them for life and resurrection, for forgiveness of sins, and health of soul and body, and enlightenment of mind, and defense before the dread judgment-seat of your Christ.[12]

Health of body and soul, life and resurrection are not torn apart here or ordered in hierarchical and dualistic ways. Rather, they belong together. The health of the body is not excluded or dismissed.

The old liturgical acclamation "Christ has died, Christ is risen, Christ will come again" is an expression of eschatological hope as well. The memorial acclamation holds the memory of Jesus' death, celebrates Christ's resurrection, and longs for his coming. This acclamation is a condensed expression of the hope that grounds the messianic meal. In many Eucharistic liturgies, old and new, this acclamation is inserted between the anamnesis (from the Greek "remembrance") and the epiclesis (literally, "appeal" or "call"). The anamnesis portion of the Eucharistic prayers remembers Jesus' life and ministry, his death and resurrection, and in some cases his ascension. The epiclesis asks for the pouring out of the Holy Spirit on either the gathered people or the gifts of bread and wine or both, that they might be transformed into the body and blood of Christ. The acclamation "Christ has died, Christ is risen, Christ will come again" in its place between anamnesis and epiclesis embodies the inextricable connection of remembrance and hope. The memorial acclamation is attested in the *Anaphora of the Twelve Apostles.* It immediately follows the words of institution. The people are supposed to join together in the words: "Your death, Lord, we commemorate;

your resurrection we confess, and your second coming we await."[13] What follows is an anamnetic portion of the prayer in which the second coming and the last judgment are evoked along with Jesus' death, resurrection, and ascension. This form of the memorial acclamation is unique. It is not to be found in the medieval Roman rite or in the prayers of the Reformers. The acclamation reappears in the *Ordo Missae* of 1969.

Eucharistic prayers portray Jesus Christ as apocalyptic, eschatological, or messianic in various ways. In the *Apostolic Tradition*, we find Jesus depicted as an apocalyptic figure who fights the powers of death and the devil. In the Preface, immediately before the institution narrative, Jesus is presented as the one who stretches out his hands to release from suffering those who believe in God:

> And when he was betrayed to voluntary suffering that he might destroy death, and break the bonds of the devil, and tread down hell, and shine upon the righteous, and fix the limit, and manifest resurrection. . . .[14]

In the *Testamentum Domini*, which draws heavily on the *Apostolic Tradition*, these images are further intensified:

> When he was betrayed to voluntary suffering that he might set upright those who had stumbled, and find the lost, and give life to the dead, and destroy death, and break the bonds of the devil, and fulfill the counsel of the Father, and tread down hell, and open the way of life, and guide the righteous to light, and fix a limit, and lighten the darkness, and nurture babes, and manifest the Resurrection, he took bread. . . .[15]

Christ is shown here as the one who brings justice, raises the dead, and nurtures infants. Giving life to the dead and setting upright those who have stumbled is only possible when the forces that bring injustice and death are opposed: death has to be destroyed, the bonds of the devil have to be broken, and hell has to be trodden down. These are apocalyptic images that present Jesus as the victor in the cosmic battle against death and the devil.[16] Theologian Denny Weaver recognizes that the *Christus Victor* motif appears throughout the book of Revelation (especially chaps. 5–7): the slain lamb as the nonviolent conqueror who has earned the right to open the seals is celebrated as victorious over the forces that oppose the reign of God. In Rev. 5:12-17, the resurrection of Jesus Christ is revealed as the ultimate and definitive cosmic victory of the reign of God over the rule of Satan and the multiple evils he produces, including war and devastation, famine, pestilence, and natural disasters. We suggest understanding the Eucharistic prayers we have just referred to in the context of that tradition.

In what follows, we want to concentrate on how the New Testament speaks about the Eucharist as eschatological meal. We will offer interpretations of some New Testament passages that lift up the hope for the coming of Christ. Special attention will be given to the hope for the reuniting of the scattered people of God, the proclamation of the crucified Messiah and his coming, the understanding of "the new covenant in my blood," and the holy meal as the celebration of resurrection.

"I Will Not Drink Again of the Fruit of the Vine…"

In the Gospels of Mark and Matthew, Jesus' words at his last meal with his group of disciples end with a logion filled with both sorrow and promise: "Truly I tell you, I will never again drink of the fruit of the vine until that day when I drink it new in the kingdom of God" (Mark 14:25). The most important change in the parallel verse in Matthew (Matt. 26:29) is the addition of "with you." The disciples will participate with Jesus in the eschatological meal. But the saying in Mark's Gospel also implicitly contains the idea of this community banquet. These words of Jesus express hope for the messianic meal, something Jesus shared with many Jewish people. Again and again, in ever new ways, they indicated that, when heaven and earth are made new, God will invite the people of God, or all nations, to a great banquet. All will eat and drink equally well in God's reign. For Jesus, God's future is in his words, the messianic banquet, a future that is already tangible as he eats with his own. When we consider the relationship of the Eucharist to the messianic meal, it becomes important who takes part in it. Who belongs in this company, now and in the future, the company included in Jesus' words?

The Gospels of Mark and Matthew say that the "Twelve" celebrated this final meal with Jesus (Mark 14:17-18; Matt. 26:20-21). This description of the disciples means that the group itself represents the twelve tribes of Israel. Now—at the time of Jesus and the Gospel traditions—the twelve tribes are scattered. Awaiting the bringing home of the dispersed is an expression of messianic hope. That hope is made visible in the company of disciples. The texts are not the least bit interested in pointing to the idea that these are twelve men who can be identified by name. "The Twelve" are referred to even when in fact—without Judas—there could only be eleven of them (e.g., Matt. 19:28). The groups of disciples are presented androcentrically and in representative fashion in the Gospels. *Androcentric* means that the community is understood as being made up of women and men, even when only men are mentioned.[17] *Representative* means that the reference is not just to individuals, but to groups that represent something: the more intimate circle of Jesus' three or four most trusted disciples; the "Twelve" representing the eschatological significance of all discipleship as a sign of Israel's return; and the broader group (e.g., in Mark 4:10) who show the fundamental openness of the group of those who followed. Likewise, the Gospels do not distinguish consistently between the content of Jesus' sayings directed to his followers and those uttered publicly.[18]

So when Jesus celebrates his last meal in the circle of the Twelve, that expression is not to be thought of as limiting: it does not exclude women and the broader group of disciples. In Matt. 26:20, the company at the meal is called "the Twelve," (see especially pp. 118-22). But Matt. 26:26 calls the same group "disciples," a term that cannot be conceived as limited to twelve men. As the narrative continues, Jesus predicts to the same group that took part in the meal that they will flee (Matt. 26:30-35; Mark 14:26-31). "All" will be unfaithful because they have—legitimate—fear of being arrested like Jesus. This prediction does not apply only to a group understood to consist exclusively of the Twelve. It speaks of the whole group of disciples, men and women, as the rest of the narrative shows.

In the Gospel of Luke, the table company (22:14) is called "the apostles."[19] But here, too, the rest of the narrative presumes that those at table are the company of *all* who follow Jesus,[20] including women and a large group of people in general.

The nonexclusive or, better, inclusive character of the group of disciples is important for understanding Jesus' words about the messianic meal. The hope of eating and drinking in the reign of God is also a hope for community, one in which all God's children participate. The children of God in past generations, represented by the ancestors (Matt. 8:11; Luke 13:28), all the prophets (Luke 13:28), and every one of God's children in the present time—all are gathered at table. Excluded, however, are those whom God has found guilty of violating the Torah (Luke 13:27).[21] The messianic meal at God's table will unite the dispersed tribes of Israel with the peoples of the world (Matt. 8:11; Mark 13:27; even though the meal is not mentioned here, this saying of Jesus belongs within this context). The community at table stands for God's future, when all people, all nations, will eat together at God's table. This hope for the festival of the nations is linked with the expectation of the messianic meal, but also with the description of the group of disciples as "the Twelve." The reassembly of the dispersed people is associated with the expectation of a larger community of nations.

With these words of hope for the messianic meal (Mark 14:25 par.), Jesus takes his leave and speaks of the vision that has guided him. It is the vision of the reign of God. The messianic meal itself is only hinted at—just as everything said about the reign of God is framed in few words. But the idea that eating and drinking will take place in God's presence is surprising from our own perspective today. The Jesus tradition, in voicing this idea, is taking up a messianic hope that was broadly recognized in Judaism.[22] One example of this tradition: "On this mountain the LORD of hosts will make for all peoples a feast of rich food, a feast of well-aged wines, of rich food filled with marrow, of well-aged wines strained clear" (Isa. 25:6).

Why did people, in that time and in the New Testament period, picture the presence of God as a banquet, a great communion feast of all nations—or, more precisely, not pictured but hinted? In the relationship between God and human beings, eating and drinking are not incidentals. People, embodied people, are God's creation. Eating and drinking signify the ability to live, to participate in God's creation, and to praise God for the miracle of life. Drinking wine in company is a festival, the climax of life's joy.[23] Jesus' vision of the reign of God gives the nations, and human bodies, a place for universal justice, rejoicing, and community.

Why did Jesus speak of this vision during his last meal? The account of the Last Supper is not meant to be an "institution narrative,"[24] and yet it is clear that this meal reflects the common meals of the Jesus community. Jesus speaks of the future in light of his approaching death. That future is the nearness of the reign of God, lived in anticipation in the community meals of Jesus' disciples. These meals give a hint of what it will be like when the human world lives together in justice, while the dead are not forgotten. "God is a God of the living, not of the dead"—Abraham and all the generations of the deceased children of God share in the community of the resurrection (Mark 12:26-27). The Eucharist unites a community in which the dead are living, because God remembers them.

We find these same traditions in the Gospel of Luke, though in a different narrative form. Jesus begins the last meal with the words: "I have eagerly desired to eat this Passover with you before I suffer; for I tell you, I will not eat it[25] until it is fulfilled in the kingdom of God" (Luke 22:15-16). According to Luke, Jesus refers twice more, in the course of this last meal, to the messianic banquet: He interprets the first cup, which is found only in Luke's account,[26] by saying: "for I tell you that from now on I will not drink of the fruit of the vine until the kingdom of God comes" (Luke 22:18). In talking with the community at table after the meal, Jesus promises his disciples that they will have their part in the reign of God: "I confer on you, just as my Father has conferred on me, a kingdom, so that you may eat and drink at my table in my kingdom, and you will sit on thrones judging the twelve tribes of Israel" (Luke 22:29, 30). The hope that the twelve tribes of the dispersion will be gathered is linked with the messianic meal and the idea that the community of disciples will give judgment for their own people.[27] Here again, the messianic meal is the model for the community banquet before Jesus' suffering. Jesus' last meal, and with it the Eucharistic praxis of early Christianity, makes present the hoped-for future. It can be tasted and felt. During the meal, the participants can both long for and get a sense of what community and justice can be.

"Proclaim the Messiah's Death until He Comes"

In 1 Cor. 11:26, Jesus' words over the cup are translated, without formal alteration, into a word *about* Jesus, the *Kyrios*. Some later liturgies transformed it by having Jesus speak in the first person.[28] But here it is a Pauline commentary on Jesus' words at the supper. Two questions present themselves: Why is the common meal regarded as the place where Jesus' death is proclaimed? What does the coming of the *Kyrios* mean?

To take the second question first: *Kyrios* here unquestionably means Jesus as Messiah, since the statement refers to his death. Paul does not sharply distinguish the image of the coming of the *Kyrios* or the "day" of the *Kyrios* that is applied to Jesus[29] from the Day of the Lord or the coming of God. This talk of the "coming" (cf. 1 Cor. 4:5) for which people "wait" (1 Cor. 1:7) takes up the biblical and postbiblical expectation of the Day of the Lord (*yom YHWH*), which plays a central role in Paul's thinking. The day of the coming of the Messiah or the parousia (1 Cor. 15:23), his "arrival," is a day of divine judgment and universal salvation. For Paul, as for the New Testament as a whole, it is inappropriate to systematize mythic concepts—for example, to ask "in what *sequence* will the reign of God, the coming of God, the parousia of Christ and the day of the Messiah come?" It is equally meaningless to try to bring notions of the final judgment (by God or Christ) into a narrative or temporal sequence with ideas about God's salvation. In the same way, 1 Cor. 15:23-28 must not be read as an attempt to systematize such ideas. All these concepts derive from biblical language about God and are briefly indicated from time to time. In each context it is clear what is being said. Likewise, the perspective that hopes for God's future can change the present may not be forced into a system. In short, we can say that Mark 14:25, Jesus' words about the messianic meal, and 1 Cor. 11:26, Paul's words about the coming of the Messiah, express the same expectation of God's salvation for the world, but each contains different mythic ideas. The eschatological language resists a dogmatic or religious-historical/motif-historical systematization. It is poetic language for hope toward justice and the redemption of the whole world. This poetic language comes from Scripture and postbiblical Judaism. It cannot be separated from the life of the people who spoke it.

The day of the Messiah is a day of judgment (1 Cor. 1:8; 3:13; 5:5) and of universal salvation that changes the present of those who believe: "For God says: 'At an acceptable time I have listened to you, and on a day of salvation I have helped you'" (Isa. 49:8). "See, now is the acceptable time; see, now is the day of salvation" (2 Cor. 6:2).

The appeal for the "coming" of God or the Messiah, waiting for the coming of God or the arrival[30] of the Messiah—these are expressions of a relationship with God. God is the future in which suffering ends, in which the injustice of some people against others ceases, in which all nations live together in peace. "Until he comes"—thus briefly and succinctly, almost as a hint, the common meal is interpreted as the present experience of being saved and as God's promise. The biblical tradition is capable of using these kind of hints because people are at home in the riches of this language about God.

Paul here expresses just as succinctly what the primitive Christian prayer *maranatha* says: "Our Lord, come." Paul concludes his first letter to Corinth with the appeal to "greet one another with a holy kiss," to curse Jesus' enemies, and finally to call out: *maranatha*, "our Lord, come."[31] As with calling God *abba* in Rom 8:16, the ordinary Aramaic language of the first group of disciples, and of Jesus himself, has become liturgical language even for people who do not speak Aramaic. In the Corinthian community, Greek was spoken. We can suppose that the conclusion of the first letter to Corinth adopts liturgical elements from that community's assembly, in which the letter is to be read aloud at the time when the Messiah's meal is celebrated. Likewise, the book of Revelation ends with the appeal to the one who comes: "Come, Lord Jesus" (Rev. 22:20)—come, Jesus, to whom we belong and from whom we expect universal justice. That is how the content of the word *Lord* here and in the Aramaic cry of *maranatha* can be described.

Why is the common meal regarded as the place where Jesus' death is proclaimed? Jesus' words at the supper repeatedly refer to his death, to his body "for you," to his blood, and to his memory (1 Cor. 11:24, 25). Moreover, the Eucharistic meal is understood to be a repetition of Jesus' last meal before his Passion (1 Cor. 11:23). Jesus was crucified by a Roman cohort's execution squad in approximately the year 33 CE. The juridical and political responsibility for the execution belongs to the prefect at the time (26–36 CE.), Pilate. Jewish leadership groups worked with the Roman authorities. Rome had clear political interests that were expressed in this execution, as in many comparable crucifixions. Political unrest in the Jewish territories, which from Rome's perspective were borderlands on the eastern edge of its sphere of interest, had to be nipped in the bud.

But from Rome's point of view, this execution turned out to be a mistake. The messianic movement that had gathered around Jesus was only briefly discouraged by his death. Their common meal became a place to remember Jesus' death. As often as the meal was celebrated, Rome's vicious deed was named as such. The remembrance of Jesus' death gave Rome's imperial oppression the name that unmasked it. It did not bring peace, but rather death. And yet, at the same time, hope itself was given a name: Jesus, Messiah, Lord, come: Judge the peoples in righteousness and unite them at God's table.

Proclaiming the death of the Messiah means telling the truth about human violence and, at the same time, seeing beforehand how it will come to an end. It cannot endure. In the Christian traditions of the Western world from which we come, the proclamation of Jesus' death is encumbered with notions of individual guilt and an orientation toward death. But those are not the ideas of early Christianity. It is no accident that 1 Cor. 11:26 links the meal, as proclamation of Christ's death, with the expectation of his coming. When the Messiah comes, he will put an end to "every ruler and every authority and power" (1 Cor. 15:24).[32] That is the deathly power of those who crucified him (1 Cor. 2:6). It is the very proclamation of the death of Jesus in the common meal that announces the end of violence that kills and oppresses human beings. The simple fact that people, through their common meal, bring a crucified man into their midst, already meant at that time the naming of that violence as injustice and anticipating its end. The proclamation of that death happens in the action of the meal with its interpretive words relating it to Jesus' death.

"The New Covenant in My Blood"

The words with which Jesus interprets the cup are found in two different versions: (1) "this (cup) is my blood of the covenant, which poured out for many" (Mark 14:24, for the most part identical to Matt. 26:28, which adds "for the forgiveness of sins"), and (2) "This cup is the new covenant in my blood" (1 Cor. 11:25, largely identical to Luke 22:20, which adds "poured out for you"). Since in the preceding chapter we have made clear how necessary it is to give an eschatological interpretation to the covenant theology of the Eucharist, at this point we need, from that point of view, to take a closer look at how these covenant statements are formulated.

In the popular mind, and in some periods of the history of the Eucharist, we find a simple identification of the red wine in the cup with the shed blood of Jesus—from which arose the widespread association of the sacrament with drinking blood. Sometimes this association is refuted by the correct observation[33] that such a notion was unthinkable in a Jewish context, against the background of the First Testament's prohibition on using the blood of animals for nourishment (Gen. 9:4; cf. Lev. 3:17; 17:10-14; Deut. 12:23). The accusation that human blood is drunk at the Eucharist[34] can be found even in antiquity, proposed by critics of the Eucharist and of Christianity, but it was always seen by the Christians as slanderous. The association is not present in the New Testament. For Paul, and in the Gospel of Luke, the interpretive words do not apply to the wine, but to the cup and the cup ritual, the prayer that encompasses the giving and drinking. This is the probable interpretation of Mark and Matthew as well. The demonstrative neuter pronoun at the beginning of the verse (Matt. 26:28; Mark 14:24) in any case refers back to the cup (*potērion*, neuter), not to the wine, which is not even mentioned. The counterargument is: "The reference to the cup can only mean its contents, the wine."[35] But both these interpretive sayings are to be understood as interpretation of the ritual, and not as referring to the elements of bread and wine with the association of eating flesh and drinking blood. The reference of the demonstrative pronoun should thus not be seen as applying directly to the relationship cup/blood of the covenant, but rather as encompassing the whole cup ritual.

It is simply inappropriate to ask of the New Testament text whether the historical Jesus could have spoken of his death and the new covenant in these interpretive words. They speak of Jesus Messiah, whom they identify with the man Jesus of Nazareth, but without any "historical" application like that of the question regarding the historical Jesus that has prevailed since the nineteenth century. Likewise, the Last Supper accounts in the Gospels speak from the perspective of early Christian Eucharistic practice.

A number of different traditions come together in the words of interpretation in the cup ritual: (1) the tradition of a covenant between God and Israel, sealed with the blood of bulls (Exod. 24:8 in Mark 14:22; Matt. 26:28); (2) the hope for a new covenant between God and Israel, as in Jer. 31:31-34 (in 1 Cor. 11:25; Luke 22:22); (3) the history of Jewish martyrs, women and men, whose violent death at the hands of imperial occupation forces frees the people from their sins before God (that is how these mar-tyrdoms were interpreted). Martyrdom breaks the power of Israel's ene-mies. In spite of the difference in formulations, these three traditions are present in every version of the words of interpretation.

Our concern here is not to engage with the sacrificial tradition, but to consider the vision that is bound up with the hope for God's covenant with Israel. However, the content of that vision is so intimately connected to the Jewish theology of martyrdom that we need first to present an exam-ple from that tradition in order to contextualize the hope for the (new) covenant. The subject of that hope is Israel, suffering under oppression. The Synoptic Gospels say that the blood of the covenant will be shed for "the many" (Mark; Matthew),[36] for "you" (Luke). In both, the reference is to Israel. The hope for Israel is in these texts, as in other Jewish texts, to be interpreted simultaneously as a hope for all nations.[37]

The Septuagint, the Greek version of the First Testament, includes a number of additions to the book of Daniel, among them the Prayer of Azariah.[38]

8 [31]	. . . all that you have brought upon us,
	and all that you have done to us,
	you have done by a true judgment.
9 [32]	You have handed us over to our enemies . . .
	and to an unjust king, the most wicked in all the world.
10 [33]	And now we cannot open our mouths;
	we, your servants who worship you, have become a
	shame and a reproach.
11 [34]	For your name's sake do not give us up forever,
	and do not annul your covenant.
12 [35]	Do not withdraw your mercy from us,
	for the sake of Abraham your beloved
	and for the sake of your servant Isaac
	and Israel your holy one,
13 [36]	to whom you promised
	to multiply their descendants like the stars of heaven. . . . [39]

Azariah is one of the three Jewish men in the furnace, in the story told in the book of Daniel. They have refused to worship the golden image erected by the powerful King Nebuchadnezzar. They remain faithful to the God of Israel, even if it cost them their lives (Dan. 3:1-20). They "yielded up their bodies" (Dan. 3:28). So the king had them thrown into the furnace of fire. Azariah's prayer in the furnace is that of a martyr, in the literary form of a "community lament."[40] The people's "we" and the "we" of the martyrs commingle. This is about the rescue of the people. After this, the book of Daniel tells how the three men were saved by God—as the rescue of the nation from the "furnace of fire."[41] All the elements of the interpretive words over the cup are contained in the Prayer of Azariah. It can be read as if it were being prayed by the Eucharistic community.

The people at prayer are lamenting that Israel, in their time, is without a king and has no Temple for sacrifice (3:38). They ask that God will accept their sacrifice "as if" they were bringing animals as their offering (3:39, 40).

This prayer is only loosely connected to the narrative in the book of Daniel, but it is an exemplary expression of the people's relationship with God in their oppressed situation, when martyrs are dying because they try to prevent the subjection of the people to a foreign power, which will destroy Israel's bond with its God. Their sacrifice[42] in the metaphorical sense makes resistance visible and frees the people from the power of their enemies over their hearts and hopes. The new covenant that Jesus has in mind when he speaks the words over the cup is the old covenant with Israel, which God maintains even now, when the people are utterly cast down.[43] It means God's mercy, the mercy God promised to the ancestors, the expression of the promise that the people will have a great progeny and a future. The hope for the covenant, for God's mercy, includes God's judgment, which falls upon the people because of their faithlessness: war and oppression. But this will come to an end.

The words "This cup is the new covenant in my blood" (1 Corinthians and Luke), as well as the version in Mark and Matthew, "my blood of the covenant," promise the suffering people that God will keep the covenant, considering that covenant as sealed with a sacrifice in the martyr's death of Jesus.

Since the new covenant has been interpreted in Christian tradition since the mid-second century as a covenant with the church that has replaced the old covenant with Israel,[44] there is need for a radical rethinking of the Eucharistic covenant theology. The new covenant is the old covenant with Israel renewed; in no possible sense of the word is covenant an ecclesiological concept. How, then, is God's affirmation that the death of Jesus Messiah effects the preservation of God's covenant with Israel to be related to the nations? People who come to Israel from the nations enter into Israel's obligation to God's Torah. They become proselytes.[45] The same is true for the church of the "Gentiles." It is equally subject to the God of Israel. The covenant, as a covenant with Israel, contains an eschatological promise for all nations and the invitation to listen, now, to God's voice. The clear consequence is the obligation to live and practice the Torah. We can, with Krister Stendahl, summarize this by saying that through Jesus members of the Gentile church have become "honorary Jews."[46]

The words over the cup speak of hope and promise for oppressed Israel. God has sealed the covenant anew. Gentile Christians enter equally into this obligation and promise. The covenant theology of the Eucharist points the Christian community to the Torah. It enters, with Israel, into God's renewed covenant, which promises community between Israel and the nations. Now this covenant promise can be made real in a common life according to the Torah.

The Eucharist as Experience of Resurrection

Eucharistic texts in the New Testament are often read with a focus on Jesus' death, not with a hermeneutic of resurrection. "In all honesty, we have to admit that we do not often feel altogether embraced by the Risen One at table."[47] But what does "the body of Christ" in the Eucharistic formula mean in the light of a hermeneutic of resurrection? And what does it mean that the participants have community (*koinōnia*) with the body of Christ and so become "one bread" and "one body" (1 Cor. 10:16-17)?

The words over the bread are "this is my body" (*sōma*; Mark 14:22; Matt. 26:26), or "this is my body for you" (1 Cor. 11:24) or "this is my body, which is given for you" (Luke 22:19). My body "for you" means: for your salvation. "Given for you" need not refer to the martyr's self-gift, but can mean: I give (see Luke 22:19, the same verb) you this bread as my body for your salvation. Reference is often made to the words over the cup in order to interpret the body of Christ as a "body of death,"[48] as the body of the Crucified. Certainly, the reference of the Eucharist as a whole to Jesus' death is clear enough, but it is striking that the words over the bread need not be read in this way. Add to this the theological clarity with which, throughout the New Testament tradition, the Messiah's death and resurrection are never separated. Whatever concerns Christ's death concerns also Christ's resurrection, and the resurrection of all women and men and of the whole creation. We look at Christ's death through the experience of his and our own resurrection, for the Risen One is "the firstborn within a large family" (Rom. 8:29), the firstfruits, the first harvest of the dead (1 Cor. 15:20, 23). In what sense do the words over the bread refer to Christ's resurrection, the resurrection of the dead, and the renewal of all creation? John 6:54 interprets the Eucharist in terms of the hope of resurrection, and it is applied in that way in Christian liturgies.[49] But here we want to ask a broader question about the relationship between the words over the bread and the resurrection.

For Paul, the community of the faithful with the body of Christ is the basis for life in the fullest sense: "God raised the Lord and will also raise us by his power. Do you not know that your bodies are members of Christ? . . . anyone united to the Lord becomes one spirit with him" (1 Cor. 6:14-15, 17). Communion with the Risen One is a bodily community. Paul does not even recoil from a comparison with sexual communion. In the concrete context the problem is that men in the Corinthian community are endangering this bodily communion with Christ by going to prostitutes.[50] The communion with the Risen One is not merely compared with "being one body," but is literally so: Believers are members of the body of the Risen One; they themselves are risen.[51] They are the temple of the power of God's spirit dwelling within them (1 Cor 6:10). They belong to the body of Christ, and that changes their own "bodiliness." We could also say that their bodies are changed, because the Greek word *sōma* refers to the physical body, not to a bodily existence outside the present reality.[28] The power of the divine Spirit that dwells in the bodies of those who adhere to Christ effects a radical change in their lives. People who serve death and violence and are used as instruments by them (Rom. 6:12-14) become risen people. The Eucharistic words over the bread concern this communion in the body of the Risen One, which is also the body of the Crucified. Eucharist, like Baptism, is a ritual that expresses this radical transformation of body and life. Bread is eaten and the meal becomes the festival of the renewal of life. That renewal is made present in the Eucharist; at the same time it is beheld, as in a vision, as the renewal of creation and the resurrection of the dead. It is experience and hope—and it has consequences for daily life.

The radicality of the renewal of life taking place in the Christ-community of the body is described in 1 Corinthians 15: What is perishable (*phthora*, 15:42)[53] becomes imperishable before God; what is dishonored (*atimia*, 15:43) becomes God's glory; what is weakness (*astheneia*, 15:43) becomes God's power. In the midst of the destruction of life by the structures of the "world" of the Roman Empire, of worldwide death and sin, there is born new life. This new life can be sensed in bodies and in a way of life; God's presence will bring it to fullness in God's future. Ordinarily, 1 Corinthians 15 is read with a hermeneutic of linear time and individualism: Individuals will rise only after physical death. The *sōma pneumatikon*/spiritual body (1 Cor. 15:44) is not a body, but the nonbodily risen existence of the individual. Claudia Janssen has convincingly shown that the death that must be died before resurrection (1 Cor. 15:36) is death to sin, not physical death. Paul speaks of God's future as resurrection in the bodies of the faithful. These bodies are bodies-in-community, now under the conditions of structural sin, and in God's future as well. The resurrection community is a new creation (2 Cor. 5:17) and includes the liberation of all people and of the earth (Rom. 8:21). When Paul quotes Jesus' words over the bread in 1 Cor. 11:24, Jesus' body is the body of the Crucified (1 Cor. 1:18) and Risen One (1 Cor. 15:12-22). Communion with this body of Christ is experienced in the Eucharist and so the Eucharist becomes the place where resurrection is experienced. In this eschatology, present and future are inseparable.

In the Gospels, as in Paul's writings, the Eucharist is in this sense an experience of resurrection. Jesus, who gives the bread, is the Crucified and Risen One. Luke 24:30-31 tells how a tiny community of two disciples, arriving at Emmaus, invites an unknown traveler into their house and to their meal. "He took bread, blessed and broke it, and gave it to them. Then their eyes were opened, and they recognized him." Jesus' last meal is, in the narrative framework of the Gospels, the meal before Jesus' death, but a separation between the "historical" Jesus and the Risen One is not in accordance with the Gospels' intent. The Last Supper itself is narrated in such a way that the eyes of those who hear the story are opened and they see the Risen One. In the Gospels, the faithful are themselves "children of the resurrection" (Luke 20:36), for God is a God of the living, not of the dead (Mark 12:27 par.). That is how God was revealed to Moses, saying: "I am the God of Abraham, the God of Isaac, and the God of Jacob" (Exod. 3:6). These words of Jesus about the God of Israel exegete Exod. 3:6 with the equally biblical idea that God calls the dead to life (1 Sam. 2:6; Pss. 71:20, 139:8; Deut. 30:20; 32:39). God is life, and in relationship to God, death, that misanthropic power, is overcome: "I shall not die, but I shall live, and recount the deeds of the LORD" (Ps. 118:17).[54] But the Western passion for order, with its corresponding linear notion of time, is not content to trust the God of the living; it wants to know with certainty: Have the ancestors already been raised? What is the relationship between their resurrection and the resurrection of the dead in apocalyptic, at the eschatological judgment? Is not the general resurrection of the dead something altogether new and different from hope in the God of the living? These questions are simply inappropriate to the First Testament and to the New Testament.

In the same way, the martyrdom texts of postbiblical Judaism see the death of the martyrs as birth to new life, and their death and resurrection as life-giving power for the whole people.[55] As a representative example of the overall biblical and postbiblical idea of God as the God of the living, we cite here from the *Shemoneh Esre*: "You, O Lord, are mighty forever, You are the Reviver of the dead, You are greatly able to save. You sustain the living in lovingkindness, You revive the dead with great compassion, You support the falling, heal the sick, set free the bound and keep faith with those who sleep in the dust. . . . Blessed are You, O Lord, who revives the dead."[56]

The whole New Testament should be read from the perspective of the Eucharist as the place where resurrection is experienced. The people whose voices are heard in these texts know themselves, in community, as the body of the Risen One. Sharing in the body of Christ as the Risen One can be perceived with the senses through the presence of the divine Spirit in the bodies present, and in the act of eating together. This experience of resurrection becomes invisible when Jesus' death is isolated. The violent destruction of life, as Jesus suffered it, does not create an experience of salvation. Isolating the death of Jesus results in a legitimation of his murder by the imperial power. Christ's resurrection and the Eucharist as ritual of resurrection—these are life's alternatives to the murder of Jesus and the structures of death that are visible in his death. Therefore in the Eucharist we experience the joy of resurrection.

"Let Your Church Be Gathered into Your Reign": Eucharist in the *Didache*

As we look back at the four dimensions of the eschatological meal in the New Testament, we can see the significance of the Eucharistic community for the church as a whole. This community sustains a living hope for the communion of all peoples. In looking at the Eucharistic community, we come to understand the church eschatologically. The early Christian writing called the *Didache*, "The Teaching of the Twelve Apostles," developed this eschatological vision of the church very clearly in its Eucharistic prayers. Hence we need to look at these prayers again (see above), because they help us to name the church's hope still more exactly and to recognize the Jewish roots of that hope.

The *Didache* is a church document from the beginning of the second century addressed to proselytes (6:2, 3)[57] in a non-Jewish environment. The *Didache* appears to polemicize against individual Jewish groups, but not against Judaism as such.[58]

This text reveals the existence of Christian communities that were not Jewish in origin and yet were thoroughly rooted in Jewish tradition. They regard themselves as those who have come to Israel through God's grace, a community who take nothing away from Israel and inherit nothing. "The holy vine of David" has been revealed to the community through Jesus (9:2). The holy vine of David is Israel, the chosen of God (Psalm 80; Jer. 2:21). The text does not say "*we* are now 'the holy vine.'" "Israel," the vine, has been revealed, like "life" (9:3) and "knowledge and faith and immortality" (10:2). "Israel" is the people of God, into whose salvation the God of Israel incorporates people from among the nations. As in Mark 13:27 and Matt. 24:31, here is hope for the eschatological healing of the community of nations: the gathering of those who are scattered. Like the hope for the restoration of the community of the twelve tribes, so also the hope for the gathering of those scattered throughout the nations (the diaspora) is an idea that was and remained proper to Israel, but then, as if by its very nature, incorporates the nations as well. Nothing is said here that in any way questions Israel's special relationship to its God. It is the ancient vision of Isa. 56:6-8:

> 6   And the foreigners who join themselves to the LORD,
>   to minister to him, to love the name of the LORD,
>   and to be his servants,
>   all who keep the sabbath, and do not profane it,
>   and hold fast my covenant—
> 7   these I will bring to my holy mountain,
>   and make them joyful in my house of prayer;
>   their burnt offerings and their sacrifices
>   will be accepted on my altar;
>   for my house shall be called a house of prayer
>   for all peoples.
> 8   Thus says the Lord GOD,
>   who gathers the outcasts of Israel,
>   I will gather others to them
>   besides those already gathered.

Didache 14:3 appropriately cites Mal. 1:11 in this same sense.

As we already saw when we discussed the covenant theology of the early Christian Eucharist, the Gentile church at this time was not seen to be separated from Israel in any negative sense. It has received honorary membership, in Krister Stendahl's sense.[59] Jesus Messiah has shown it the way to the God of Israel. Israel's ancient hope for the healing of the community of nations is expressed again here.

The *Didache* clearly expresses the eschatological character of this church of the Gentiles in communion with Israel: "As this (broken bread) was scattered upon the mountains, but was brought together and became *one* bread, so let thy Church (*ekklēsia*) be gathered together from the ends of the earth into thy kingdom (*basileia*)! For thine is the glory and the power forever!" (*Did.* 9:4). The breaking of bread in the Eucharist indicates the wholeness of the bread and the healing of the dispersion. After the meal, the prayer continues: "Remember, Lord, thy Church, to deliver it from all evil and to make it perfect in thy love, and gather it together in its holiness from the four winds to thy kingdom which thou hast prepared for it" (10:5). This language, like Isaiah 56, contains no imperialistic undertones— neither toward Israel nor toward the Gentile world. The Eucharist is the feast of imagining the longed-for community of nations. The blessing of bread and wine (9:3, 2) connect to the Jewish blessing of God at meals and so interpret the Eucharist as a festival of creation: "Thou, Lord Almighty, didst create all things for thy Name's sake, and didst give food and drink to human beings for their enjoyment, that they might give thanks to thee, but us hast thou blessed with spiritual food and drink and eternal light through thy Child" (10:3).

The texts of the *Didache*, like the meal texts from the New Testament, illuminate the crucial point as if under a magnifying glass: It is clear that the Jewish blessing of bread and wine furnishes the basis for the Eucharistic words. It is easy to miss this in the brief indications in the meal narratives, "he said the blessing. . ." (1 Cor. 11:24, 25 "also"; Mark 14:22, 23 and its synoptic parallels). It is obvious that the Eucharist is a meal, not only the symbolic indication of a meal. *Didache* 10:1 speaks explicitly of being satisfied with food. The "spiritual" meal is a holy meal that satisfies. Those who pray there rejoice in the creation, which brings forth bread and wine and all the foods not named that may be included in the word "bread." The meal revealed in the *Didache* is often incorrectly regarded as an *agapē* meal (or something similar), to be distinguished from the Eucharist proper. Rather, it shows us how deeply the Christian hermeneutic of early Christianity was shaped by later Christian developments, such as the separation of meal and Eucharist. The Eucharistic prayers in the *Didache* could serve us today as teachers, to show us how to renew the Eucharist, a joy in creation, focusing on eating as the gift of God, and on human bodies. This is how the church will become the place of eschatological hope and will not remain trapped in the prison of a long-shattered ecclesiastical imperialism. In view of the suffering of the nations from military power, the Eucharist can be the place where we can practice hope for the healing of the community of nations.

Chapter 3
THE BREAD OF LIFE
IN TWO ECONOMIES

THE EUCHARIST CAN BE UNDERSTOOD as an eschatological meal that invites participation in the body of Christ as a resurrection experience. This celebration of resurrection has fragmentary character. It is a foretaste. It is not triumphalist. When it breathes sacramental permeability, it will release a sense of joy that connects with the world as the body of God. It will not suppress the realities of life; rather, it will juxtapose faith in Christ as the bread of life with the ambiguous "bread realities" that surround us.

In this chapter we consider what it means to speak of the bread of life in two economies and how the Eucharistic life is entangled in it. We reflect on the market economy and the economy of grace,[1] for example, God's economy, as it shines through the market exchange. We assume that these are not two separate realms; they rather influence and affect each other. When we come to the table, we come as people who suffer or profit to different degrees from the market exchange economy. It affects all of us; we cannot withdraw from it. We will speak about eating disorders and global food politics, about Jesus' hunger, and about the temptation to live by a "bread alone economy." The contemporary perspectives as well as the biblical stories point to the destructive effects of alienated eating practices and hunger. With the story of the multiplication of the bread we will attend to the eschatological imagination of a starving people. Reflecting on these issues in the context of the Eucharist, we point to sacramental permeability. We draw connections between all these ambiguous experiences with food and its absence. Finally, we are interested in the deeper economic logic that shapes our choices and how we see ourselves as economic agents: we will dig deeper into the imagination of the *Homo oeconomicus*, which is hostile to eschatological imagination. We will ask how liturgical actions such as thanksgiving, returning of gifts, money collections, and interceding hold the potential to overcome the mimicry of market exchange.

The Bread of Death: Dieting America and Global Food Politics[2]

... the enjoyment of food
(and the rituals that codify and often intensify that enjoyment)
is knit into the very fabric of society,
acting as a civilizer,
a bond between peoples,
a celebration of life itself.[3]

One cannot deny the bodily responses to starvation,
and that is part of the reason, some nights,
I sat in the basement of the dorm;
locked in a bathroom, catching myself in the mirror
as I stuffed candy bars, chips,
like a vending machine
anything into my mouth,
and then threw it up.[4]

For while fifty million Americans
are currently dieting to lose weight,
nearly half that many are collecting food stamps
and/or standing in line at the local food pantry.[5]

Eating and drinking can be a delicious pleasure or, as the French chef Jacques Pepin says, it can be a celebration of life itself. It can give joy. Sharing a table and sharing a meal can provide community and deepen friendships. Eating together can reveal the sacramentality of life, our dependence on sun and rain, fertile soil and the mystery of growing life, the labor of people we do not know. The very profane act of eating and drinking can disclose the goodness of God:

"God pervades the world in the same way as honey in the comb," wrote Tertullian. Eating is the most intimate, sensual act; it is how the world enters into us and how we become part of the world. We also share food with others; we give pleasure to others and their delight transforms us. Food is revelatory of the goodness and the joy of the earth; it is also how we come to taste the language of grace and love; it is how we come to know community. Food opens up in us the visceral channels of knowledge. It enables us to experience love before we have a name for it. God comes to feed us, to fill us, to love us. We know grace first through our bodies."[6]

Eating is a fundamental necessity for the preservation of human life, yet it is also experienced as a menace to life. Eating and drinking embody sacramental permeability but also the shadows of alienation. Psychoanalytical research focuses on this ambiguity from the very first moments when we begin to breathe. On the one hand, the first experiences of eating can mediate for the newborn the deepest feeling of security and support. Eating and being fed can be considered the original form of affection. This sentiment can also be applied to early childhood eating habits, when the child cannot recognize the boundaries between subject and object but rather feels oneness with the provider, who is most often the mother. On the other hand, the refusal of nourishment provides the deepest experiences of despair and subjection. Hunger is a total, elemental, and basic experience. It is an experience of urgent need and can have brutalizing effects because it constricts and diminishes human imagination; it "cuts off the freedom to transcend, which is human."[7]

Understanding these experiences in early childhood as formative for the human person allows us to recognize why nourishment is connected with rituals of holy eating in various religions and cultures throughout the world. It can be a key to understanding the ambiguous symbolization of death and life taking place in rituals of holy eating.[8] This psychoanalytic dimension belongs to the fabric of our imagination along with awareness of the sociopolitical realities surrounding nutrition that produce eating disorders on a large scale as well as unjust, unecological food production, distribution, and consumption.

The ambiguity of people's experiences is at hand. Many North Americans no longer have access to the pleasure of eating. The struggle with food consumption can lead us on a horrible journey. For many, eating appears to be a dangerous and shameful activity, an obstacle, especially for women and girls, to the search for the perfect body:

> In particular, consumer-media culture's prevailing ideals of womanhood, along with the self-correcting disciplines that these ideals inspire (e.g., dieting and exercise), are the icons and rituals by means of which a vast number of girls and women organize and manage their daily hopes and fears. For many of them, a network of symbols, beliefs, and rituals centering on bodily appetites and appearances constitutes an ultimate frame of reference—a "secular" salvation myth—despite its seeming banality.[9]

Michelle Lelwica, in her study on the spiritual dimensions of eating problems, draws the conclusion that the commodification of the female body according to super-exaggerated standards of slenderness becomes the center of the desire to be saved and to find ultimate meaning in life. Lelwica claims that those who struggle with bulimia and anorexia do not represent an isolated minority. Rather, women and girls who have to deal with extreme forms of eating disorders reflect a larger problem deeply ingrained in society. The formation of the female body through dieting is supposed to give life meaning and direction. These body practices and images function in a quasi-religious way.[10] Counting calories, indulging in "Culture Lite," is accompanied by a powerful call to exercise and fitness.[11] Lelwica captures the religious dimension of these cultural phenomena in an ad for running shoes in the magazine *Avia*:

> This is not about guilt. It's about joy. Strength. The revival of the spirit. I come here seeking redemption in sweat. And it is here that I am forgiven my sinful calories. Others may never understand my dedication. But for me, fitness training is something much more powerful than exercise. It is what keeps my body healthy. It is what keeps my mind clear. And it is where I learn the one true lesson. To believe in myself. *Avia*.[12]

This obvious usage of traditional Christian language is infused in these dieting and fitness rituals: redemption in sweat, joy instead of guilt, and the forgiveness of sinful calories can be found in excessive fitness programs. The faith that is generated is self-referential: believing in oneself is the goal. This explicit connection between dieting, fitness, and salvation also prevails in many evangelical circles. R. Marie Griffith analyzes, for instance, how the teachings of the evangelical Christian women's organization Women Aglow reproduce classic norms of female slenderness. Now it is only God and not the male society that needs to be pleased. A thin body proves faith in God and obedience to God's demands. Jesus is introduced as someone who overcame carnal appetite; he becomes the savior of women by serving as a model for self-control and modesty in food consumption.[13]

In some cases anorexic women refer to mystics who had refused to eat in order to prepare for special revelations. The desire to "know what was beyond ordinary living" is expressed:

> I wanted to be praised for being special ... to be held in awe for what I was doing. I found out that it was hard to be recognized by other people as an enlightened person. ... I didn't want anybody to know it, but I was

convinced that one day I would get the mystical insight—I was waiting for the day of the great Revelation.[14]

In addition to these plain statements we find many examples from the rites of dieting America that do not use explicitly Christian language. Lelwica quotes the "vow" of the diet club Happy Losers in which dieting becomes a divinized activity:

> The diet is within me; I shall not cheat
> It leadeth me to choose the legal food whenever I have the urge to eat
> Yea though I may wish to eat sweets or cake
> I shall eat them never
> For the diet is with me
> And I shall reach my goal
> And remain slim forever. Amen.[15]

The struggle with eating disorders and the obsession with dieting and the perfect body stand in a crass tension with the growing poverty in the United States:

> Despite the relatively strong economy that had until 2001 produced a boon for millions of citizens, there remained 31 million people in the United States who experience either food insecurity or actual hunger. *Food insecurity* is defined as lack of access to adequate supplies of nutritional food acquired without recourse to emergency resources like food pantries and soup kitchens.[16]

In the United States, as in many other countries, issues of poverty and food consumption, such as food insecurity, malnutrition, and hunger are intimately connected with racism. According to the U.S. Census Bureau, the rates of food insecurity and the estimated percentage of people exhibiting moderate and severe hunger are two to three times higher for African Americans and Hispanics.[17] "Amartya Sen has shown that the mortality rate for U.S. African Americans is higher than the mortality rate for people in China or the state of Kerala in India. The mortality rate for African American men in Harlem is higher than the death rate for men in Bangladesh."[18] Issues of race and food consumption have to be looked at in a systemic way. Poverty and racism are intertwined; they have an influence on all basic human needs such as nutrition, access to housing, education, healthcare, safe ecological environments, and so forth.

If we look globally, hunger is still an issue of overwhelming magnitude: 828 million people on this globe are hungry, malnourished, and in danger of starvation. "Every day more then 31,000 children die from hunger and other related, preventable causes. Nearly 160 million children are malnourished worldwide."[19]

The 1980s and 1990s were an era in which food production increased worldwide while the price of food decreased. This development, however, did not help to solve the severe issue of hunger: "Hunger today is less a problem of general food availability than of access."[20] The authors of the study *Ending Hunger in our Lifetime* report that, for instance, "India achieved its national goal of food self sufficiency and even exported food in the 1990s, yet continued to have more undernourished people than any other country on earth."[21] Ending hunger in our lifetime is perhaps the largest political conundrum we face.

Facing the facts with regard to world hunger politics—especially the denial of access to food for everyone for the sake of securing the wealth of the rich countries of the Northern Hemisphere—is the biggest challenge for a Eucharistic practice that fosters the eschatological imagination that all can be fed.

In the beginning of this chapter we said that hunger can have brutalizing effects because it constricts and diminishes human imagination and has destructive influences on the social and ecological environment. We turn now to the New Testament, which already reflects a similar experience, as illustrated by one of the strangest texts in the Gospels of Mark and Matthew.

The Hope of the Hungry in the New Testament

Jesus' Hunger

Mark 11:11-25 (and Matt. 21:10-22) tell a disturbing story about Jesus' hunger. Jesus and his companions have traveled from Galilee to Jerusalem. It is becoming apparent that he will be persecuted and killed by the Roman occupying force as a political offender. The governing elites of the Jewish people also regard him and his success among the people as a threat, and they are cooperating with Rome's representatives. On their first evening in the capital, the Jesus people simply visit the Temple and take a look around. They will spend the night in Bethany, a village near the city. The next morning, Jesus and his friends return to Jerusalem. The text laconically remarks that "he was hungry." From the distance he sees a fig tree full of leaves. He goes to the tree and looks for fruit on it, but he finds none, "for it was not the season for figs" (v. 13). The hearers are meant to understand that his behavior is completely irrational: he looks for food where he must know he will not find it. And now his behavior becomes disturbing: He curses the fig tree, and through his curse makes barren a tree that would have been able to bear fruit only a few weeks or months later.

This story was told by people who followed Jesus. It was important to them. For these people, hunger was a daily reality—as it had been in Jesus' time. In the first century CE, the Jewish people in Palestine suffered at an escalating rate from famines, debt, and sickness. Extrabiblical sources, as well as the Gospels, narrate these circumstances with intense interest. Only a tiny elite group among the nations within the Roman empire enjoyed hygiene and a good life. The majority experienced increasing poverty. When we read the story of the cursing of the fig tree against this background, it becomes clear that it is no accident that Jesus is said to be hungry, and it is not just that he had not had breakfast, whereas the disciples with him were not hungry.[22] Their hunger is not mentioned in the story, but it is taken for granted as a normal circumstance of life. This is apparent also in other stories about hunger in the Gospels. In Mark 2:23-28 (and the corresponding parallels in the other Gospels) we read that the disciples pluck grain on the Sabbath and eat it. Jesus defends their violation of the Sabbath with the argument that David did something comparable when "he and his companions were hungry" (Mark 2:25). So it would be inappropriate to conclude from the story about the disciples' plucking grain that Jesus was not hungry. The narrative about Jesus' curse of the fig tree tells of his hunger because, for Jesus as for most of the people around him, every day was a struggle against hunger.

When we thus consider the life context within which this text belongs, we are struck by the fact that the story does not appear to criticize Jesus in any way, even though by cursing it he made a fig tree barren, a tree that otherwise would have borne fruit soon thereafter. Jesus' curse destroys food. The people who told this story were not surprised by it, nor were they angry. Why not? We can see from the story how Jesus is driven by hunger and how disappointed he is (Mark 11:13). He speaks in anger and destroys what he will so desperately need. Stories about hunger in the ancient world repeatedly tell of such desperate actions: Mothers even kill their children. Viewing the destruction of Jerusalem in 70 CE, a prophet laments:

> Happy the man who was never born,
> Or the child who died at birth.
> But as for us who are alive, woe to us,

> Because we see the afflictions of Zion,
>
> And what has happened to Jerusalem.
>
> ... Sow not again, you farmers;
>
> And why, earth, should you yield your crops at harvest?
>
> Keep to yourself your goodly fruits.
>
> And why any longer, vine, should you produce your wine?
>
> For no offering of it will again be made in Zion,
>
> Nor again will they offer first-fruits from it.
>
> ... And let not the *married* women pray for children,
>
> For the barren shall rejoice above all. . . . (*2 Bar.* 10:6-14).[23]

Jesus' curse expresses the same feeling: We have no future. The life of the nation is in danger. Jesus' curse is a ritual whose effect is destructive and thus revelatory. It is a cry to God for help, a cry that makes visible the crisis of the whole nation and the destruction of its very life.

Throughout the history of Christian interpretation, the social-historical context has often been left out of account; anti-Jewish models of interpretation have been used instead. So arose the fixed reading that makes the fig tree symbolize the Jewish people (or their leadership).[24] Jesus is said to curse the tree because the people have not accepted him. The consequence of the people's rejection of Jesus' messiahship was God's judgment on Jerusalem in 70 CE Christian anti-Judaism has endured stubbornly in biblical interpretation. Social-historical questions are useful for overcoming it.

The barren fig tree stands at the beginning of Jesus' Passion as a visible sign of the hunger of the suffering city, Jerusalem. Jesus and the people of his time, and those in the decades after his death, could read the symbolism as a sign of the approaching end of the suffering, the longed-for coming of God to renew the earth. It is not a self-contradiction that in the Jesus tradition he teaches people to see a fig tree in the spring as a sign of the coming of God (Mark 13:28-29). Jesus continually illustrates his own critical need and that of his people and teaches us to see that we must not cover up our despair with acceptable lies; we must keep our sight clear so that we may work for change. God gives us the strength for it, because God is near.

In the wealth of exegetical literature on the cursing of the fig tree we found nothing but an endless repetition of the anti-Jewish interpretation. Finally, after finishing our search, we came across a voice from Latin America that teaches us how to read this story. René Krüger writes of it: "Jesus' anger is fully expressed at the situation of extreme poverty and hunger— that's all. It is not necessary to turn to other explanations . . . [about] symbolic condemnation of sterile Israel. . . ."[25] Kruger shows that Jesus himself is one of the poor, and therefore the slogan "Jesus' option for the poor" should rather be "Jesus' solidarity with his people," his impoverished people. Then it would no longer be possible to misinterpret it in a paternalistic sense as alms from the wealthy.

Bread Miracles and God's Economy

The New Testament tells many stories about God's economy, the economy of grace. It does so, as the story about Jesus' hunger has shown, in the midst of experiences of the economy of death. In Mark 6:30-44, we find one version of the story of the bread miracle (there are six in all). This very multiplicity shows how important the story was for the first Christian generations. People told about how hungry the people were, and that Jesus distributed a few loaves of bread and a few fish and they were all satisfied: five thousand men (Mark 6:44; Luke 9:14; John 6:10). Matthew specifies that these were men "besides women and children"—that is, five thousand men, not counting the women and children, which means at least fifteen thousand people. The fifth and sixth versions of this story in Mark and Matthew tell of another bread miracle for four thousand (Mark 8:9), or four thousand men "besides women and children" (Matt. 15:39). These huge numbers are mentioned in order to make clear that God's bread is sufficient for all, no matter how many: the whole nation, the whole of humanity must be satisfied, and all creation must enjoy its fullness. Even the fragments that are left over after the meal make clear what abundance the divine economy creates: "And all ate and were filled; and they took up twelve baskets full of broken pieces and of the fish" (Mark 6:42-43; there are corresponding accounts in the other versions).

The fragments are enough for all, for the whole nation. This is not just about those who are present; it is true for everyone. The "Twelve" again recall the longed-for community of the nation that is now dispersed.[26] In a globalized economy in which the strong wage a war of distribution against the weak, the fragments are to be thrown away. The strong and the wealthy are to consume, to have an excess and to throw it away; this drives the economy. This kind of economy had already been criticized by the story of the manna in Exodus. God gave manna to those starving in the wilderness. "They gathered as much as each of them needed" (Exod. 16:18). But some could not stop competing with others for their share, and they tried to collect an extra supply for themselves. Their supply spoiled overnight. The biblical tradition, for millennia, has distinguished in simple, clear stories between the violent economics of the distributive struggle at the expense of the weak and the economy of God. In the stories of the bread miracles all eat what they need, and there is really enough for all, even for those who are absent. That is why there is a surplus.

Are these only dreams? The reality looks different, then and now. We are attempting to read the stories of the bread miracles with the question: What possibilities for action are they trying to demonstrate? They were told in order to teach those who would imitate Jesus. The stories of the bread miracles begin by talking about hunger:

> Those who had been sent out gathered around Jesus, and told him all that they had done and taught. He said to them, "Very good! Now come away to a deserted place all by yourselves and rest a while." For many were coming and going, and they had no leisure even to eat. And they went away in the boat to a deserted place by themselves. But many saw them going and word got around about where they were going. And they hurried there on foot along the shore from all the towns and arrived ahead of them. (Mark 6:30-33)

Mark's Gospel contains a number of comparable scenes (1:32-38; 2:2; 3:20). The people, the crowds, are in need and hope for help from Jesus and those with him. In Mark 6:34, Jesus sees their affliction: "they were like sheep without a shepherd" (cf. Num. 27:17). The people have a failed political leadership, and that means violence, sickness, and increasing poverty. In their affliction, the people press upon Jesus and his companions. They can no longer get any rest, and they have neither the time nor the opportunity to eat. They have a few provisions with them, as the text later says: five loaves of bread and two fish (6:38). Jesus shows tender concern for his companions, who have been on the road for days, healing the sick and interpreting the Torah. They need to rest and recuperate, and Jesus himself needs food and rest. But their quiet meal is disrupted by the people's need. Instead, they share what they have brought with the people. There are situations in which a withdrawal into private life, no matter how necessary, can no longer be justified. The five loaves and two fish would have provided only a minimal meal even for Jesus and his group. We are not told how many disciples were with him—there certainly were more than twelve. The hungry crowd cannot be satisfied with what is on hand. The disciples suggest that the people be sent away so they can find food for themselves—if they have the money. But the suggestion is illusionary, a shirking of responsibility. Jesus now incorporates his community of followers explicitly in his responsibility: "You give them something to eat." The group gives Jesus a precise calculation of how delusional his suggestion is: It would cost two hundred denarii, a year's wages for an agricultural laborer. Lack of money is the ultimate obstacle. The experiences expressed in this text are easy to recognize. Fertile land and a sea full of fish surround them, but the people are dependent on money. Others have the grain and fish at their disposal. The crowd is dependent on work, and on the money others permit them to earn.

Jesus asks the crowd to sit down formally in groups of diners (each containing fifty or a hundred people), just as Israel had done in the wilderness (Exod. 18:21, 22), even though the situations are somewhat different. In the earlier case the issue was dividing power, laying it on many shoulders and enabling a system of justice that was close to the grassroots. As with the people in the wilderness before them, here again the ordering of the people expresses their community with God. Jesus blesses the bread just as it was blessed at Jewish meals: "Blessed are you, Adonai, our God, King of the universe, who bring forth bread from the earth." Jesus breaks the bread, and the disciples distribute it to the groups. "And all ate and were filled." After the Enlightenment in Europe, such narratives were called miracle stories because they tell of something that, in terms of scientific knowledge, cannot have happened. Therefore one must "believe" in them, contrary to reason. But inasmuch as the story tells of God's multiplication of bread, contrary to the logic of the economy then in place, it is the story of God's economy, which certainly does *not* require a spectacular intervention contrary to reason. Through their community, people can transform their situation of affliction. It is, in fact, small steps taken in community, that give everyone a new perspective and make everyone independent of the economics of violence. Why should I not be able to imagine that all people shared the little they had brought with them, and that, through a just division, it proved to be enough for all? People only had to follow the model provided by Jesus and his companions.

As these stories were told, and told again and again, the groups that made up the communities of Jesus' followers were celebrating the Eucharist together. The common meal, with prayers and remembrance of Jesus' death and resurrection, is the *Sitz im Leben*, the life-setting, of these bread stories. In the Eucharist, too, the group's resources are shared, as we hear in 1 Cor. 11:17-34, but also in Acts 2:42-44; 4:32—5:11. We will return to these passages. In the Eucharist as well, the abundance, the wealth of God's creation is experienced. The longed-for messianic meal is close enough to grasp: "For now we see in a mirror, dimly, but then we will see face to face" (1 Cor. 13:12). There is a connecting thread running through Scripture from the manna in the wilderness, through Jesus' multiplication of bread, to the earliest Christian practice of the Eucharist and its anticipation of the messianic meal of the nations in God's just world, the *basileia tou theou*. That connecting thread becomes visible in the narratives of the bread miracles, and it is the basis of Eucharistic practice. Here, God's economy unfolds.

"Not by Bread Alone": Jesus' Temptations (Matthew 4:1-11)

The story of Jesus' temptations reflects the conflict between the economy of violence ("bread alone") and God's economy. Jesus' temptations are also those of his followers. They, too, know the power of hunger, the danger of death and the apparent omnipotence of imperial rule. Therefore we will set alongside the three temptations another three references from the Gospels that make it clear that Jesus' experiences of temptation should not be understood as isolated events: Matt. 6:25-34 (about the power of economic affliction), Matt. 10:28-32 (about the fear of death), and Matt. 22:15-22 (about the Roman Empire's claim to rule). Jesus is tempted like Abraham and other pious people.[27] His own companions also know this despairing hour of temptation: "If you are God's child. . . ," says Satan to Jesus, twice. He is not talking about a status as child of God that is unique to Jesus but rather the condition and child-of-God status of all men and women for whom the *Shema Israel* is the foundation of their life. This becomes clear from the content of the temptation narratives.

What does it mean to be "tempted"? Before narrating Jesus' temptation, Matthew writes of his baptism. The voice of God had addressed Jesus: "This is my Son, the Beloved, with whom I am well pleased" (Matt. 3:17). After this, the divine power of the Spirit takes Jesus out to the desert, where Satan tempts him. Two theological questions arise already: What does it mean to say that God "tempts" people, as the Lord's prayer says ("lead us not into temptation")? And why, as in this case, do people tell stories about Satan, the devil, or demons?

Texts that speak of God's tempting or testing people are about human situations of conflict. Peter's "betrayal" can serve as an example. After Jesus' arrest, Peter follows him to the place where he is being examined. Peter is recognized. If he were to acknowledge that he is a follower of Jesus, he would be arrested and executed in the same way. That was the usual procedure Rome followed in dealing with people who disturbed Roman order, and with those who confessed their allegiance to those who were arrested or condemned. Peter did not do that, and we hear in the texts how despairing he was afterward (Matt. 26:57-75 par.). Did he do wrong? It was the kind of situation in which he could have played the hero and so helped nobody. But the brothers and sisters needed him. Therefore people pray, "Lead us not into temptation"—stand by us when we get into conflicts in which we have a hard time knowing what is right and are in danger of doing wrong. Biblical texts call that being tempted by God. They are not saying that God caused the conflict. The situation is a consequence of humans' violent deeds. But in the aftermath the children of God who told the story of Peter recognized the hand of God, who protected Peter and gave him the strength to make the right decision. So we can say that God tempted Peter, but Peter withstood the temptation.

When we take these stories about temptations from God—or, for that matter, the Lord's Prayer—out of context and couch them in general language divorced from concrete experience, the result is an image of God that does not correspond to the biblical tradition: God is seen as testing arbitrarily, in authoritarian fashion, making use of human misery for educational purposes. It is important to start from the concrete situation and to ask what is the experience of God in it and who is talking about it. The experience of having rightly resisted violence is called withstanding a temptation from God. It is an experience of resistance that can look like what happened with Peter.

Why do the biblical texts speak of Satan or the devil? Here, too, the subject is experiences of suffering, of crises caused by human beings. These experiences often occur for their victims in and through anonymous structures. Social pressure to subject oneself to an unjust order is usually brought by other people who themselves function as cogs in the larger machine. It was no different then than now. People speak to us in the biblical texts, people who give a name to evil, breaking through its anonymity. They call it Satan. The power that is at enmity with life receives a name that does not personalize its structural effectiveness, but makes clear its structural character. In Matt. 4:1, the divine power of the Spirit leads Jesus into the desert, and he is tempted by Satan. Those who remember these harsh hours for Jesus are not saying that God is the ultimate cause of the conflict. But from the beginning it was clear to the audience that Jesus would have the power to resist. God stands by him, because the power of God's Spirit is in him. Satan is called the source of the temptation because the experience of evil in Jesus' world must be called by its name.

The first temptation portrays the pressure in Jesus' world, the world of the Roman Empire at the beginning of the imperial period, to subject oneself to an economy of violence. Indebtedness, impoverishment, and sickness tormented the population of the countries ruled by Rome. The temptation to act as an accomplice in the rapid exploitation of the poor was omnipresent. Even slaves were subject to that pressure, as the parable of the "talents" (Matt. 25:14-30) tells. The slaveowner expects his slaves to take care of his money during his absence. They are supposed to make it grow. He would not have been satisfied if they had put it in the bank at interest (Matt. 25:27). He wants bigger profits; he wants the original sum doubled. That kind of profit could be obtained by lending money to families of small farmers who, as a rule, very soon lost their land because they were unable to repay such debts.[28] Two of the slaves behave like their owner. They have made themselves the agents of violence. Only the third slave resists. This parable makes clear how dependent persons were drawn into the structures of the power of money and the kind of strength that is needed to resist it.

The first temptation names accommodated egoism: changing "stones into bread." In the face of this pressure—so the text says—Jesus thinks of the miracle of the manna for Israel. He quotes Deut. 8:3, and so the quintessence of the manna miracle (Exodus 16). The people are starving in the wilderness and so grumble against Moses and Aaron. They wish themselves back at the fleshpots of the time of slavery. God does not let the people starve. Manna rains like bread from heaven. This divine bread can only be used according to God's economy. It satisfies all according to their need; some need more, some less. But it cannot be hoarded, because it spoils. The Torah calls this experience an exercise in God's economics: being tempted by God. The people have learned something, and they will continually remember it. The memory is summarized in Deut. 8:3: "one does not live by bread alone, but by every word that comes from the mouth of the LORD." Jesus recalls this memory in the face of his urgent need to stand fast against pressure, to resist the economy of egoism and hold to God's word. Here that word means participating in an economy oriented to human needs, a manna economy. Jesus' hunger makes him vulnerable. He thus shares the vulnerability and need of the people around him, whose daily concern is: What shall we eat, what shall we drink, what shall we put on? (Matt. 6:25-34). They must hold to God's word; the *Shema' Israel* (Hear, O Israel) must shape their daily lives. Their relationship with God is realized in the small decisions of every day. The first temptation is about the pressure of the economy of death, which desires to bring even the least members of society within the scope of its violence.

In the second temptation, Satan tries to destroy Jesus' trust in God. He challenges him to jump to his death from the dramatically high angle[29] of the Herodian temple in Jerusalem, trusting in God to save him. In the context of Jesus' life and that of those around him, this is a plausible temptation. Many had the same questions as Peter: Should I revolt now? Should I, for example, refuse to pay taxes to Rome? Should I proclaim myself a follower of someone condemned to death for political insurrection? Should I fear the perpetrators of violence or not? "Fear not those who kill the body.

They cannot destroy life . . . every hair of your heads is numbered" (Matt. 20:28-33). But in the concrete situation it is necessary to decide whether resistance is necessary and reasonable. Playing the hero is the wrong choice. Instead, one has to walk a fine line of concrete decision making. In this second temptation, Jesus again recalls Israel's time in the wilderness. He quotes Deut. 6:16, "Do not put the Lord your God to the test." In the story of the second temptation, the text teaches Jesus' followers the same thing a rabbi expressed in different words: "A man should never stand in a place of danger and say that a miracle will be wrought for him, lest it is not. And if a miracle is wrought for him, it is deducted from his merits" (b. *Shabb.* 32a).[30]

The third temptation throws a spotlight on the political situation. "All the kingdoms of the world and their splendor"—that is a short summary of Rome's imperial self-definition. The emperor Augustus wrote in a propaganda text[31] near the end of his life about how he had imposed the *pax Romana* on one kingdom after another. Augustus's *Res Gestae* can be read as a commentary on Satan's brief summary of the world empire of that time. Rome's splendid edifices or, within the sphere of Roman influence, Herod's magnificent buildings, stood triumphantly on view. Even the Herodian temple in Jerusalem was part of this imperial splendor. The people who told the story in this text were convinced that such world power is only made possible by worshiping the devil. Satan here tempts Jesus in grand style, but people's everyday experiences also challenged them to betray God. They were not offered world power for their betrayal, but only their own survival. That is what is at stake in Peter's denial (Matt. 26:69-75). Jesus teaches in Matt. 22:15-22 how to deal with Rome's imperial power. Here we see the alternative to Satan's temptation: not the desire for power and sharing in rule, but a clear limitation on the power that belongs to each one in his or her own life. "Give therefore to the emperor the things that are the emperor's, and to God the things that are God's" (Matt. 22:21). The boundary drawn around the imperial power again comes from the *Shema' Israel.* All of life, one's whole existence, belongs to God. Only when no damage is done to that tie can the emperor demand taxes and make laws. The treading of that line on the part of those who know themselves as children of God was a daily exercise of strength. It was necessary to study the Scriptures together with others in order to discover responsibly what could be given to the emperor, day by day, today and tomorrow, and what could not.

Satan wanted to get Jesus to adopt the perspective of the imperial power, to make it his own.

When Jesus' followers gathered and ate the Eucharist together they brought with them the conflicts reflected in Jesus' temptations. Those were their daily reality. Blackmail, rape, and danger were written in their hearts and bodies. The Eucharist has a place; it does not happen in a vacuum. The temptation story helps us to see and recognize that place.

The Holy Meal and the *Homo Oeconomicus*

The biblical examples offer us glimpses of how the economy of grace breaks through and transforms economic circumstances based on unjust distribution of food in a money-driven market economy. These examples likewise demonstrate the destructive power contained in experiences of hunger. The Gospels depict even Jesus as someone who is familiar with these issues, who knows about the struggle for the bread of life in the midst of these two economies. Issues of poverty and property threaten and challenge the Eucharistic life and affect the ways the holy meal is celebrated.

Now we turn our attention to ancient and modern depictions of the *Homo oeconomicus*, the mythological figure of the property owner, the person whose life is centered on possession and whose major interest is in the accumulation of money (gold and silver).[32] The terrain of the *Homo oeconomicus* is the market exchange in which goods are exchanged for money. That exchange produces abstract relations between producers and consumers, relations not based on fulfillment of the basic needs of the individual or the community but on the multiplication and accumulation of money.

The following stories and theoretical deliberations illustrate the assumptions—in most cases hidden—about the mechanisms of the money-driven market economy. These shape our thinking and our ethical orientation with regard to economic exchange. They appear natural, the only choice we have. We will demonstrate how this invisible logic opposes and destroys practices of eschatological imagination. In an indirect way, paying attention to the imagination of the *Homo oeconomicus* is also crucial for how we see the economy of grace unfolding in the celebration of the holy meal and in the Eucharistic life.

Although the theory of the *Homo oeconomicus* is a creation of modern classic and neoclassic economic theory, we can find already in antiquity an interest in the question of what kind of economic reasoning people should follow. We discover in ancient literature a strong suspicion of and reservation against the social effects produced by market exchange.[33] We are fully aware of the differences in the circulation of money then and now. However, we assume that it is possible to mark points of convergence between the ancient and modern critiques of the *Homo oeconomicus*. Those points of convergence offer the potential to open a window through which we can see our contemporary situation in a new light. Sketching out those critiques, we will seek to discover in the holy meal practices implicit alternatives to the logic assumed by the *Homo oeconomicus* theory. Those alternative practices may disrupt the worldview that market exchange logic is the only rational or "natural" way of engaging in economic affairs. Paying attention to the different forms of economic imagination the two economies provide will help deepen our understanding of sacramental permeability with regard to economic exchange and Eucharist.

The Imagination of the *Homo Oeconomicus*

In the *Metamorphoses,* Ovid tells the story of the god Bacchus, who decides one day to grant Midas, the King of Phrygia, a wish. Without any hesitation the king desires that everything he touches should be converted into gold. Bacchus fulfills his wish.[34] Ovid describes Midas's ecstasy when he recognizes he can break a green branch from an oak tree and it will turn into gold. He would grasp a rock and touch the earth underneath his feet and it would turn into bright, shimmering gold. But when his slaves serve him a delicious meal with fruits and vegetables, meat and bread, Midas has to realize that to bite on gold is disgusting; it neither satisfies his hunger nor tastes good.

Besides Ovid there are various ancient authors who describe the social effects of the introduction of a money-driven economy. They describe in systemic terms how, for instance, the development of usury causes injustice, and how those who do not profit from the circulation of money are exploited. They also describe the microcosm of the human mind: How hearts are enslaved by the desire to accumulate and how relationships are corrupted since money is placed between people like a self-contained power. Pliny the Elder speaks of the compulsion to accumulate as *pleonexia* (from Greek *pleon echein,* "to have more").[35] *Pleonexia* is greed not solely as a moral habit of the *Homo oeconomicus* but as a structural force that keeps the market exchange going. It compels people to rummage Mother Earth in the search for silver and gold. Pliny in his *Natural History* describes work in the silver mines as a violent penetration of the earth, which is imagined as a female body.[36] He also draws the connection between this devastating exploitation of the earth and the money-based economy. The greed thus stimulated is a voracious appetite for gold, expressed in unjust practices of usury.

The philosopher Dio Chrysostom emphasizes the limitlessness of the greed that emerges from *pleonexia.* He describes people who live for only seventy years yet create reserves that will survive for a thousand.[37] *Pleonexia* produces the illusion of infinite life as the endless consumption of goods. The desire for eternal life is expressed through the accumulation of goods that suffice for a thousand years. The critique of *pleonexia* can also be found in the New Testament. The story of the rich young man (Matt. 19:16-23) who is not able to follow Jesus because of his attachment to his property, as well as the so-called vice catalogues, all reflect the problem of *pleonexia*.[38]

Modern theories about the *Homo oeconomicus*[39] are inspired by the insights of the philosopher Adam Smith (1723–1790). Smith understood the complex processes of economic exchange as the product of countless individuals who make rational decisions according to the best available information. Under the given conditions they strive to optimize their own self-interest and become what he calls "rational egoists." From the actions of rational egoists derives an anonymous mechanism Smith identifies as *the invisible hand*. The invisible hand describes a state of balance that causes social integration, the harmonization of interests, and social welfare. The invisible hand refers to the rules of the market, but it also enters the realm of religion. The invisible hand echoes the activity in the world of God, whose providence does not permit total imbalance.[40]

For Smith the rational egoists are not callous creatures, but are able to express empathy. In his *Theory of Moral Sentiments*[41] Smith reflects on sympathy as part of the given human nature. Human beings are—in the literal sense of the Greek word *sympathein*—able to suffer with and feel the pain of others. Due to their aptitude for imagination, human beings are able to put themselves in the position of others and to enter, so to speak, the body of the other who bears pain.[42] According to Smith, the affection of sympathy is crucial to the world of ethics. The immediate affection of sympathy needs, however, to be accompanied by rational reflection. Smith does not develop further the manner in which the order of economics and the realm of ethics are related, but this is a crucial point.

In current debates there is concern that these anthropological assumptions about the *Homo oeconomicus* are far too constrained. For example, Birger Priddat asserts that such a view does not consider seriously the common human experience of failure—that is to say, humans' inability to put into practice decisions made on the grounds of rational thinking.[43] Human experiences of suffering that reflect the gap between rational intention and practical failure cannot be explained solely in terms of miscalculation. They are part of the human condition. Therefore the anthropological assumptions about the *Homo oeconomicus* need to be complemented by other theories that talk about the identity of a person against the background of the experience of failure and uncontrollable suffering. Those theories speak differently about the value of a human person, beyond the language of optimizing the competence to make better-informed decisions. According to Priddat, this is the realm of moral discourse that cannot be gained in the arena of economic theory such as rational choice. However, it is necessary for human beings to be able to recognize themselves as persons with value, independently from the results of their actions.[44]

Coming back to Adam Smith, we see another problematic aspect in his theory. He believes that *pleonexia* and the striving for justice and the well-being of all people are not mutually exclusive. He assumes that the elimination of *pleonexia* would have serious economic disadvantages; *pleonexia* and prosperity are inextricably interwoven.[45] The desire of consumers for more articles to consume is the driving force of the capitalist economy. Without this desire, economic exchange could not exist.

In the next section we summarize our concerns with regard to the *Homo oeconomicus* theory from a theological perspective, focusing on aspects that are critical for our question of how to understand Eucharistic life within the eschatological imagination.

Our first criticism is directed against the understanding that the *Homo oeconomicus* has the power to imagine life as endless. Infinity and eternity are equated with the possibility of limitless accumulation. The circulation of money is envisioned as an endless stream.

Various historical developments could be analyzed that fostered this myth of infinity. With regard to the *Homo oeconomicus* theory, the correlation of money and time is crucial.[46] It was probably in the late medieval period that people in Europe began to relate time to space. The future was envisaged as a space in which economic business takes place. Especially through the increase of long-distance commerce, traders dealt with goods that had to be financed before they were purchased and then sold again. Merchants had to develop the capacity to put the coordinates of time, space, and money in a frame of reference. A calculating consciousness of time surfaced from that necessity. The emergence of mercantilism was accompanied by drastic changes in language systems, particularly in the grammatical constructions of tenses. The introduction of the *future perfect* made it possible to articulate the accomplishment of economic projects that were to be completed in the future. The sentence: "Next year the ship that carries spices will have returned from the colonies" reflects the calculation of money that is already invested, for example, in the infrastructure that will be increased after the ship's return.[47]

In European modernity the progression of the money-driven economy led to an anticipation of the future as something completed. The image of future was connected with the calculation of presence by means of money. The creation of such an anticipation of future has . . . to be described as an achievement of the imagination that shapes reality. Thus the temporal mode of the future perfect can be described as monetary fantasy. . . . The myth generates a reality ruled by images.[48]

The progression of the business of lending[49] as well as later speculation in currency on the stock market can be interpreted in this sense as belief in the infinite possibilities of the increase of wealth in the realm of the future. This kind of anticipation nourishes the illusion that the future can be domesticated and controlled. The fantasy of infinite accumulation is a product of this attempt to control the circulation of money.[50]

In sketching our understanding of eschatological imagination we have critiqued this illusion of infinite life. It has deadly consequences for those who do not profit from the circulation of money. Immortality of the soul may be construed in this context as the further extrapolation of the idea of endlessness. As we develop our eschatological imagination in the context of the Eucharistic life it is crucial for us not to corrupt our thinking with the logic of unlimited accumulation that the *Homo oeconomicus* offers.

Our second concern is with the fact that the *Homo oeconomicus* is exclusively about the realization of self-interest. As Adam Smith said, we do not expect our food from the charity of the butcher, the brewer, or the baker. We rather expect them to realize their own interest. We do not appeal to their humanity, but to their self-love.[51] Smith proceeded from the assumption that if everyone would just follow the impulse of realization of self-interest, economic balance in the social order would be realized. Everybody should just strive toward this goal. The invisible hand he saw at work echoed God's working in the world, which would not allow drastic imbalance. However, what we have to realize is that exactly this drastic imbalance is operating in economic exchange processes all over the world. It cannot be proved that human beings "naturally" develop a healthy sense in articulating self-interest. Thus many people do not have access to economic resources to realize this kind of self-interest, and their power to be potent agents in the market exchange is significantly constrained. This imbalance in terms of access to resources seems to be essential to the ability to accumulate. Furthermore, this understanding of self-interest in the context of market exchange diminishes relationships to a utilitarian form. Solidarity and community are then reduced to corporate identity or to a sense of family that efficiently reproduces the work productivity of its members.[52]

One of the highest goals of the *Homo oeconomicus* is the accumulation of capital. This is his terrain of ultimate concern; this is what determines and shapes his existence. This compulsion is not to be understood as a moral failure of the individual. It rather describes the structural logic of the capitalist economy as well as the logic of individual socialization. This compulsion shapes images of the world and the body. *Pleonexia* imprisons human desire and relationship to others in the world. Plutarch says in his treatise *Of the Love of Wealth* that the desire for more money cannot be satisfied by silver and gold, and the greed that derives from the processes of accumulation never ceases to desire more.[53] The desire for more gives birth to a craving for objects that moves the *Homo oeconomicus* away from the satisfaction of the basic bodily needs of all people. His inner clock ticks according to the news of the stock market. He does not start with bodies or bread. He does not take seriously the physical, psychological, and spiritual needs of bodies as a prerequisite that is valid beyond the logic of economic calculation. Men, women, and children are considered human capital. They are primarily valued from a utilitarian perspective; care and well-being are perceived from the perspective of the regeneration of human work productivity. Thinking about human life beyond the framework of economic benefit does not belong in his frame of reference. A similar utilitarian lens is brought to the exploitation of natural resources, which reveals the potential of irrationality. As rational choice theory emphasizes the rational behavior of the *Homo oeconomicus* on the market, the compulsion to accumulate destroys rationality.[54] The myth of Midas demonstrates exactly this irrational force that undergirds the multiplication of money. The desire to turn everything into gold will finally lead to the king's starvation: gold cannot be eaten. Nonrenewable energy resources cannot be depleted endlessly; oil reserves will be exhausted. The only question is when this will happen.

Our third concern is the divinization of money exchange. The *Homo oeconomicus* is involved in idolatry, in worshiping the idol of capital accumulation.[55] This idol becomes his God. Jewish and Christian traditions witness to the fact that *pleonexia* leads to idolatrous worship. The alternative between mammon and God describes a line of conflict that can be discovered in the New Testament as well as throughout the history of Christian churches.

Economists and philosophers of the nineteenth century were particularly interested in analyzing the mysterious power that seems to be attached to the circulation of money. Karl Marx, for example, recognized the religious dimension of money circulation in his reflection on the fetishistic character of goods.[56] It is market exchange under the conditions of capitalist economics that leads to a perception of particular exchange mechanisms as determined by an external power. Those processes cause the utility value of goods to disappear; the only relevant dimension seems to be their exchange value. It is no longer important to determine the usefulness of a product so much as what that product could generate in profits. The exchange-value character of goods is the actual stimulating factor of production. The goal is to sell and to accumulate money. The accumulation of money makes the processes of production invisible. The human agency of workers and capitalists is made invisible in the sense that suddenly the prices of goods on the stock market seem to be the subject or agent of power. We hear things like: "The coffee price dances on the market." Our very language reveals this phenomenon.[57] It seems as if we would have to obey the movements of money. Marx uses the term *fetish* in an ironic sense. When he was writing his *Critique of Political Economy*, ethnologists had just discovered the native religions of African and Melanesian tribes. Those religions were characterized as fetishistic in their ritual practices. A fetish was believed to exercise power over those who lived under its spell; it demands submission, but in the eyes of "enlightened" European researchers and colonizers, this fetish was a *nothing*. Even so, according to Marx, these same "enlightened" people attribute this very fetish character to goods in such a way that they transform human activities into incomprehensible life circumstances that alienate and dominate.[58] The sociologist Christoph Deutschmann stresses that it is not only the twofold character of the goods (as exchange and in their utility value) that produces the imaginative dimension of money. It is the money itself, with its capacity to produce assets, that gives money its mythological gestalt. The ability to produce assets refers to *potential* wealth, not to real, tangible goods. It "embodies an imaginative dimension of actions; it evokes dreams and fantasies in the owner. Since it dominates not only goods but also work, it represents the bridge between reality and potentiality."[59] The horizon of potentiality is most intensely expressed in capital as the most abstract form of money. This horizon penetrates all forms of communication, including those that do not function explicitly in economic terms. This potentiality exercises powerful pressure on our actions: They ought to be convertible into actual money.[60]

It is the capacity to represent potentiality and access to all of life in the mode of abstraction that evokes the religious quality of money circulation. These qualities appeal to the *Homo oeconomicus* in his idolatrous worship of accumulation.

We bring our journey into the imagination of the *Homo oeconomicus* then and now to a close. Looking at the traces of how the *Homo oeconomicus* imagines his world, we come to the conclusion that major aspects are in sharp contradiction to our portrayal of eschatological imagination. This is especially true for the depiction of eternal life as limitless opportunity to accumulate money, the exclusive focus on realization of self-interest, and the divinization of money exchange.

Let us now reflect on Eucharistic traditions that respond to the eschatological imagination. We are pondering whether holy meal practices and theologies might have the potential to reveal ritual objections to the omnipotent claims of the *Homo oeconomicus*, at least in an implicit and fragmentary way. This is a question of interpretation of tradition as well as of current practices. We are searching for liturgical traditions that do not duplicate the logic of market exchange but point to the traces of an economy of grace. We want to ask how this economy of grace is embodied in holy meal traditions. What are the objections to an understanding of future as endless opportunity for economic growth? Can we discover the symbolization of exchange processes that transcend the utilitarian framework of realization of self interest? Where can we find voices that challenge idolatrous divinization of market exchange? We are interested in Jewish and Christian worship traditions that give an implicit or explicit response to the seemingly omnipotent claim of the *Homo oeconomicus* to present the only rational choice to communicating life. The economy of grace, as we see it, celebrates the creatureliness of human beings in which the gifts of life are shown to be gifts of God.

The Alternative Economics of Eucharist
Eucharist as Gift Exchange

> *What have you that you did not receive?*
> *If then you received it,*
> *why do you boast as if it were not a gift?*[61]

In the following we propose two theoretical approaches that might give impulses for an interpretation of the Eucharist in the context of an economy of grace: deliberations about gift-exchange theories and consideration of economic theories that stress the criterion of sustainability with regard to human and natural resources. Through the centuries, we can find aspects of gift exchange practiced in Eucharistic liturgies. It is important to emphasize the connection between gift exchange and Eucharist. Under-standing the holy meal in this horizon also helps to resituate the debate about sacrifice and Eucharist.

Many ritual theorists and some practical and liturgical theologians con-sider rites of gift exchange as a basic genre of ritual action. The French Roman Catholic theologian Louis-Marie Chauvet, the North American Roman Catholic theologian David N. Power, and the German Lutheran practical theologian Hans-Martin Gutmann are all engrossed in an inter-pretation of gift exchange for an understanding of the "economy of grace" as it is particularly expressed in the Eucharist. From a Roman Catholic perspective, David N. Power understands the sacraments in general as the basic language of God's giving:

> The sacramental elements of bread, wine, oil, and water are already an expression of gifts received. Humans receive them from the earth, and through them they receive life and communion together. To express his own self-giving, Christ took what by creation and earth's bounty are already gifts given. Through this medium, he gave sacramental form to his own self-giving. . . . The Eucharist is an economy of gift, where the gift is from God, of and through Christ and the Spirit, and the com-munion table is the central rite, not the consecration nor any gift made by the Church to God.[62]

These theologians are all interested in exploring the symbolic order in which religious communication is expressed beyond the logic of market exchange. All refer to Marcel Mauss's classic essay *The Gift*,[63] in which he develops the thesis that there are two major forms of gift exchange: the agonistic and the nonagonistic. Mauss studied the first form as it is embodied in the potlatch. In the Chinook language, *potlatch* means "to nourish" or "to overspend." Potlatch refers to a ritual practiced by various Native American tribes such as the Tlingit, Haida, and Kwakiutl living on the northwest coast of North America. Potlatch indicates a form of social communication and distribution of goods in which those who lav-ishly spend all their riches during particular celebrations earn the highest reputation within their community. The agonistic forms of gift giving, as the example of the potlatch shows, are filled with competitive and aggres-sive energies; giving gifts is about making the receiver feel ashamed and getting him or her into a position that makes it impossible to respond to the gift with a bigger present in return. The nonagonistic forms of gift exchange seek to foster relationships between families and clans just by living out generosity and hospitality beyond the framework of aggressive competition. Commitment is here understood as the winning of friendship by means of a gift.

It is crucial for both forms of gift exchange that they produce relationships with strong commitments. Their purpose is to sustain social peace within a group and to regulate the aggression and potential violence that threaten the relationships between tribes. Mauss believed that the compulsion to accept a gift was motivated by the nature of the gift: In the understanding of the Maori, for example, gifts are animated by a spirit, the *hau*, that represents a part of the life of the donor. Because of the *hau* the receiver is obliged to offer a gift in return. That means the economy of gift exchange does not know abstract objects as gifts; rather, all gifts exist in a relationship with the giver.[64]

The act of gift-giving creates certain kinds of obligations. Mauss distinguishes four types of responsibilities: the first three are the obligation to give gifts, to accept gifts, and to respond with a gift in return. The exchange of gifts is a binding action that produces relations of mutuality, yet not necessarily equality. The fourth category of obligatory gift-giving is the sacrifice, which includes gifts to the dead and to the gods. Sacrificial rituals of gift exchange follow the *do ut des* logic in which people make a gift, an offering, or a sacrifice to a deity in order to receive a gift in return—a restored relationship with God or simply good weather for the next harvest.[65] Direct offerings may be given to praise, please, and placate divine power; those offerings are often destroyed in the ritual process in order to provoke a bigger gift in return. Sacrifices acknowledge that the deities are the actual proprietors of the gifts and in doing so they reveal the origins of life.

Mauss's theory received challenging responses, especially from post-structuralist and postmodern philosophers. The major challenge is formulated in the critique of Jacques Derrida,[66] who questions whether true gifts cannot be exchanged. Bernhard Waldenfels[67] tries to develop Mauss's theory further by distinguishing between *responsive giving* and *exchange giving*. Giving in the realm of gift exchange focuses on the other's need, which has to be accommodated and balanced. Responsive giving, however, acts out of the acknowledgment of a surplus that existed before one's own gesture of giving. Responsive giving acknowledges the prior reception of an extraordinary gift. One's own gift-giving takes place in the awareness that one has received beforehand; the line between giving and taking begins to blur, and in this way the reciprocity in the gesture of giving is emphasized. Praise and thanksgiving might be understood accordingly as responsive giving.

Hélène Cixous[68] concentrates on the character of the activity and asks what the giving effects. This question seems to be most fruitful as it can be asked in concrete contexts. Does the gesture of giving strengthen friendship, evoke joy, pacify conflicts? Or does the activity of giving cause shame and a feeling of inferiority in the recipients? Is there giving that is self-destructive and giving that causes bad dependence? There seem to be good gifts and bad gifts, or more precisely good giving and bad giving, good and bad waste, good and bad emptying of the self, total exhaustion that brings peace or death. And are there gifts that do not need a return gift as a response? These questions seem to be crucial in determining what the symbolic order of the economy of grace is about. It is highly significant for our understanding of gift-giving that derives from the celebration of the meal and is directed toward the poor. We need to ask about traditions of collecting and distributing money and other gifts that do not reproduce patterns of unctuous charity.[69]

For Louis-Marie Chauvet, the distinction between market exchange and symbolic exchange is crucial. As the money/market system concentrates on accumulation and calculation, it produces abstract relationships and focuses on possession. Symbolic exchange, on the other hand, does not rely on having but on being, since it is not values that are exchanged; the subjects who enter into communication exchange themselves. It is not so important *what* is exchanged; it is in the very act of exchanging that human beings recognize themselves as subjects. Symbolic exchange belongs, for Chauvet, to the domain of gratuitousness and generosity. He emphasizes that symbolic exchange is also vital for societies that are dominated by market exchange. Chauvet conceives symbolic exchange as a form of communication that encompasses not only gift exchange but also other forms of communication: "And since all properly human, that is, signifying acts are encompassed by language and, as a consequence, undergirded by speech, we must recognize that *the subject constantly lives in and from symbolic exchange.*"[70]

With regard to the sacraments, Chauvet writes that the position of gift is occupied by God's gratuitous action. It does not belong to the order of value or merit but to the domain of gratuitousness and generosity:

> Under this aspect of gratuitousness, God's grace is not something due and its measure is not that of human merit. Grace comes from God's pure initiative, that of love.... Then the *reception* of God's grace *as* grace, and not as anything else, requires (relation of implication) the *return-gift* of faith, love, conversion of heart, witness by one's life. We have said it before: in the sacraments, God alone, and not faith (no more than

the other subjective conditions of the authentically Christian life), is the measure of the gift. In other words the "validity" of the sacraments depends on God; its "fecundity" depends on the believing subject.[71]

Following Chauvet's argument about the reception of grace as gratuitous gift, we can say that the liturgical response and social agency of believers can be understood in the sense of Waldenfels's notion as *responsive giving*. This responsive giving is enabled through the two dimensions of grace: its gratuitousness and graciousness.

> God's grace is gratuitous, that is to say, it is not necessitated by anything and it is God who has the initiative. . . . But if one considers grace only under this aspect, one isolates the first term from the structure of exchange and causes it to function *imaginarily*. Indeed, if this were the case, a human being would be "alienated" from God. Too much generosity alienates. To overwhelm someone with gifts so gratuitously that one takes away from the other even the possibility of giving in return is to treat that person as an object, because, by denying her or him the possibility of being a subject of duty, one deprives her or him of the dignity of subject, period.[72]

Chauvet makes an interesting point here: The return gift (thanksgiving, witness, love) from the believer needs to be given in order that she or he may be fully recognized as a subject and not only as an object of reception and in order for the true nature of the divine gift to be recognized in its fullness. This necessity does not belong to the realm of the market economy. It reflects the quality of the human-divine relationship and the sociopolitical and liturgical activity that does not make people feel inferior or small in view of the divine generosity but makes them fully responsive.

In this sense we can interpret the Eucharist as a ritual of gift exchange, an exchange initiated by God's giving. We celebrate the encounter with the living God who provides enormous gifts. We receive the gifts of creation that sustain our bodily existence. And in Christ, God offers God's self as pure grace. Through Christ's life, death, and resurrection we receive the incredible gift of the promise of a future for creation. The power of sin as the global force of alienation, which causes destruction, death, and segregation, will not forever dominate human communication. This is the gift of grace that is given in Eucharistic celebrations. It opens the space of eschatological imagination in which we receive a foretaste of the resurrection of our bodies and the redemption of the whole creation.[73]

Gutmann refers the gift-exchange theory to Martin Luther's theology of the *happy exchange* (*fröhlicher Wechsel*). Luther describes the *commercium* of faith as an intimate interaction between Christ and the soul of the believer in which righteousness is exchanged for sin. Luther compares this exchange with the relationship between bride and groom.[74] Although Luther fundamentally attacks the Roman understanding of the Mass as a human *sacrificium* or *meritum,* he is able to speak of the faith of believers within the framework of gift exchange.[75] In this gift exchange, which takes place in the Eucharist, God commits God's self to her friends, as is told in John 15:13: "No one has greater love than this, to lay down one's life for one's friends." Jesus' death as a sacrifice may be understood in the sense of the Hebrew notion of *natan,* as a gift that provides friendship and love. This exchange occurs in the Eucharist. Being freed from sin, people are enabled to give thanks to God through their prayers and hymns. The exchange of gifts enables the participants in the Eucharist to join in the play of a just distribution of bread and wine and of the sanctification of life. The Eucharistic celebration represents the creation of committed relationships between God and God's people and among those who share the bread and those who are absent.

Hence the economy of grace is about an exchange of gifts in which not accumulation but spending is the primary action, and in which is established an order of gratuitous wasting and not of calculation. But how can lavish spending be the paradigm of the economy of grace in our age, marked by threatened ecological systems and poverty in the Two-Thirds World?

Sustainability: Abundant Love and Limited Resources

He will turn the hearts of parents to their children.[76]

The second aspect crucial for our attempt to sketch out the economy of grace as an alternative to market exchange is that of sustainability. Concepts of sustainability embrace human mortality and finitude. They envision the future as an imaginary space centered on the well-being of the next generation.

Within the ecological movement of the last twenty years, more and more economists and ethicists have challenged the paradigm of endless growth as the basic dynamic of economic exchange. Attempts have been made to offer a different model. Theories that focus on the notion of sustainability see as the major goal not growth but a sustainable practice with regard to natural resources.

Steven Rockefeller defines sustainability as follows: "Patterns of production and consumption are considered to be ecologically sustainable if they respect and safeguard the regenerative capacities of our oceans, rivers, forests, farmlands, and grasslands.... [S]ustainability includes all the interrelated activities that promote the long-term flourishing of Earth's human and ecological communities."[77] According to this definition, an activity can be understood as sustainable when it can be continued indefinitely. This sense of indefinite activity has to be distinguished from *Homo oeconomicus*'s notion of limitless access to resources. In contrast to the attitude of the *Homo oeconomicus*, this position takes into account the life of prospective generations of children, men, and women, as well as the future well-being of all creatures and plants that inhabit the planet Earth. This imagination of future life is supposed to shape current economic production and consumption of goods. It might be interpreted as the modern version of Luke 1:17: "He will turn the hearts of parents to their children." This turning, which sees the life of future generations as pivotal to our current activities, implies a radical paradigm shift: it departs from the attitude of dominion over natural resources and moves toward a consciousness of the radical interrelatedness of all beings, including the human species, within the ecological system. This paradigm shift further takes into account that there is no such thing as waste.[78] The garbage we produce has to go somewhere; all the waste we produce does indeed affect the environment. Since the Western system is so much based on the value of increased consumption as the provider of happiness, it will take a revolution in the economic system as well as a revolution in our thinking to abandon this mindset. This tremendous challenge exists even though the evidence that high consumption correlates with happiness is very weak.[79]

> Given that a shift away from fossil fuel dependency will be nothing less than traumatic for the continuing functioning of our modern and particularly our American society, we are most reluctant and exceedingly poorly equipped to simply become sustainable, to carry out those tasks which would either make us sustainable or at least improve our sustainability ratio.[80]

This paradigm shift is in the deepest sense a spiritual task. It calls forth a refocusing of resources of reason and sciences. A new focus on the relation between economy and ecology is needed. This shift requires from us a sincere questioning of our own lifestyle. We need to revisit our sense of place by cultivating a stance of awe and humility toward the natural resources that sustain our whole existence. How can our praise of God as the creator of all things ring true when the "average resident of an industrial country consumes 3 times as much fresh water, 10 times as much energy, and 19 times as much aluminum as someone in a 'developing' country?"[81]

If the economic-ecological crisis that is based on our non-sustainable way of living destroys our sense of holiness of life, we have to revisit our God images as well. We have to ask if the God language we use in our public worship services is just a bad mimicry of the consumer God or if we are able to express the economy of grace in its eschatological breadth and depth.

What is needed in order to make this happen? We think that the language of "wasteful" generosity and gratuitousness as it is expressed in the symbolic order of gift exchange in the Eucharistic celebration has to be complemented by a language of abundance that displays a healing sense of sufficiency. When we talk about the abundance God provides for us at the table, or about divine love as abundant love, we need to take into account that abundance in the consumer society is connected with *pleonexia*, with the compulsion to have more than before.[82] The abundance of supersize XXL is paradoxically driven by the myth of scarcity, which generates the fear that there might be not enough to consume in the future.

Thus life-embracing abundance needs to be understood within the ecological model of sustainability. As Sally McFague writes:

> The ecological model, then, suggests a new vision of the "abundant," the good life. It is not and cannot be the consumer model of individual gain; it must be a shared life where "the rich must live more simply, so that the poor may simply live. . . . We must envision models of the abundant life based not on material goods, but on those things that make people really happy: the basic necessities of food, clothing, and shelter for themselves and their children; medical care and educational opportunities; loving relationships; meaningful work; an enriching imaginative and spiritual life; and time spent with friends and in the natural world.[83]

This good life is grounded in the words "there is enough"; it focuses on basic needs as the source of spiritual life.

Biblical as well as liturgical traditions offer examples of this understanding of abundance as "there is enough." The witness of the Hebrew Bible to

God's abundant giving starts with the recognition in Genesis 1 that everything God created was indeed very good. The sense of God's abundant love as it is realized in creation is expressed in Psalm 104, which can be read as a commentary on Genesis 1. "The psalmist surveys creation and names it all: the heavens and the earth, the waters and springs and streams and trees and birds and goats and wine and oil and bread and people and lions."[84] The psalmist goes on and on until arriving at the words that sound like a table prayer: "You give them all food in due season, you feed every body."[85] Here a sense of abundance is displayed that has reached its goal in the eschatological vision that everyone will be fed.

However, this trust in God's abundance experiences rupture in times of crisis. The Hebrew Bible and the New Testament give manifold witness to this. The manna miracle in Exodus 16 demonstrates the fear of scarcity. Afraid of not having enough to eat, the people of Israel experience God's generosity as trickling from heaven as bread. They receive God's generous gift in the form of nourishment that will suffice for the day. However, since Israel had come to believe only in the scarcity of food, the people responded by hoarding the bread.

> When they tried to bank it, to invest it, it turned sour and rotted, because you cannot store up God's generosity. Finally, Moses said, "You know what we ought to do? We ought to do what God did in Genesis 1. We ought to have a Sabbath.' Sabbath means there's enough bread that we don't have to hustle every day of our lives."[86]

The manna economy displays an abundance that does not serve the purpose of accumulation. It serves the purpose of nourishment for the day, of fulfilling the basic needs of the community. As we have already shown, the bread stories in the New Testament show a similar logic. The story of the multiplication of the bread, with its "sacramental" underpinnings,[87] refers to an understanding of abundant food as a sharing of small resources that can only be understood against the background of the gospel of the poor.[88] In that sense we can discover a connection between the manna story, the multiplication of the bread, and the celebration of the Eucharist.

The language of God's abundance, as the expression of the eschatological vision that what God provides is enough, finds its way into liturgical practice. In the Jewish Pesach Seder we find a song of praise called *Dayenu*. It follows the recital of the ten plagues, during which each of the participants removes a drop of wine from her or his individual cup with a fingertip. The song *Dayenu* (it would have been enough for us) conveys that if God had performed only one of his many deeds on behalf of the Jewish people when he brought them out of slavery in Egypt, it would have been enough. The people sing the refrain in a very lively melody: "For that alone we would have been grateful." It concludes the enumeration of each of God's blessings.

Had he brought us out of Egypt
And not fed us in the desert,
Brought us out of Egypt,
Well then—Dayenu!
Refrain

Had God fed us with the manna,
And not then ordained the Sabbath,
Fed us with the manna, well then—Dayenu!
Refrain

Had God then ordained the Sabbath,
And not brought us to Mount Sinai
Then ordained the Sabbath, well then—Dayenu!
Refrain

Had God brought us to Mount Sinai,
And not given us the Torah,
Brought us to Mount Sinai, well then—Dayenu!
Refrain

Had God given us the Torah,
And not led us into Israel,
Given us the Torah, well then—Dayenu!
Refrain

Had God led us into Israel
And not given us the prophets,
Led us into Israel, well then—Dayenu!
Refrain.[89]

The Mimicry of Market Exchange

Christian worship, especially the celebration of the Eucharist, cannot be exclusively interpreted as a realm embodying the economy of grace. It is rather that the two economies that are in conflict in the sphere of commerce and everyday life found their way into the worship life of the churches as well. Thus, throughout the centuries, we can find examples of liturgy that can be understood as mimicry of market exchange.

In the first three centuries of the Christian era, however, we might assume that the symbolic order of gift exchange prevailed in many Christian communities. The Eucharist was mainly understood as a celebration of thanksgiving.[90] Thanks were given to God the creator, who gives food and sustenance as well as the covenant, the Torah, and faith in Jesus Christ. The prayers as well as the offering of material gifts represented a kind of gift exchange as the worshipers responded to the gifts God had bestowed on God's people. Those gifts expressed gratitude for all that was received beforehand. The gifts rendered at the Eucharist, food as well as money, were presented before God and then distributed among the poor and marginalized.

> At the outset of the third century, in North Africa, an intimate relation was seen between the presentation of bread and wine by the faithful and the central act of the Lord's Supper. This presentation was considered symbolic of their co-offering of the Eucharist with the chief celebrant. Since the dead were regarded as members of the Church, it was natural that they should be drawn into the fellowship of the earthly worshipers by gifts offered " in their name."[91]

The gift exchange that occurred in the Eucharist thus had as its purpose the constitution of the community of the faithful; the offering of the gifts demonstrated membership in the body of Christ. It was taken for granted that the dead were included in the Eucharistic community. In that sense gift giving functioned in an obligatory manner; it strengthened the commitment among the members. Worshiping God meant the consecration of the fruits of one's labor. Practicing social justice was considered responsible worship of God.

In the history of Christian worship, however, we find not only traces of the economy of grace that embodies Jesus Christ as the bread of life. We also come across traditions that can be considered mimicry of particular aspects of market exchange—for example, those in which gift giving became exclusively an expression of the realization of self-interest. Edward Kilmartin sketches how in the West from the sixth to the ninth century the Eucharistic sacrifice came to be understood as something accomplished by the priest as representative of the people of God. The Mass became a means to obtain certain favors for the living and the dead:

> Recompense came to be expected for a gift given to the church or the priest. This custom had its roots in German law, in which it belonged to the essence of a gift to be sealed by a recompense. . . . The church or the priest was expected to provide in some way for the care of the soul of the donor and his or her intentions. At first, mention in the prayer of petition was considered to be a fitting remuneration, but by the end of the eighth century, Masses were brought into the sphere of ecclesiastical recompense.[92]

The understanding of an exclusive, individualized share in the benefits of the Eucharistic sacrifice corresponded with the value of the gift. In a certain sense the benefits of redemption could be bought. From our point of view, this logic leaves the terrain of sacrificial offering as a form of gift exchange and enters the realm of calculation of benefit in a way that mirrors the money-driven economy. It found one of its crassest expressions in the sale of indulgences in the Reformation period.

No longer was the gift offering of the whole community crucial for the Eucharistic celebration; rather, it represented the satisfaction of individual concerns. "The priest was said to offer 'for the people' and the people were described as offering 'through the hands of the priest.'"[93] The role of the community was diminished by this understanding, which simultaneously put the priest in the central role of mediator between the people and God in the performance of the Eucharistic sacrifice as well as mediating people's needs and desires before God.

There are certainly more historical examples that could be given to demonstrate how the mimicry of market exchange was infused into the theology and practice of the Eucharist. We can conclude from the variety of liturgical exchange practices that there is no "essence" of ritual, in the sense, for example, that it is always liberating. It is rather the case that rituals can also sustain and foster the order of dominance. As always, everything depends on the context.

Dissent from the Omnipotence of the *Homo Oeconomicus*

Let us return to the question of implicit ritual objections against the omnipotent claims that come with the economic imagination of the *Homo oeconomicus*, and look at particular ritual actions within Eucharistic liturgies.

Giving Thanks

And we call this food "thanksgiving."[94]

Very early the holy meals were called *eucharistia*, as the act of thanksgiving was central to the consumption of bread and wine. The first Christians were immersed in the Jewish tradition of saying a blessing over the bread and wine and with the *birkat ha-mazon* at the end of the meal. These were domestic table prayers spoken at ordinary meals.[95] For the twentieth century, the Jewish scholar Leo Hirsch describes how the ritualized meal at home should look. We assume a similar practice for the first century and afterward:

> Pour clear, clean, fresh water into a glass or jug, twice wetting the right hand and twice the left hand. While drying the hands, speak the blessing "for washing hands," and utter no other words until *hamozi* has been completed. Sit at table, cut or break a piece of bread, dip it in salt, and say the blessing: "Blessed art thou, O eternal, our God, king of the universe, who brings forth (*hamozi*) bread from the earth," and eat the bread. Now the meal has begun, and one may eat without speaking the other special *berakoth* (blessings). . . and after the meal again pour water over the fingers. Then follows the *benschen* (*benedicere*), the table thanksgiving (the lovely German version of which by Franz Rosenzweig is here quoted). All the remaining food is removed, leaving only bread and salt on the table as if to show what one thanks God for. . . .

> > So, when there are three adults at table the speaker begins:
> > Gentlemen, let us give thanks.
> > The others reply:
> > May God's name be blessed, now and forever.
> > Then the speaker, after repeating the reply, says:
> > By the will of the Lord:
> > Let us offer praise the One from whose storehouse we have been fed,
> > And from whose goods we live.
> > This the speaker repeats and continues (the one who bensches alone begins here):
> > Praise HIM, praise his name.

Now praise and honor to you, O God, thou our God and king
of the universe.
Daily he invites his universe
To the meal
In love, in kindness and gentleness.
He shares bread with all creatures,
For his love is without end.
And because of his great goodness
There is never a lack, nor do we lack
Food at all times,
For the greatness of his Name.
For he feeds and cares for the whole universe,
He does good for the whole universe,
And he gives food to every creature
        That He has made.
Praise be, therefore, praise be to Thee, O God, who feeds the
universe.
So we thank you, O God, our God,
That you provided for our ancestors
A land beautiful, fruitful, and vast,
And led us out, O God, our God, from the land of Egypt,
And delivered us from the house of slavery,
And for the covenant you marked in our flesh,
And for your Law, that you taught us,
And for your ordinances, that you made known to us,
And for your life, your love, and your kindness that you
bestowed upon us,
And for the table you set for us.
And you are the one who cares for us forever,
Every day, at all times, in every hour.[96]

This tradition of giving thanks and praising God in the context of
domestic meals was a source of inspiration for the development of Eucharistic liturgies.[97] In the *birkat ha-mazon* God is blessed for creating the
world and for nourishing his people with goodness, grace, kindness, and
mercy; God is the nourisher of the universe. Jews render thanks for the land
that bears the produce to be eaten, for the covenant and the Law, for life
and food. People bestow thanks on God as the one who feeds in the literal
and the metaphorical sense. Being fed by the goodness of God is pivotal for
religious conviction and practice.

Thus the act of thanksgiving is intimately connected with the acknowledgment of God as the giver of life in its very basic physical sense. We can discover a similar understanding in many texts. The *Didache,* for example, is obsessed with praise and thanksgiving.[98] Prayers of thanksgiving are spoken over the cup and the bread. Thanks are given to the Father for Jesus the child as the revealer of the holy vine of David, the revealer of life and knowledge, faith and immortality. The example of the *Didache* demonstrates that in the very act of thanksgiving and then of eating and drinking, revelation takes place through Jesus the child of God. The practice of thanksgiving flows into doxology: *Glory be to you, O God.*

David Power writes about the relationship between praise and thanksgiving:

> Praise is given in virtue of wonder. It allows the sheer wonder of the gift/presence of Word and Spirit to stand forth, as they are contemplated in the events of grace in the actions of all the *dramatis personae* of salvific action. Thanksgiving comes as it were in second place, by way of acknowledging the origin of these events and their grace in God and in God's love.[99]

The doxology is like the deep breath that has to be taken when one encounters sheer beauty; the thanksgiving is a way of seeing and looking behind things: since they come from God they are not our own. Praise is the recognition of this generosity in amazement; gratitude implies, besides the awe that flows out of the doxology, the readiness to articulate the commitments and obligations that are connected with the reception of gifts. Eucharistic liturgies often close with prayers of praise and thanksgiving. One beautiful example is Per Harling's *Gloria,* a doxology with a wide perspective:

> With space full of mystery and buds that burst open,
> with meadows, with forests, and seas,
> we cry out in joy to you, nurturer of all:
> Gloria! Gloria! Gloria!
>
> With cells that divide in continuing patterns,
> in flowers, in children, and birds,
> We cry out to you, who became human:
> Gloria! Gloria! Gloria!

With the people who seek and are woken by the wind
Of truth and freedom and justice,
We cry out to you, our creator:
Gloria! Gloria! Gloria![100]

The *Didache* describes the ability to give thanks as a work of God's creation: "You, almighty Master, created all things for the sake of your Name,
and gave food and drink to mankind for their enjoyment, that they might
give you thanks."[102] Eating and drinking as enjoyment are part of God's
creative work. It is not primarily moral obligation, but rather enjoyment
that is the basis for gratitude.

There are more aspects to the act of thanksgiving. The anaphora[26] that
is attributed to Hippolytus names Jesus as the one through whom believers
give thanks. Jesus, portrayed as the apocalyptic Christus Victor who breaks
the chains of the devil and tramples down hell, gives thanks at the Last
Supper. Because of his redemptive work the celebrants are enabled to thank
him for their ability to worship God in honor.[103] In this anaphora Jesus is
pictured as the mediator who enables the thanksgiving of the faithful and
engages in thanksgiving to the Father through the *birkat ha-mazon*, and
he is simultaneously the reason why genuine worship is possible.[104] The
discovery of the Christus Victor motif[105] in the context of the Eucharistic
prayer leads to the question, What is meant here by the chains of the devil?
What kind of redemption is pictured when Jesus tramples down hell, the
place of the dead? If redemption has to do with the overcoming of death as
a structural entity it definitely encompasses the destruction of hunger and
poverty. Those experiences were certainly considered chains of the devil in
the context of the *pax Romana*. As we have said before, believing in the
resurrection of the dead was, among other things, about the eschatological
vision of full stomachs.

In his *First Apology*, Justin the Martyr describes the acts of solidarity
that flow from the common meal with its prayers of thanksgiving. Those
who are absent and cannot partake in the holy meal receive part of the
bread, the wine, and the water that were shared by the community.[106] Those
who are sick or in prison, as well as the widows and orphans, receive the
gifts given by the wealthy. The president of the congregation takes care
of those people according to their needs.[107] Justin's description of the gift
exchange that takes place demonstrates that it is not exclusively reciprocal; it embraces those who are absent from the meal and those who are
stigmatized as "the others" in their everyday experience. The thanksgiving thus has a twofold direction: toward God and toward those who are

in need. It has consequences for liturgical practice, which transcends the Sunday morning celebration and includes those who have to stay at home. It also embraces the further social demand that the *leitourgia*, the work of the people, should address the physical needs of those who live at the margins.

For Luther and other reformers, giving thanks was also at the heart of the Eucharistic celebration.[108] Luther was convinced that we cannot express anything other than our praise and thanks to God since we have received everything from God: grace and the Word, the gospel, our faith, and all things. The Eucharist is the place where *free* thanksgiving is made possible, since we join Christ through whom thanksgiving to God the Father happens. In the holy meal, giver and gift are identical: "This is my body." According to Luther, this is the perfect expression of God's love.

We could add numerous examples from the Jewish-Christian traditions that connect the reception of food with the act of thanksgiving. In what sense can we speak of this ritualization of gratitude as a subversive practice that challenges the omnipotent claims of the *Homo oeconomicus*? Three basic assumptions about life are defied in the practice of thanksgiving that leads into an ethics of gratitude: the illusion of infinity as endless accumulation and its reverse, the focus of the affluent on scarcity, the "commodification" of the world, and the invisible practices that the fetish character of goods produces.

The appreciation of the givenness of life as it is expressed in this kind of prayer acknowledges the limits to total accumulation and "thingification" or "commodification" of human productivity and natural resources. By "thingification" we mean a sense of being in the world that turns everything into an object for use.[109] Consequently, the right to exploit people's work and the globe's resources can be claimed as the unreserved realization of self-interest. The recognition of the givenness of the gift, however, puts limits on its use. What is given to me is not earned by me; it is not my exclusive possession. The gift rather refers back to the giver and the relationship it constitutes. The relationality that is implied in the act of gift giving conveys a sense of obligation with regard to the gift itself and what it effects in a particular environment. Or, as Paul F. Camenish states:

> With gift language, the Christian points to the unearned, undeserved character of the many benefits we all enjoy, including existence itself. These benefits, it is asserted, are given out of the benevolence of the giver and with the intention of enriching the recipients' lives. They are not boons from the blue resulting from natural or historical

happenstance. Because of this, the Christian also uses gift language to point to, to ground, and to specify the resulting obligations which come to bear upon the recipients in relation both to their conduct toward the giver and their uses of the gifts themselves. Gift and gratitude language also point the Christian toward the general stance toward existence and the world which is appropriate in the light of God's overwhelming generosity.[110]

Praising and thanking God can also be understood as an act of resistance against economic marginalization. It can be a powerful ritual action in the symbolic order of the gift exchange economy. We find this kind of ritualized protest against the omnipotence of the *Homo oeconomicus* in communities of faith who live at the margins. The doxology "God is good," which is proclaimed, for example, by African American Christians not only on Sundays but through the whole week can be understood as the imaginative window that pictures a counter-reality against the background of poverty and racism. The experience of economic marginalization that excludes from the benefits of the money-driven economy is challenged by the praise and thanksgiving that juxtapose the goodness of God with the experience of social, economic, and racial injustice. We conclude this section with a portion of a sermon the Reverend Dr. D. Mark Wilson gave just before the Thanksgiving holiday in 2004. It reflects exactly the spirit of this tradition:

> As we count our blessings in the land of plenty, some of us may ourselves sound a bit like my grandmother who would pray at every family get-together during holidays like Thanksgiving. And when she prayed, I mean, she really prayed. She not only prayed for the ancestors, aliens, wandering Arameans whose names she didn't know, but she prayed long prayers for all the multitude of blessings in her family—as instructed in her Hebrew biblical theology. She started with her children, then prayed for her children's children: "Lord I want to thank you for my eight children, Bettie, Landers, Melissa, Mary C., not to be confused with my granddaughter Mary E., Deborah, Idella, William (nicknamed Bad), and Sherman (nicknamed Good), then Lord, I want to thank you for my forty-plus grandchildren," then she would start to call all of our names, Bettie's six children, Landers' eight children, etc., then "Lord, I want to thank you for my sixty great-grandchildren, go down to Mississippi, and look on Mary's twelve children, and their children's children, go on up to Detroit and look on James' seven children, go over to Oakland and look on Bettie's twelve grandchildren," and we'd be saying,

"Come on grandma, the food is getting cold," and with one eye open and the other shut, she'd look at us and say, "Shut up, I'm still praying." Why? Because she had so much to be grateful for, when you come up from the land of segregation, poverty, with memories of grandparents from slavery at seven, when you've raised eight children on your own, notwithstanding taking care of young critical thinking babies destined to be preachers like me, when everything and everyone was against you and still you found a way to build community, to make family, to live and see the future, you've earned your right, grandma, to say thank you and what else there is you want to say.[111]

Returning Gifts

Indeed, Chrysostom urged his hearers in that very church
to know that the only way to put food into the mouth of God
is to put it into the mouth of the poor,
which he called "sacrifice" or "offering,"
and the givers he called "priests."[112]

Another powerful movement in the economy of gift exchange that the Eucharist embraces is the returning of gifts, traditionally called the offering. We will present our own reflections on the significance of this particular ritual action, which has undergone various changes in liturgical history. It has the potential to make visible the economy of grace in which food and money exist for sustenance and not so much for accumulation.

When we give thanks to God as the giver of life we reject the invisible mechanisms that come with the fetish character of goods. Acts of thanksgiving are the fertile ground for the returning of gifts. Truthful thanksgiving names God as the source of all that is given to us, yet it also makes visible the ways in which the concrete products we consume are fashioned. Truthful thanksgiving is not naïve with regard to the sufferings the market economy produces; it rather speaks against the seemingly autonomous dance of coffee prices on the market, and against the invisible exploitation of human labor that is attached to the picking of the coffee beans. Enrique Dussell emphasizes:

The first thing to realize is that the bread of the Eucharist, the bread prepared for the sacrifice, is *real* bread, it is *really* the product of someone's work, in time, specific human work. This means that offering something to God not only has a sacramental meaning (if by sacrament we understand an "outward-material-sign of grace" indicating the man-nature relationship—water, oil, salt, bread . . .) but also an economic meaning. Giving, offering, presenting something to someone, or exchanging it with him, or stealing it from him is an economic relationship. Offering God a piece of bread ("We have this bread to offer, which earth has given and human hands have made") is an act of worship, of *theological economy*.[113]

The bringing of bread and wine and other gifts to the table during the Eucharistic celebration embodies the economy of grace. This ritual action has traditionally been called the offering, or the offertory. Following our interpretation of Eucharist as gift exchange in which we receive first God's gratuitous gifts of grace—the fruits of creation, and life in light of the resurrection—it seems inappropriate to us to speak of offering. The modern usage of "offering" something implies that I give something away that belongs to me. Bringing the gifts of creation to the table actually points to the opposite: We bring what we have received from God through the hands of working people. We bring gifts that have been offered to us by others. In that sense we rather return the gifts to the table, and by doing so we are engaging the circle of the economy of grace. We do not bring the gifts to God's table so that they might be transformed into something particularly sacred, but rather to lift up the sacredness that they per se inhabit. We then use the food for the nourishment of the assembly during the meal. This is again a movement in the economy of grace. What is left over, as well as additional gifts, will be brought to those in need. Gordon Lathrop writes:

> None of it is "offering." All of it should go to our neighbor. None of it solves the world-hunger problem or even the local need. It only bears witness to the Gift of God and to the truth of the world and to our acknowledgment of our insertion in the widespread, aching need. We can only call these gifts "offering" metaphorically, using the wrong word and thereby destroying all offerings. It is such a metaphor Chrysostom is using when he calls the poor "the mouth of God." Certainly, there are other ways to speak the metaphor, to see our religious gesture broken to the service of the Gospel.[114]

And for the liturgy of our ordinary lives: Returning the gifts to the table could be part of the effort of making visible the circle of production that is attached to this particular food. Analyzing the circle of production and the oppression attached to it is another task that belongs to the Eucharistic life. This task expands liturgical practice. It is a spiritual exercise we can practice in the supermarket when we buy coffee or tomatoes, or when we fill up our cars with gasoline: what is the circle of production that is hidden behind those things? The Eucharistic life gains concrete forms when we challenge the firms who make big profits, for example, from the Iraq war and its aftermath, or when we choose to buy strawberries that have been picked by immigrant workers who receive a just wage for their labor and are not exploited as slave workers, as is frequently the case on the strawberry fields in southern California.

Lifting up the good gifts of creation, which are indeed the bread of life for us as well as the redemptive work as it is expressed in Jesus' life, death, and resurrection, sustains our eschatological imagination. The eschatological imagination that comes with the returning of gifts can enter the sphere of the hidden mechanisms of market exchange and provide light where idolatry is supposed to reign.

However, the returning of gifts not only implies this critical momentum of lifting up the hidden idolatry. It also gives those who celebrate a chance to express themselves in their desire, gratitude, and neediness. David Power reflects on the assembly that brings gifts in gratitude:

> They bring gifts that express themselves, the urges and the needs of life, expecting to encounter the urges and the needs of others. Though gathering to receive from God, they obey the urge to bring something of their own, even if only in this way to bring themselves more fully. They place their gifts in the basket, putting them there, alongside those of others, confiding them to the caring Church. What they bring will be blessed, shared and increased by God's own giving. In the blessing of the gifts, it is life itself that is given increase. An exchange, an economy, is opened up in which God's initiative outstrips humanity's and brings about a new order.[115]

The following feminist litany makes a strong connection between God's own work as creator, the labor of the people—here in particular the labor of women—and bread as a symbol of resurrection. In God's own self is eschatological yearning that brings forth the magnificent creation. It is out of that divine yearning that the call for all to be fed from the gifts of the earth arises. In the labor of the women who plant the seeds, who reap the harvest, who crack the wheat, who pound the corn, and who bake the bread is prayer and song. The litany plays with the structure and with single motives from the creation account in Genesis 1. It can be performed with drums that mimic the heartbeat of God's and the women's labor; the whole Eucharistic celebration could be sustained by that drumbeat, especially when the people move to the table and when they share the gifts:

Speaker ("S") 1: In the beginning was God

S 2: In the beginning the source of all that is

S 3: In the beginning, God, yearning

S 4: God moaning

S.1: God labouring

S 2: God, giving birth

S 3: God rejoicing

S 4: And God loved what she had made

S 1: And God said, All this is good.

S 2: Then God, knowing that all that is good is shared

S 3: Held the earth tenderly in her arms.

S 4: God yearned for relationship.

S 1: God longed to share the good earth

S 2: And humanity was born in the yearning of God.

S 3: We were born to share the earth.

S 4: In the earth was the seed.

S 1: In the seed was the grain.

S 2: In the grain was the harvest.

S 3: In the harvest was the bread.

S 4: In the bread was the power.

S 1: And God said, All shall eat of the earth.

S 2: All shall eat of the seed.

S 3: All shall eat of the grain.

S 4: All shall eat of the harvest.

S 1: All shall eat of the bread.

S 2: All shall eat of the power.

S 3: God said, You are my people

S 4: My friends

S 1: My lovers

S 2: My sisters

S 3: And brothers.

S 4: All of you shall eat

S 1: of the bread

S 2: and the power.

S 3: All shall eat.

S 4: Then God, gathering up her courage in love, said

S 1: Let there be bread.

S 2: And God's sisters, her friends and lovers, knelt on the earth

S 3: planted the seeds

S 4: prayed for the rain

S 1: sang for the grain

S 2: made the harvest,

S 3: cracked the wheat

S 4: pounded the corn

S 1: kneaded the dough

S 2: kindled the fire

S 3: filled the air with the smell of fresh bread,

S 4: And there was bread!

S 1: And it was good!

S 2: We the sisters of God, say today,

S 3: All shall eat of the bread,

S 4: And the power

S 1: We say today,

S 2: All shall have power

S 3: And bread

S 4: Today we say,

S 1: Let there be bread.

S 2: And let there be power!

S 3: Let us eat of the bread and the power!

S 4: And all will be filled

S 1: For the bread is rising!

S 2: By the power of God

S 3: Women are blessed.

S 2: By the women of God

S 3: the bread is blessed.

S 4: By the bread of God

S 1: the power is blessed.

S 4: By the power of bread,

S 1: The power of women,

S 2: The power of God

S 3: the people are blessed

S 1, 2, 3, 4: The earth is blessed.

Celebrant: And the bread is rising![116]

Presenting the gift of bread in this way is one possible way to engage in an act of eschatological imagination that is permeable for God's and the people's labor. So far we have sketched out our own interpretation of the returning of gifts. In the following we want to take a brief look into the liturgical tradition of offering gifts in order to ask to what extent this tradition offered an alternative to the implications of market-exchange logic. The presentation of gifts at the Eucharist has a complex history with changing meanings attached to it.[117] According to Edward Kilmartin, the basic official meanings of the Lord's Supper determine the interpretation of the gifts presented at the Eucharist.[118] As long as the Eucharist was mainly understood as a celebration of thanksgiving, gifts were signs of gratitude. They were also an expression of the social justice concerns of the early church. This was the case in the first three centuries. However, the more the Mass was seen as the sacral sphere dominated by priests, the more the intention of gift giving as a means of obtaining recompense came to the foreground.

Early on we find a variety of hints related to offerings at the Eucharist. In *1 Clement*, probably written around 96 CE, the writer criticizes Corinthian Christians who reject people for the episcopate "who have blamelessly and holily offered its sacrifices."[119] Justin the Martyr refers to the bringing up of gifts at the beginning of the Eucharist.[120] He speaks of bread and wine mixed with water brought to the president just before he begins the prayer of thanksgiving. Tertullian speaks of the faithful who bring their gifts, and he describes their gift giving as an offering directed to God.

However, quite early there were objections to the offering of material things. In Irenaeus we find the argument that God *does not need* sacrifices, but that it is nevertheless fitting to offer him praise and thanksgiving as well as bread and wine. He, like many church fathers, cites the "pure offering" of Mal. 1:11. This reference was used as part of an anti-Jewish polemic that considered sacrificial offerings as only an outward and ritualistic action not performed by the heart. In Irenaeus we find strong polemics against the Jewish sacrificial cult. At the same time he emphasizes that Jesus taught the disciples to offer the first fruits of creation to God. In spite of this emphasis on the pure offering of prayers of thanksgiving, Irenaeus and Tertullian both stress that the "elements" of bread and wine are part of the created order. They react against Gnostics who talk about offerings as entirely non-material. Thus Irenaeus emphasizes the resurrection of the body as a material experience flowing out of the sustenance the Eucharist provides. Bodies are given life through the Eucharist by being drawn into communion with the body of Christ.[121]

The *Apostolic Tradition* instructs the deacons to present the offerings to the bishop, who lays hands on them together with the presbytery and gives thanks.[122] Although the context of the Eucharist is not explicitly mentioned, we find further prayers of thanksgiving and instructions to offer the first fruits of creation. The new fruits are to be offered to the bishop. He blesses them and names the donors, saying:

> We give you thanks, O God, and offer to you the first fruits which you have granted us to receive; you nourished them by your word, and ordered the earth to bear all fruits for the joy and the nourishment of men and for all animals. In all these things we praise you, O God, and in all the things with which you have helped us, adorning for us the whole creation with various fruits; through your child Jesus Christ our Lord, through whom be glory to you for the ages of ages.[123]

This prayer refers to Gen. 1:11 and 29. The oblation is an act of recognizing the gifts of creation, which are there to be joyfully consumed. The oblation thus points back to the origin of the gifts; they are an adoration of the Creator and, in offering them, we value the gifts as good creation.

The instructions for the Eucharist on the occasion of the ordination of a bishop are followed by instructions for the offering of oil, cheese, and olives. Again the thanksgiving for these gifts demonstrates how the oblation of material things makes God's healing power and love transparent to the faithful.[124] We might assume a connection to the baptismal Eucharist, since oil and milk were part of the rite of baptism. If this is true, baptism as well as Eucharist point to the profane experience of daily nourishment. The *Apostolic Tradition* already reflects the hierarchy that is attached to the gift bringing. It is not the whole people of God who bring their gifts to the table, but the deacons and bishops who serve as mediators between the faithful and God. They are the ones who offer on behalf of the community.

A different picture is presented by a mosaic of the church excavated at Aquileia, reflecting the Constantinian era. The mosaic depicts an offering of gifts that is not restricted to bread and wine; it shows men and women bringing bread and wine, grapes, flowers, and a bird.[125] However, as early as 393, the Synod of Hippo states clearly that at "the Sacrament of the Body and Blood of Christ nothing is to be offered except bread and wine mixed with water."[126] In the *Apostolic Canons,* we find ordinances that the bishops and priests are not to offer anything but bread and wine at the altar during the Eucharist. All other gifts must be given to the deacons and other clergy.[127]

Richard Kieckhefer stresses the complex history of offertory processions:

From at least the third century, the laity were expected to make offerings of bread and wine for use at the eucharist. Not only bread and wine but also oil, wax, and candles could be presented, and monetary offerings eventually became common. Yet lay offerings did not necessarily imply a lay offertory procession: they could be collected by the clergy (or in modern times by ushers) rather than brought forward in procession. Still, lay offertory processions did develop, at different times in different regions. They might take place only four or five times yearly, on the great feasts of the church year, perhaps on the anniversary of a church's dedication or on its patronal feast day. Sometimes the gifts were still bread and wine; sometimes other gifts were brought. . . . In ninth century Gaul the laymen and then the women, followed by priests and deacons, moved forward to the altar after the Creed in an offertory procession that was compared to the procession at Jerusalem on Palm Sunday. Even when a procession was made with offerings, it did not necessarily occur at the liturgical offertory: in a given region it might take place at the Kyrie, before the gospel, or even at communion time. From the later Middle Ages we hear of processions in which the priest blessed each person making an offering, but elsewhere the clergy went on with the liturgy seemingly oblivious to the laity who processed forward.[128]

Joseph Jungmann concluded in his reflections on the offertory procession of the faithful that from the eleventh century onward the giving of gifts was more and more diminished to the offering of money: "So, since the twelfth century, in explaining the offertory, the enumeration of offerings usually begins with gold: Some offer gold, like the Wise Men from the East, others silver, like the widow in the Temple, still others *de alia substantia;* only after that are bread and wine mentioned as gifts of the clerics, who have always formed the last in the rank of offerers."[129]

The offertory processions came under scrutiny during the Reformation era, which challenged the idea that during Mass people could offer anything at all to God. The reformers emphatically rejected the understanding of the Eucharist as a sacrifice performed by the priest and stressed instead God's redeeming activity in liturgy and life.

In summary, we can say that the offertory traditions were in danger of turning into mimicry of market exchange when they were attached to narrow and individualistically defined concerns for one's own salvation. When salvation could be bought with money, one's own concern to be saved became an isolated issue that could be separated from the larger social environment.

We conclude this section with a reflection on an engraving by John Everett Millais that depicts the parable of the bread-baking woman, an artifact that breathes sacramental permeability and suggests a parallel between the kitchen table and the altar, the kneading of the bread and the blessing of the bread. We see here a woman in the priestly role and at the same time as a maid who kneads bread.

"The kingdom of heaven is like yeast that a woman took and mixed with three measures of flour until all of it was leavened" (Matt. 13:33). In 1864, John Everett Millais published a series of engravings inspired by New Testament parables, including this one of the parable of the leaven.[130] We see an older woman

Fig. 2. Sir John Everett Millais, The Leaven (published 1864). Relief print on paper, 140 x 108 mm. Tate Gallery, London. Photo: Tate Gallery / Art Resource, N.Y.

and a young girl in a kitchen, both barefoot and simply clothed. We can see the face of the girl, who looks pale and tired. The kitchen is reduced to necessary and simple things: the table dominates the picture; on its surface are a couple of bowls, on the right side sheaves of wheat lean against the table. In the background is the brick arch of the oven. Doug Adams offers the following interpretation:

> Many painters featured important people in their works, such as national leaders or the wealthy or highly educated or moral exemplars like clergy; but Millais features two poor females who hardly counted in their own nineteenth-century culture, any more than women did at the time of Jesus. At the very center of the engraving is a billowing piece of fabric around the woman's waist—a feature like the billowing loincloth around the middle of Jesus on the cross in many art works. The woman's hands could be kneading the bread or blessing the bread, and the latter action is one which is like so many art works of Jesus' hands on the bread. We may see the table as a communion table at which a woman

not only is present but also presides. At the time of this engraving, the priest at the altar stood with his back to the congregation in celebrating the Mass as this woman in Millais' engraving stands with her back to the viewer; but in most churches only men officiated. The girl, too, holds a loaf in her hand and could be thought of as a server of the communion or an altar girl at a time when there were only altar boys.[131]

Before the offering of gifts such as bread can happen, the bread has to be kneaded. Millais's engraving inspires us to think that the work of women's hands cannot be separated from the blessing that is spoken over the bread. The woman's body bowed down in exhausting labor mirrors the body of Christ. Here is the place of eschatological imagination that yields sacramental permeability.

Consecrating Private Property

The task of integrating money into the relationships between people in the early Christian congregations was recognized from the outset. Money makes relationships abstract and anonymous. It creates its own world according to the logic of the economics of violence. Early Christianity was faced with the necessity of using money and private property. The problem posed by this task was how to change the rules.

The oldest account of the early Christian common meal is that of Paul in 1 Cor. 11:17-34. For the content of the prayers at the meal and its connection to Jesus' last meal, Paul appeals to tradition handed on to him; he says it was given him by the *kyrios* (11:23). *Kyrios* here refers not to God ,but to Jesus Christ. Paul had not known Jesus in person, but of course there were people, followers of Jesus, who handed on this tradition to him and welcomed him to share their community meal. He says nothing of that in detail. We may assume that Jesus died in about the year 33 CE The first letter to Corinth was written in about 55 CE We can therefore suppose that the community meal had been practiced by messianic groups of Jesus' followers from the time of his death onward, and that it represented the heart of the communities. It continues Jesus' community meals during his lifetime, and it is part of the history of Jewish meals. The prayers and the form of the meal stand within Jewish tradition; if the prayers of the Christian tradition (e.g., 1 Cor. 11:24, 25) are assumed to be familiar ones we can insert them into Jewish tradition. In Paul's account (11:24), the blessing of the bread is only mentioned, not quoted. Jesus "gave thanks," or more precisely he blessed God with the words: "Blessed are you, Eternal One, our God, king of the universe, who brings forth bread from the earth. . . . In the same way"

(11:25) he prayed before passing the cup and blessed or thanked God.[132] But then Paul quotes Jesus' words that give a messianic interpretation to the bread and cup that are shared. These, then, are additions to the Jewish table prayers.

This oldest account is part of Paul's reaction to a conflict in the Corinthian congregation over the community meal. He quotes the account of the meal in order to counter the meal practices of a group of Christians in Corinth. It is not a question of a conflict between Paul and the Corinthians, but rather a dispute between groups within the Corinthian community (11:18, 19); in his letter, Paul sides with one of the groups. The image of the apostle and his opponents has shaped the history of interpretation of the Pauline letters, but it is an ecclesiological one. Its starting point is the assumption of the continuity of a genuine or correct Pauline church that flows into the contemporary church, on the one side, with, on the other side, opponents, sectarians, and schismatics—then and now. This dualistic contrast does not do justice to the multiplicity of community praxis in early Christianity; in addition, it attributes to Paul an absolute authority that he neither had nor claimed. He was a teacher and apostle among many women and men who together lived the gospel and who discussed and disputed the correct interpretation of the Torah in their situation.

In exegetical discussions, the internal Christian conflict in Corinth is interpreted almost unanimously (although usually as a conflict between Paul and his opponents): According to Hellenistic-Roman custom, the meal would have consisted of food brought by the diners. But there were major social differences among the people who made up the community (cf. 1 Cor. 1:26). The well-to-do had better food and different meal customs from those of the day laborers and slaves. The former regard themselves as part of the Christian community and come to the community gathering, but they eat the food they have brought more or less separately from the others, as a private dinner (11:21, 33). They pay no attention to the poorer people who could bring very little, and whose food was also of lesser quality. The result is inequality: some are hungry and others are drunk (11:21, 22). The rich justify their behavior by saying they are hungry (11:34, 22). This practice is seen by other members of the community (11:18) and by Paul as despising the community and the poor (11:22) and as a wounding of the holiness of the body of Christ (11:29).

In 1 Cor. 11:30, Paul says that the meal practices he and others are criticizing have already led to sickness and death in the community. This idea that bad behavior in the community and before God can be dangerous and even fatal is alien to modern thinking. But it is crucial for understanding early Christian meals that we comprehend the significance of holiness for the very existence of community.

What is presumed in 1 Cor. 11:17-34 is a law of possessions that we also find in Acts 2:42-45 and 4:32—5:11. The congregation is a community sanctified by God, with a common property consecrated to God (*koina*, Acts 2:44; 4:32). The notion opposite to common property is private property (*idion*, Acts 4:32; 1 Cor. 11:21). The two forms exist alongside one another. For example, someone who owns a piece of land and becomes a member of the community is still the owner of the land, but is in principle ready at any time to sell the land for the benefit of the community, if the congregation decides to do so. The goal of the community is to prevent economic need on the part of individual members and to level economic inequality. The congregation is to be a holy community. Justice is an essential part of that holiness. According to the Acts of the Apostles, just as for 1 Corinthians 11, the community meal is based on that same holiness and justice. The well-to-do in Corinth did exactly what Ananias and Sapphira had done: They treated community property consecrated to God as private property; more precisely, they treated as their private property something that had already become common property devoted to God. Ananias and Sapphira had "kept back" (Acts 5:2) something dedicated to God,[133] thus risking sickness and death. They had had the opportunity to keep their private property for themselves (Acts 5:4). The wealthy in Corinth could have eaten at home (1 Cor. 11:22, 33), but in doing so they would have withdrawn from the congregation and its holiness. Sharing in the meal meant sharing in justice, holiness, and communion *(koinōnia)* with one another and with Christ. "Wounding the integrity of a community presumes a break between the human being and the divine."[134]

To the modern mind, the death of Ananias and Sapphira is as offensive as 1 Cor. 11:30. But it also happens today that people throw away their lives or put them at risk when they destroy their right relationship to other people and to God. We find parallel material in the First Testament and in Hellenistic-Roman literature for the notion of divine property that underlies both 1 Cor. 11:17-34 and the accounts in the Acts of the Apostles of the so-called community of goods: Josh 7:1-26; 2 Macc. 4:32-50; Lucian, *Philopseudēs* 20. Lucian writes of an iron statue of Pelichus, a Corinthian general.

> At the feet of the statue a number of pence were laid, and other coins were attached to his thigh by means of wax; some of these were silver, and there were also silver plates, all being the thank-offerings of those

whom he had cured of fever. Now we had a scamp of a Libyan groom, who took it into his head to filch all this coin under cover of night. He waited till the statue had descended from its pedestal, and then put his plan into effect.[135]

The groom was found out, and the statue forced him "to wander about in the court all night long, unable to find his way out." When daylight came, then, he was caught with his booty. He was flogged for the theft, and ultimately died of the beatings the statue gave him every night thereafter. Ananias and Sapphira, like the wealthy in Corinth and this slave, violated divine property. At any rate, Paul and Acts interpret such an act as *hierosylein*, even though they do not use the word in this context (but see Acts 19:37; Rom. 2:22). Lucian calls the coin thief *hierosylos:* one who stole from a divinity.

The story of Achan in Joshua 7 helps us to understand that a crime against God's property endangers the whole community, not just the perpetrators in the strict sense—as in 1 Cor. 11:30. We are not supposed to think that it was only the well-to-do in the Corinthian community who were stricken with sickness and death; it happened to other members as well. The community, its relationship to God, its holiness—all this was injured.

We may assume that the blessing of the bread turns private property into God's own. We can see from other early Christian traditions also that private property was not given away at random; there was a formal, public act of handing it over to become God's community property. This has a name in Acts: private property is "laid at the feet of the apostles" (4:35, 37; 5:2). Justin (*Apol.* 1, 67) says that it was laid "away" with the presider, presumably "away" from one's own possessions. It is therefore deceptive in this context to use concepts that come from present-day methods of giving donations. In all cases of early Christian "charity" for the poor, it is clear that this is not a matter of donations by the rich for the sake of the poor, but that the property of the well-to-do and of those not so well off became the property of the community and was then distributed by the community leaders. The food at the Eucharist also comes from dividing and sharing (*metalambanein*, Acts 2:46; Justin, *Apol.* 1, 67) in community. Participation in the meal and receiving money from the community do not make the recipients the objects of charity.

This is most obvious in the case of the "collection" Paul took up in the new communities made up mostly of people who were not Jewish in origin, destined for the "saints" in Jerusalem (Gal. 2:9, 10). When we put together the fragmentary information about this collection in Paul's letters and in

Acts, we get the following picture: The collection derived from an agreement between Paul, as apostle to the Gentiles, and leading figures in the Jerusalem community (Gal. 2:9, 10). It was agreed upon in the individual Christian congregations (Acts 11:29). The money was donated in the community assemblies (1 Cor. 16:2). These acts of giving also seem to have been understood as the bringing of a sacrifice to God (2 Cor. 8:12). The collection was meant to bring about equality in the sense of the manna miracle: All the communities are to receive as much as they need (2 Cor. 8:13-15; Exod. 16:17, 18). It achieves equality through the exchange of gifts (Rom. 15:27; 2 Cor. 8:14). Thus the poor, the communities in Jerusalem, are not only recipients; the gift is understood on both sides as an expression of God's caring (2 Cor. 9:12-15). Giving makes the givers righteous (2 Cor. 9:9, 10) as they imitate Christ's self-gift.

Here, as in the texts previously discussed, we see with what care and reflection the messianic communities treated their economic responsibility for one another and for those outside. Here again their praxis is in continuity with the synagogal tradition.[136] There, too, a gift from a wealthy person to a poor person was seen as problematic. Unfortunately, the language of private donation has dominated the Christian tradition of translation and interpretation of these texts, but this is not about "charity." It is about justice.

We began with the connection between 1 Corinthians 11 and the legal concepts in Acts as applied to the community of property. The question remains: What does the Eucharist have to do with the economic responsibility of Christian communities for each other (the transregional collection) and toward their members (community of property)? In its distribution of food, the Eucharist derives not only from the idea of God's property; the meal itself is an expression of economic and ecumenical responsibility. It is not a trivial thing that all eat what they need. The community meal was part of their necessary nourishment. When Justin says that food was likewise brought to members of the community who were not present, he means not only that they were thus brought visibly into the community, but that they were fed. These are not just symbolic pieces of bread; this is a meal. The word *bread*, as always, comprehends the whole meal, since in our culture bread is the most important food.

Interceding

Marjorie Suchocki's reflection on the radical interdependence of all things that constitute our being in the world reflects the impact that prayers of intercession potentially have on the environment surrounding us and on the people who are far away from us:

All things relate to all other things. In this interdependent world, everything that exists experiences to some degree the effects of everything else. We are so constituted that very, very little of all this relationality makes it to our conscious awareness. But we are connected, nonetheless. Praying lifts these loose connections to our conscious awareness in the context of God's presence. We begin to feel an echo of that divine meeting and weaving, no matter how distant the one for whom we pray.[137]

Suchocki says that prayers of intercession create a "channel in the world through which God can unleash God's will toward well-being. Prayer puts you in the way of the channel, and you will become a part of God's rolling waters."[138] These images, nurtured by insights from process theology, help to overcome the habits that result in the "thingification" of the poor, the marginalized, and all those who are in need. "We" do not pray "for them," thereby making "them" into mere recipients and objects of our and God's care. Rather, all who engage in intercessions enter into the co-creating process, in which God can unleash God's will toward well-being. Interceding can open us to God's possibilities that are yet to be uncovered. It can foster our apocalyptic sensitivities and eschatological imagination. Prayers of intercession unfold the desire that is directed toward the well-being of the "other"; they expand the realm of narrow self-interest and in that way de-center the desire of the *Homo oeconomicus*. We stop believing that the poverty of two-thirds of the world's population, who are victims of the logic of capitalist market-exchange, is a natural effect, that it cannot be different, that those things simply are as they are—unchangeable. The practice of interceding reveals and brings to light what is supposed to be hidden and unnamed: that the hidden effects of market exchange that create economic injustice are conceived to be part of the nature of human existence and history.

Prayers of intercession are a spiritual exercise that helps to overcome the "frozen apathy" the logic of market exchange produces in our hearts, minds, and emotional expression. They are an exercise in empathetic perception of the world in all its fragmentariness. Compassion is by no means something that comes naturally; it has to be nurtured. We have to be formed into compassionate disciples. This thought is thoroughly developed in Dorothee Sölle's theology of prayer. Sölle says of frozen apathy:

> We have inverted the relationships between love and suffering. . . .
> Our highest goal is to remain free of it right up to the moment of
> death. . . . The apathetic freedom from suffering, this freedom from
> want and from pain and from commitment to people has been

promoted to our highest value. . . . The goals of being capable of love
are subordinated to the goal of getting through life "well," which is to
say getting through unscathed, untouched.[139]

The practice of interceding is an initiation into the melting of frozen
apathy; it cultivates local and global imagination about the *basileia*. It also
fosters consciousness of our involvement in the global economy.[140]

In the Swedish *Sofia-mässor*, we find the following intercessions after
the Lord's Prayer, right before communion. These intercessions are intimately interwoven with the breaking of the bread:

> We break this bread for sisters and brothers
> who live in lands where war prevails
> as a sign that we all share
> both in the pain of war and in the longing
> and fight for peace and justice.
> We break this bread for brothers and sisters
> of differing beliefs and religious affiliation
> as an expression of the fact that we are all part of
> the same humanity
> and share this life on earth and with one another.
> We break this bread for our wounded earth,
> for fields, forests, and seas,
> as a sign that we belong together
> with the whole of God's creation
> and want to take responsibility for the healing of the earth's wounds.
> We break this bread for the division
> and brokenness we experience within ourselves
> and in relationships between people
> as an expression that we want to open ourselves
> To wholeness and life
> when we share the bread that is the body of Christ.[141]

The intercessions of the Swedish *Sofia-mässor* stress the interconnec-
tion with those for whom the people pray. In this sense they overcome the
danger of objectifying "the others." They also rise above an anthropocentric
perspective by focusing on the wounded earth as well, revealing another
dimension of interdependence.

What could be highlighted in such a prayer is the complicity of those
who pray. If those for whom we pray are indeed connected with us, we are

reminded not to romanticize this connection but to ask about our complicity in the effects of the global economy. The Eucharistic life that flows out of the practice of interceding invites us to be honest with ourselves and to inspect our privileges and the disastrous influence they have on the social and ecological environment. This kind of self-inspection can be seen as a result of the hard work of interceding for our enemies. If we delve into the truth of radical interdependence, we cannot avoid recognizing that our enemies are part of our own lives, and those of us who enjoy First World privileges as white middle-class Westerners are enemies of the life of others.

The praxis of interceding is grounded in the insight that we are not omnipotent; we are finite, and our access to the resources that let us live is not limitless. The expression of our finitude and the limits of our own agency in the world as it occurs in prayers of intercession can become a subversive practice. It has the potential to challenge the omnipotent illusions that come with the myth of the *Homo oeconomicus* who dreams of life eternal as realization of eternal health and limitless ability to accumulate wealth.

Interceding is a process in which we become aware of the limits of our own agency and the needs of the people that still must be met. We become aware of the things we cannot change, as in the case of terminal illness. We voice the helplessness that emerges from those ordeals and offer them to God. We also become aware of our limited perception of the overwhelming suffering of people and God's entire creation on this planet. We recognize only marginal bits of it. There are so many voices we will never hear and who deserve to be heard; there are so many victims of poverty and warfare whose names we do not know. The practice of interceding confronts us as well with the disastrous forms of misinformation as they are conveyed through the media, especially in the United States. The greater our desire to speak as concretely and clearly as possible, the more we recognize how fuzzy our perception and analysis of life circumstances are, for example, in the Middle East. Those hindrances to our ability to intercede may motivate us to revisit information politics with regard to those places. In this way interceding may become a critical spiritual exercise in global empathy.

Some people might respond that this is ridiculous, because God does not need to be informed about matters of global world economy. But we believe that this radical interconnectedness also has an impact on God. In many intercessory prayers, God is asked to remember God's people. What is assumed here is that interceding is a way of tapping into the memory of God. Don Saliers describes interceding as remembering the world to God and an act of solidarity with Christ, who is constantly interceding for the pain of the world.[142] Saliers draws our attention to the fact that prayers of intercession were initially "prayers of the faithful"; only those who had been baptized could join Christ's intercessions. Those prayers were spoken in one of two places: either at the end of the service of the Word, just before the gift offerings were brought to the table, or as an integral part of the Great Thanksgiving itself. "In some cases very long intercessions were prayed in the presence of the eucharistic bread and wine. This is especially true of the Jerusalem liturgy (St. James), the Byzantine Liturgy of St. Basil, and still today in the orthodox liturgy of St. John Chrysostom."[143] In some of those prayers the intercessions can be understood as "an expansion of the *epiclesis* upon the congregation to include within the Eucharistic action those for whom they pray."[144] The prayers of the faithful for the world gain their power through the invocation of the Holy Spirit.

Intercession was made for the living and the dead through the so-called *diptychs*. Diptychs[145] were writing tablets that contained lists for the living and for the departed.[146] The liturgy of St. John Chrysostom, for example, contains extensive diptychs commemorating the Virgin Mary, John the Baptist, all who have fallen asleep, the holy, catholic, and apostolic church, the emperor and Christ-loving empress and their court and army, the city in which we dwell and all cities, and the archbishop. The Lord is asked to remember those who do good works in the church as well those who are at sea, travelers, the sick, prisoners, the poor. In the liturgy of St. John Chrysostom, these diptychs are placed right before the Lord's Prayer and following the prayers of inclination, elevation, and fraction.[147]

Interceding is understood as remembering the world to God; it includes the departed, the church, and the cities, those who have political, military, and ecclesiastical power. The prayer for those who are in political power is a prayer for peace, that they might use their authority for the well-being of the people.

Our journey through the two economies and how they are related to the Eucharist comes to a close. We have seen how biblical and liturgical traditions through the centuries give witness to the violence the market economy produces. We have introduced spotlights of eschatological imagination in which God's economy breaks through. We have offered the symbolic order of gift exchange and the concept of sustainability as a framework that might help us to rethink issues of economic exchange, liturgy, and Eucharistic life.

Chapter 4
THE BODY POLITICS
OF EUCHARIST

"This is my body,"
says someone.
And presently the same person says,
or almost says,
"This is my blood."
What is going on?[1]

Real Bodies at the Meal[2]

Bodies are the divine presence on earth,
they are sacramental and are often profaned.[3]

THE EUCHARISTIC LIFE IS ABOUT the real stuff: bread and hunger, food and pleasure, eating disorders and global food politics, private property and the common good. The Eucharistic life is about the real stuff in the light of sacramental permeability. It is about holiness and resurrection; it is about gift exchange, sustainability, and the economy of grace. When we share the holy meal together, when we bring our gifts to the table, when we intercede for the world, when we collect money, and when we give thanks we are entering the realm of eschatological imagination.

At the center of all these things we do is the body. In their book on body theology, Lisa Isherwood and Elisabeth Stuart ask:

> What more than the human body and its needs makes us present in the world? What reminds us constantly of the demands of relationships more than our body selves? In what other ways can we really become

aware of the divine than by looking deeply and bravely into the face of divine matter? This looking does not make something descend that is not otherwise present; it rather makes demands and offers empowerment in the light of divine indwelling.[4]

We begin with a Eucharistic liturgy that was offered by the Reverend Colette Jackson, in which she expresses how she, as a queer African American woman, sees the connection between body politics and holy eating:[5]

"Witness God's Welcome": A Communion Celebration (Colette Jackson)
(*The sound of perhaps a single heartbeat from the drum is heard out of the silence. The four voices are placed in different corners of the room. They speak in turn. The voices may be more than one person each. The speakers hold the elements.*)

Fire voices:
> The church is on fire. Let it burn till we are free.
> The table set two thousand years ago waits for us.

Wind voices:
> A tornado has hit my house. Let it whirl until the betrayal of my family has been witness.
> The table set two thousand years ago holds a place with my name on it.

Earth voices:
> The earth quakes beneath the courthouse. Let it rock until the laws protect my people.
> At the table set two thousand years ago there is a plate filled with food for all.

Water voices:
> There are floods in the city of God. When we come together and the flood joins the river of justice, then we will eat.
> The table is set. It is time now.

Two thousand years ago there was a table set to witness our welcome.
The meal speaks truth:
That all are welcome, all are loved.
> we know that there is no force that can stop this witness of welcome
> we know as Jesus knew that this is the meal to which all are invited
> we know that no church law can take this meal away from

any who come

we know that not even torture of our minds can take this
meal away from us

we know that not even death can take this table away from us
and we know why this bread was broken for all

and we know in the breaking of this bread we are the Body
of Christ.

It is our bodies.

It is the body of the poor,

it is generations of Han,

of legacies carried in the bodies of African Americans,

of Native Americans,

of Jews.

It is the children's bodies breaking in fields of labor across
the nation;

it is the bodies of women killed across the planet in domestic violence;

it is the bodies of all peoples who have suffered at the hands
of a crucifying culture.

It is God's body breaking with us.

(Breaking the bread at each station and the words of institution.)

And so

we witness today that God has put us in the center of this
justice movement;

we witness today as so many have done before that we will
not turn back from this table of righteousness;

we recognize that when we witness the welcome of queer
people,

when we put ourselves at the center of this communion,

we witness the welcome of all marginalized people;

we will witness to every denomination the river of justice
that is God's plan.

(Raising the cups at each station and at the words of institution.)

So as we drink from this cup we are aligned in the great cosmic
moment of crying out for love in the same way that Jesus raised the
cup two thousand years ago to witness to the world that all people are

welcome here and not even death will change that truth.

We must know that we are not only welcome at this meal; we are this meal. In these times of queer bashing and queer youth suicide and a history of Homosexual torture God speaks through us.

We are not to allow ourselves to wait on the edge, linger on edges waiting for acceptance.

God has put us at the center of this movement for a reason.

God works through those who have been the most marginalized, the most oppressed. And we are the new voice of justice.

Will you pray with me:

We pray to you, O God, great spinning earth spirit.

Break this bread grown from your great dark soil.

Fill it with your spirit, God, so that we will fill also with the strength of the earth

for this journey we now take on

God, great Mother/Father God,

move through the elements prepared today with the mighty force of your wind.

Break this bread in our hearts

so that we will know the urgency of speaking as queer Christians and allies,

so that we can save the lives of hundreds of young queer sistahs and brothers

who will not need to take their lives now that we have witnessed to their welcome today.

Great Spirit, move as the flames of justice as we take these elements.

Let us know the flames that surge inside us.

Let us spit fire into the fears of old closets and burn shame to ash

so that we speak and act from this time forward inside your burning bush of truth.

And God,

as we drink, move like the great river of justice through our souls, joining our spirits with the spirits of all marginalized and oppressed people throughout the world.

Give us the breath and blood of a people who can witness the welcome of all beings,

and let us know in this great thanksgiving that we are cherished and loved forever and ever.

     So be It, Amen.

     We are the voice of God today.

We now sit in the seat of civil rights
and this is the meal that will sustain us;
this is the meal that will fill our souls
with the righteous indignation of Jesus.
This is the meal that will let us walk through the valley of the shadows
of death and hatred.
This is the meal that God has given us.
So no one can tell you you are not welcome at this table.
No one can tell you you cannot serve at this table.
This is the table of God
and we are God's messengers today.
Everyone is welcome. *(Instructions.)*
(Serving the meal.)

The body is at the heart of the Eucharistic celebration.[6] We enter into the mystery of communion with the tortured and risen Christ in the Eucharist through the physical activity of eating and drinking. The Eucharist is a messianic meal in which the resurrection of the body is celebrated.[7] It is also the celebration of resurrection in which sins are forgiven and we partake in the mystical body. Last but not least, those who are gathered around the table are the body of Christ in the world; their actual, individual bodies are temples of the Holy Spirit. Our bodies are sacred places through which God acts in the world. Being the body of Christ in the world also takes into account the fact that our physical bodies are porous; they are connected with the environment every second of our existence. The Eucharist is the feast of radical empathy with the most vulnerable.

Over centuries theologians have pondered how to speak about Christ's bodily presence in the Eucharist. This presence is at the heart of the Eucharist as a resurrection meal. During the history of the church many quarrels have arisen over the interpretation of the presence of Christ in the Eucharist. The Roman Catholic view, that the elements of bread and wine are transubstantiated into Christ's real blood and flesh, was challenged in the Protestant traditions.[8] Reformed Christians emphasized the work of the Holy Spirit, who mediates Christ's real presence through the sacraments. Some, like the Genevan Reformer Zwingli, focused on the act of remembrance that takes place in the celebration of the Eucharist. Zwingli denied the presence of Christ's human nature in the sacrament.[9] A study of the question of Christ's presence suggests that, since the time of the Reformation in Europe, three models for describing Christ's presence in the Eucharist have dominated: transubstantiation, spiritual presence, and the Lutheran view, which emphasizes the real presence of Christ in both natures, human and divine.

We find in the theology of the Reformers as well as in the works of theologians of the early church intense reflection on the connection of the Eucharist with incarnation: "as in Ignatius the Eucharist serves as the place where the believer meets the fleshly Christ of the resurrection after his ascension, in Justin the Eucharist is the place where the incarnate Logos is remembered."[10] Irenaeus of Lyons emphasizes that there can only be salvation of the flesh in the Eucharist because of Christ's incarnation: "Now if there is no salvation for the flesh neither did the Lord redeem us with his blood, nor is the cup of the Eucharist a communion [*communicatio*] in his blood, nor is the bread which we break communion in his body" (cf. 1 Cor 10:16).[11]

Martin Luther stands in the tradition of the church fathers who see the redemptive activity of God at work in the bodily presence of Christ, which is in the sacraments attached to physical things.[12] Redemption is situated in the corporeal world:

> But we trust our God, who has willed to be born of Mary spiritually and physically but not to be eaten and drunk by her physically or spiritually. By the shepherds and Simeon he wanted to be seen spiritually and physically but not born and not eaten. So, according to his pleasure, he has permitted himself to be physically and spiritually handled, seen, heard, born, suckled, carried, touched, and the like by whomever he willed. But here in the Lord's Supper he wants to be neither born nor seen nor heard nor touched by us but only eaten and drunk, both physically and spiritually.[13]

How this happens remains a mystery, but Luther insists that we should not set bounds and measures to God's word and promise.[14] The Eucharist reveals a complex bodily reality: the tortured body of Christ, the resurrected body, the body given for us, the spiritual body we incorporate into our own body. The Lutheran tradition stresses the corporeity of the sacraments, which infuse God's promise and life by giving *word* to the material world of water, wine, bread, and bodies. Luther was very much concerned with the real presence of Christ in the Eucharist. He followed Paul's theology that the body has to be redeemed just as much as the soul. It is time to realize that we bring our real selves—that is to say, our bodies—to the table.

If we put our reflection on bodily presence in an ecclesiological perspective and focus on the gathered community, we can realize that a baffling variety of body realities connected to the holy meal emerges: The assembly as the body of Christ is radically interconnected with the sufferings in the larger world. When we partake in the holy meal, our bodies are lifted up as temples of the Holy Spirit. Our individual bodies that congregate around the table are sites of social power struggles and containers of memory. Our bodies are the most intimate places in which we live out our lives. They are the most intimate places from which we connect ourselves with the world, from which we form relationships. We cannot separate ourselves, our minds, or our spiritual lives from our bodily existence. In that sense, it is really true that we do not have bodies—rather, we *are* bodies.

We come to the table as aging and differently abled bodies, constantly changing in inward condition and outward appearance. We come as dying bodies, as pregnant bodies, as bodies carrying different forms of cancer, as bodies infected with HIV. Our bodies are "archaeological sites" holding innumerable body memories of pleasure and ecstasy, illness and pain, as well as joyful memories of being fed and filled, memories of hunger, violence, and alienation.[15] We come as eating bodies with ambiguous experiences around the consumption of food. We come and hide that we are anorexic or bulimic. We come as bodies who have been raped. We come as bodies that hold this overwhelming variety of memories even as we are invited to enter into the existential act of remembering another "body story." We come with gendered bodies—as female, male, transgendered, or in between. We come with sexualized bodies, as queer or straight, and with racialized bodies that are White, Black, Asian, Hispanic.[16] We are particular bodies that are "seen" into existence by others. The normalizing gaze has given our body identity by means of measuring and modern scientific reasoning.[17] Social power struggles are inscribed in our bodies, our skin, our genitals.

In the Eucharistic celebration we are immersed in the narrative of Christ's life, death, and resurrection, and we become one in Christ. This proclaimed oneness in Christ does not mean that we should ignore the politics of difference and the power struggles that are inscribed in our bodies. The notion of community that the body of Christ metaphor implies is not naïve or romantic; it rather acknowledges the painful experiences of privilege and exclusion.

Our bodies are not physical entities per se. In their very physical appearance they are seen into existence by others and by our own practices. Those practices encompass the rituals in which we engage. The ritual theorist Catherine Bell speaks of the ritualized body that comes to know his or her body-self by employing certain practices.[18] Ritual actions such as eating and drinking in particular ways, standing, kneeling, or bowing, any and all of which are accompanied by words, the pulse of prayers, and the lyrics and sounds of spoken and sung words, physically engage the ritualized body. Those practices performed in peculiar ways not only communicate specific religious convictions; they produce ritualized bodies onto which particular ways of knowing the divine are imprinted.[19] Catherine Bell emphasizes that "the molding of the body within a highly structured environment does not simply express inner states. Rather, it primarily acts to restructure bodies in the very doing of the acts themselves."[20] Thus we become ritualized bodies by celebrating communion.

In what follows, we explore the diversity of "body realities" that emerges from the Eucharistic life and related body politics. We begin with the issue of body and metaphor. We are interested in a metaphorical understanding of the body of Christ that embraces the physical reality of our bodies, and so we highlight the presence of actual bodies at the meal as the place of sacramental encounter.

The Body as Metaphor as Body . . .

The sacraments state that
the word of God wants to enter our bodies.[21]

It was in the Chapel of the Great Commission in Berkeley, California, on December 3, 2001, that the Reverend Jim Mitulski presided at the table.[22] He broke the bread, lifted it up with his left hand, and pointed to his own body with his right hand, saying, "This is the body of Christ. The body of Christ has AIDS." He paused for a moment. Then he opened his arms, embracing the congregation with his body and his words: "Please join me: We are the body of Christ. The body of Christ has AIDS." I heard voices in the room more stammering than in full confident unison: "We . . . are . . . the body . . . of Christ. The body of Christ . . . has AIDS." The atmosphere was loaded with earth-shaking electricity generated by this one gesture of a man who dared to point to his own body and then embrace the whole congregation—with the consecrated bread in his hand. He, a pastor infected with HIV, presented his body as the body of Christ.

This was a deeply sacred moment for me. All of a sudden I had a deeply "felt" sense for what I have understood on a cognitive level for quite a while:

Our individual bodies are temples of the Holy Spirit, and the assembly around the table *is* (in the flesh and not only representationally) the body of Christ. Christ's presence in the Eucharist is manifested not only in bread and wine but in the actual bodies as they come to the table.[23] It was at this worship service that I was fully immersed, with all of our senses, into this mystery.

We suggest calling this gesture an *embodied metaphor*. The gesture opened a space that resonated with a multitude of meanings. It was not self-absorbed—Jim Mitulski did not say, "I am the body of Christ," nor was he solely pointing to his body. He included the food and the assembly that was about to commune. This gesture as embodied metaphor illuminated how dangerous and shocking it can be to speak about the body of Christ in this way.

A couple of years later, Jim Mitulski talked about what it means to him that real bodies come to the table, that real bodies are places of sacramental encounter.[24] He spoke about the denial in which many religious communities engage. People with HIV and AIDS might be considered objects of religious welfare at the receiving end of Christian charity, but associating infected bodies with Christ's body is appalling for many. With regard to the Eucharist, many liberal U.S. Protestants tend to favor a disembodied understanding of the Lord's Supper. Many are not interested in—indeed, they are afraid of—inquiring into an embodied presence of Christ that qualifies our own corporeality.

Metaphors in the context of ritual are embodied expressions. They are embedded in performative practices:

> The sacraments, which inscribe the faith in the body of the participants, symbolically give a role to play to all these modalities of the human being as "speaking body": the body of desire is given a role through the "enjoyment" of the complaint or the jubilation, of the cry or the silence, of the prostration or the hand lifted up to the heavens; . . . the body of nature is given a role through the play of light and darkness, the play of seasons which punctuate the liturgical year, the play of death and life in the baptismal water, the play of food and drink in the Eucharist and so on.[25]

The sacraments as event inscribe faith into the body of the participants; they transform human beings into "speaking bodies." This is how Jim Mitulski became a "speaking body" to me, in a concrete moment in time, on the occasion of the observance of World AIDS Day in Berkeley, California, in the year 2001. By qualifying this experience in time and space, we insist that embodied metaphors have to be understood in their context; they do not hold meaning in an essentialist way.

Metaphors in the context of ritual are embodied expression. In time and space they are embedded in energy, flow, movement, gesture and, last but not least, language. Language is not to be separated from the body. We think and speak bodily; we are in that sense speaking bodies.[26] Our embodied knowing is highly subjective and, at the same time, creates a shared horizon. With regard to this example, we do not know what the other worshipers saw when Jim Mitulski pointed to his own body during the Eucharist. I had a sense, however, that at least the energy in the room, the atmosphere in the sanctuary, referred to a shared horizon.

Gail Ramshaw reflects on the metaphorical quality of language in liturgies. She defines metaphor as "that use of speech in which the context demonstrates that a factually or logically inaccurate word is on the deepest level true. The wrong word is seen to be the right word; to talk about X, we use the image of Y."[27] A metaphor is neither a comparison nor an analogy (for example, God as mother). According to this distinction, a metaphor is a figure of speech more fully true, a simile one only partially appropriates.[28] Metaphors express something that is literally not true: The liturgical assembly is not a body, nor is God a rock or a father. Yet metaphors express something that is on a different level true. They stimulate our imagination. We can imagine all kinds of bodies. Ramshaw refers to Paul Ricoeur's statement that metaphors expand human imagination by layering, in human thought and communication, what is with what is not. Thus lifting up the metaphorical quality of liturgical language is a way of expanding our imagination; it invites ambiguity, surprise, dissent, and perhaps laughter at our attempts to narrow and identify God's name in one-dimensional ways in our worship services.

Gordon Lathrop insists on the metaphorical usage of the body metaphor as a means of critical interpretation:

> The danger remains that we will take the metaphors literally, forgetting their core reference to liturgical assembly and to the central matters of liturgical assembly. This literal spirit is especially problematic when it brings along practices that do not accord with the root ecclesiology of the liturgy. "Body of Christ" can be used to support a monolithic, closed, and hierarchical organization, where each of us are cells of the whole and the rulers are closer to the "head." The metaphor will be healthier, more authentically related to its origins, [see 1 Cor. 10:16-17]

if it is genuinely taken as metaphor and not metaphysical reality, and
if it is always set next to the Eucharist and always used to name an
open, diverse, and centered assembly. Then calling that assembly "body
of Christ" will be stunning.[29]

We want to add that the body metaphor was frequently used to legitimize male dominance in the ordering of the ministries of the church as
well as legitimizing male patriarchal power as God-given in marriages.[30]
Body rhetoric in political discourse in antiquity was a means to proclaim a
fictional unity in social environments that were severely segregated through
slavery, patriarchy, and class differences. In current U.S. political discourse,
the slogan "United We Stand" probably serves a similar purpose.

Lifting up the metaphorical quality of our talk about the body of Christ
serves the purpose of critical deconstruction of hierarchies, of a perverted
understanding of unity, and of communities and organizations as closed
systems. Besides the task of critical interpretation, metaphors can inspire
our imagination in worship. We can speak metaphorically about the body
of Christ in ways that appreciate our corporeality without letting the reality
of actual bodies disappear. We turn now to Paul's multilayered understanding of *sōma* (body), to a nondualistic interpretation of the resurrection of
the body, and to a consideration of how it relates to the Eucharist.

"This Is My Body"

At the center of Jesus' words of interpretation in the Synoptic Gospels
and in Paul's letter stands the statement: "This is my body (*sōma*)." Jesus
adds these interpretive words to the Jewish blessing over the bread. Thus
he would have said: "Blessed are you, Eternal One, our God, King of the
Universe, who brings forth bread from the earth. This is my body that is
given for you."[31] During the prayer, or immediately after it, Jesus takes
bread in his hands, breaks it, and shares it with the company at table. The
application of the statement about the body, the "this is" (*touto estin*) is not
absolutely clear from the words themselves. The parallel in the words over
the cup, which do not mention the wine in the cup, seem to indicate that
we should not apply the phrase to the bread. It applies, rather, to the whole
action (see above, pp. 58–62). Likewise, the phrase "my body" is not absolutely clear. Certainly it applies to the body of Jesus as the martyr who will
die and rise. But what Paul says in various places about the body of Christ
and the reference to the new covenant in the words over cup both look to a
different level of interpretation, namely, that of the people of God. Before
we examine more closely the multidimensional nature of the idea of the

"body of Christ," we need to take a look at the social-historical context. The following story is told of Hillel, a Pharisaic sage (d. 10 CE):

> So it is written (Prov. 11:17): "Those who are kind reward themselves." Such (is) Hillel the elder, who in the hour when he took leave of his disciples (after concluding the lesson) went on walking with them (for a little while). Then his disciples said to him: Rabbi, where are you going? He said to them: To fulfill a commandment. And they said to him: What commandment is it? Then he said to them: To bathe at the bathhouse. They said to him: And that is a commandment? He said to them: Yes, (for) if in the case of the images of the kings that are set up in the theaters and circuses, the one who is placed over them (i.e., the images) cleans and washes them, and they (i.e., the officials) pay him (for doing so), and he can even claim for himself a share in the royal aristocracy, then I, who am made "in the image and likeness," for it is written (Gen. 1:26-27; 9:6) "in the image of God he created human beings," then how much more![32]

The statues of kings in theaters and circuses were treated like living persons, because the ruler they depicted, and his power, were present in them. Caring for the statues was an expression of cultic reverence and political loyalty. The conclusion from the lesser to the greater at the end of Hillel's parable indicates that I, as a human being created by God, am more worthy of reverence than the rulers. Bathing my body shows honor to God's creature. This little parable tells us, in a few words, how Hillel regarded bathing his own body as an expression of his relationship to God, and how he also placed the action within a political context. The bodies of human beings, created by God, were the objects of acquisitive political power; to put it more bluntly, of every form of violence that put human beings at the disposal of others. The Roman emperor regarded the bodies of those subject to his power as his own property. The poll tax was a kind of rent: people paid for the privilege of using someone else's property.[33] The word *sōma*/body could be used to refer to slaves.[34] The owners' possessive relationship was often expressed in violent seizure and abuse of human bodies: blows and sexual abuse, and in the case of slaves, torture as well.

In Rom. 3:9-20, Paul laments the alienation of bodies, the alienation of human beings from themselves.[35] "Their throats are opened graves; they use their tongues to deceive. The venom of vipers is under their lips. Their mouths are full of cursing and bitterness," the bitterness of the violent power of slaveowners. "Their feet are swift to shed blood; ruin and misery are in their paths." These words are spoken from the perspective of the victims of such violence. But Paul does not leave the victims in a stance of innocence. All have participated in violent deeds: "There is no one who is righteous" (Rom. 3:10-12). Paul's lament traces the outlines of the body. Bodies are beaten, and the victims, in their own bodies, take an active part in the systems of violence. One of Jesus' parables speaks of this: The slave whose owner makes him an overseer in charge of his fellow slaves beats those who have been placed under his protection (Luke 12:45). Here, slaves are both the victims of violence and participants in it.

Object of political power grabs and very frequently of violence, marked with suffering and complicity—that is the body Jesus speaks of in his interpretive words over the bread. It is also the body Hillel speaks of, the body that bathes and experiences itself as God's creature. In both cases the political context is a more than obvious part of the message. The Last Supper traditions and Paul both mention Jesus' final meal and thus his execution by Roman soldiers: "On the night when he was handed over. . .".[36] All the sources place the words of interpretation in the context of the narrative of Jesus' Passion. The suffering man Jesus, who has been judged guilty,[37] is present in the meal; his *sōma/body* is present.

The German language distinguishes between *leib* and *körper*, while English has only one equivalent: *body*. We are using both in the same sense here, and treating them as having the same meaning. We will return to the problem of theological dualism, but for the present we can say that "body," as the translation for the Greek word *sōma*, describes the whole human being, the person with its history and its mortal body. It is the body created and loved by God, with its history, that through Jesus' words of interpretation is made central to the Eucharist. Hillel's parable can make clear for us what Jesus, as a Jewish person in the context of the Roman Empire, means when he speaks of his body.

So what does it mean for Jesus to say "this is . . ."? The interpretive words presuppose the practice of repetition in the Christian community meal. Whenever the words of interpretation are repeated in the community of the congregation, the body of Christ is present. It is clear that *the body of Christ is the body of the martyred Jesus*. But the concept has further dimensions: It incorporates all that is signified by the people of God (made explicit in the words over the cup), and it incorporates the individual bodies of the participants. In 1 Corinthians, Paul developed these dimensions of the concept of the "body of Christ" very explicitly. In 1 Cor. 12:12-24, he speaks of the *congregation that is the body of Christ*. This is not about equating it with an organism,[38] but about the congregation's living its identity as the body of

Christ. The many, altogether, are Christ (1 Cor. 12:12). The Spirit of God transforms people so that they become part of the body of Christ. This takes place through baptism and "drinking" the Spirit of God. The people who copied Paul's letters in the early centuries were already disturbed by this formulation in 1 Cor. 12:12, and inserted a clear reference either to baptism or to Eucharist into the phrasing.[39] But the oldest text would have had this puzzling formula. We understand it to be a reference to the community meal. Baptism and community meal are not in a logical competition, as if one could ask: When, then, do the believers receive the Spirit of God? Both rites are experiences of the Spirit, experiences of transformation of the body, of the people who trust in Christ. Together with others, they become Christ. Together, they are his body (cf. Rom. 12:5). Paul thus imagines *the relationship of individuals to Christ* as a physical communion. This is clearest when he tries to persuade the Christian men in Corinth not to go to prostitutes, as was customary in that society. Paul sees sexual congress with prostitutes as an attack on physical communion with Christ: A Christian "is united to" (*kollōmenos*) Christ and is "one spirit" with him (1 Cor. 6:17). Sexual intercourse with a prostitute is, for him, like adultery toward Christ. According to Paul, a Christian man can have intercourse with his wife without wounding Christ (1 Cor. 7:1-5). He thus pictures the relationship to Christ as a relationship between the human body and Christ's body. Paul was not systematic about such ideas, something they are not really suited for. The Spirit transforms individuals, men and women, into members of the body of Christ, or as Paul will also say, their bodies are temples of the Spirit, places where God is present (1 Cor. 6:19).[40]

The three dimensions of the concept of the "body of Christ" in Paul's writing (Christ's body, the people of God, individual human beings/bodies) are so intimately related that in some texts it is impossible to distinguish them. In 1 Cor. 6:19, the "body" that is the temple of God can mean an individual person (which fits the literary context) and/or the congregation (1 Cor. 3:16). In 1 Cor. 11:29, it is practically impossible to distinguish among the various dimensions.[41]

The three dimensions are inseparable in Jesus' interpretive words, "my body." The community becomes Christ, the body of Christ. Whoever takes hold of it is touching the body of Christ. It is the body of Christ as community, and the individual members are parts of the body. The consecration, the transformation into the body of Christ—the body of Christ dead and risen—takes place through the repetition of Jesus' words of institution.

The New Testament traditions about the resurrection are still burdened with dualistic misunderstandings. The cross and the resurrection are separated (see above, pp. 62–65). The resurrection of the "body" is limited to the future, in the sense of linear time, and thus is separated from real, mortal life.

In 1 Cor. 15:44, Paul calls the resurrection body *sōma pneumatikon*/spirit body, spiritual body. What does he mean by that, and what does the "spirit body" have to do with the Eucharist? Traditionally, this expression and the whole account of the resurrection in 1 Corinthians 15 has been interpreted dualistically. People must first die.[42] They will rise beyond death, outside their bodies, in God's future, which is radically separated from the human present. It is true that the early Christian hope in the resurrection of the body was retained, but in the process the body became unreal, not identical with the mortal body whose decay we experience daily. People did not want to think dualistically, but somehow or other the resurrection body was transformed into the immortal soul.[43]

When we deliberately free the early Christian hope of resurrection from its dualistic interpretation, the separation between mortal body and resurrection body cannot be maintained. This mortal body is transformed by the divine Spirit into the *sōma pneumatikon*, now, in the midst of the drama of violence and mortality that shapes our lives. The transformation effected by the Spirit to a *sōma pneumatikon* also occurs in the Eucharist. The resurrection body, the human being transformed by the divine Spirit, lives a new life and hopes for a future with God, even after death. That people have to die is a part of their life and is not the subject of this hope of resurrection. The death of creatures is not the experience of separation from life and from God that Western culture has made it. For the people whose words and thoughts are expressed in the New Testament, "death" is primarily something humanly caused, death is violence that deforms all life and destroys creation. This death is swallowed up in Christ's victory (1 Cor. 15:54-57).

When Jesus' interpretive words are repeated, the great miracle occurs in the transformation of the community at table. Jesus' body, tortured and risen, is present. The table community is Jesus' body. These people are surrounded, in the midst of life, by resurrection—to adapt the words of one of the church's hymns ("In the midst of life we are surrounded by death").[44] They are transformed into Spirit-filled beings (*sōma pneumatikon*). Jesus was the victim of violence among human beings. The table community does not stand at a secure distance from such violence. It is threatened, just as Jesus was. But the violence has lost its legitimation. The faithful are no longer enslaved by it, and now it can be resisted.

The Body Politics of the State

Making the Tortured Body Visible

> *Just as liturgy is not a merely "spiritual" formation*
> *which then must be applied to the physical world,*
> *torture is not a merely physical assault on bodies*
> *but a formation of a social imagination.*[45]

In the night when Jesus was handed over, he took the bread. The Eucharistic celebration leads us into the imaginary realm of the night before Jesus was tortured and killed. It does not lead us directly to the place of torture, Golgotha. It is the night before all of these things happen. We speak or sing diverse words: This is my body given for you, broken for you; this is the covenant in my blood, blood shed for you, blood poured out for you.[46] The words carry sacrificial connotations for many people who listen to them. They need to be heard in the context of the events that followed the Last Supper. The Eucharistic celebration does not directly expose a tortured body but points implicitly to it, a body that carries the marks of violence, impossible to imagine,[47] unbearable to behold. This is seeing and not seeing.[48] Many Christians have a hard time making these words their own.[49]

At Pacific School of Religion in Berkeley, where we have taught the "Holy Eating" class, conflicts have arisen around communion. Some students want to abolish the Eucharistic narrative because they find the blood imagery too disturbing. They see it as glorifying violence, and they reject the idea that there could be a connection between violence and redemption. Others recognize in this argument a sanitized image of Jesus that seems to be an expression of white middle-class religion. In particular, some African American students in our courses point to the fact that, in the context of slavery, the songs about the blood of Jesus had redemptive power. They claim that this is still true for the present, and they celebrate the motif of blood-shedding as a vision of victory for African-American people. Jesus at the cross, the "tree," is strongly connected with thousands of lynchings of African Americans who have also been hung from trees. Blood-shedding becomes an image of hope and resistance: *"The blood that gives me strength from day to day will never lose its power."*[50] But there are also voices, especially of Black women, who do not agree that these traditions are still liberating for them. The Womanist theologian Delores Williams gives voice to their concerns. She claims that it is not at Golgotha that Black women can find salvation; it is rather in the wilderness, where God's angel appears to the slave Hagar and shows her the path of survival.[51]

The most radical critics address the issue of interpreting Jesus' death. Atonement theologies such as those of Anselm of Canterbury are discarded.[52] Sacrificial theologies, which are thought to be at the core of the holy meal, do not seem to make sense for many liberal Christians. Feminist theologians seek to expand the range of images as a means of reclaiming the Eucharist. It is the feast of our lives,[53] in which Jesus' dedication to life in fullness is celebrated. The holy meal is understood within the framework of God's hospitality, inviting the stranger and renewing community.

Some Mennonites reclaim nonviolent atonement theologies that shape the sacrificial language that permeates many Eucharistic liturgies. The forgiveness of sins, celebrated in the meal, is interpreted against the background of the "Christus Victor" motif.[54] Forgiveness of sins is situated in the context of God's cosmic battle against the powers of evil that enslave individuals.

Conflicts arise around how to understand the words about a body given for us in the Eucharistic liturgy. The Eucharistic narrative points to the tortured body of Christ. What does it mean to remember and in an aesthetic sense to "see" this body in a lifegiving way that does not glorify violence?

In his book *Torture and Eucharist*, William T. Cavanaugh reflects on the Eucharistic narrative as a story that does not suppress the reality of torture. Reflecting on the role of the church during Augusto Pinochet's dictatorship in Chile, he claims that the Eucharist was the church's "counter-politics" set against the politics of torture.[55] He describes

> the logic of Eucharist as an alternative economy of pain and the body. Torture and Eucharist are opposing *disciplinae arcanorum* using different means and serving different ends. Where torture is an anti-liturgy for the realization of the state's power on the bodies of others, Eucharist is the liturgical realization of Christ's suffering and redemptive body in the bodies of His followers. Torture creates fearful and isolated bodies, bodies docile to the purpose of regime; the Eucharist effects the body of Christ, a body marked by resistance to worldly power. Torture creates victims; Eucharist creates witnesses, *martyrs*. Isolation is overcome in the Eucharist by the building of a communal body which resists the state's attempt to disappear it.[56]

Cavanaugh asserts that torture, as the body politics of the state, is a kind of perverted liturgy itself, "a ritual act which organizes bodies in the society into a collective performance, not of true community, but of an atomized aggregate of mutually suspicious individuals."[57] It separates people from each other; it is based on the principle of fear. The liturgy of torture produces fragmentation and isolation. The world of the victim shrinks to a minimum; the immediacy and power of pain inflicted on the body leaves the sufferer in agony; the violated body is the only world that can be experienced. The ability to envision past and future is destroyed; the sense of space is diminished. Cavanaugh quotes Sheila Cassidy, an English doctor who was tortured in Chile in the infamous Villa Grimaldi: "It was as though I was suspended over a pit: the past had no relevance and I could see no future. I lived only for the minute that was and in the fear of further pain."[58]

The "liturgists" of torture put themselves in a quasi-divine position. After having destroyed the sense of self in the way just described, they can proceed with their self-revelation as the omnipotent takers and givers of life. They seek to create a sense of absolute powerlessness in their victims. The climax of the liturgy of torture is the confession of the sufferer that she or he is guilty of disobedience against the state powers. Often people are pressed to reveal the names of friends, colleagues, and comrades: "In torture the state borrows the voice of the victim to double its own voice. Through his terrifying and desperate insistence on confession, the torturer pulls pain from the suffering body of the victim, objectifies it and gives it voice."[59] In Chile under Pinochet, many tortured persons were among those who disappeared. Many families never knew for certain whether their loved ones were still alive or not. The politics of disappearance kept people in a realm of agony between hope and despair. Making tortured bodies disappear gave the liturgy of torture a tremendous—almost mysterious—power.

We seek to sketch an embodied Eucharistic practice that understands itself against this background as a resisting response to the body politics of the state:[60] Practicing Eucharist makes the tortured body visible. When we tell the Eucharistic narrative we do not suppress the reality that Jesus was going to be tortured; we have the chance to make the tortured body visible and by doing so to powerfully disrupt the body politics of the state. This act resists isolation because it creates *koinōnia* (community) among those who gather around the table and is a genuine encounter with the resurrected Christ. The Risen One is incorporated into our bodies; this is the most intimate possibility of communion.

If genuine communion is created in the Eucharist, pain can also be shared and transformed into resurrected life: "Pain is incommunicable beyond the limits of the body, and the sufferer must suffer alone. Christians, nevertheless, make the bizarre claim that pain *can* be shared, precisely because people can be knitted into one body."[61] Practicing Eucharist offers space and a sense of time that values acts of remembrance (*anamnesis*) that generate hope for the future.[62] Celebrating the Eucharist gives space for eschatological imagination that is inhabited by memory and hope. The particular "body story" we remember makes visible the violence of state politics. Remembering violence against the body is dangerous memory. It is painful. It is an entrance into the political and spiritual exercise of deep empathy. It creates *martyrs* who give witness to the violence and to the justice of God, who has overcome the logic of torture and the humiliating body politics of the state by resisting it fiercely in the resurrection of Jesus.

If we read Amnesty International's annual report, we have to admit that torture and Eucharist remains a crucial topic. The pictures of Abu Ghraib reveal the connection of war and torture. When we reflect on the U.S. prison in Guantanamo, we cannot help but think of bodies disappearing, bodies being delivered into a realm of total despotism. It is important for us to stress that an embodied sense of the Eucharistic life will not suppress these realities but will bring them to light.

But how can we do that in the liturgy without producing voyeurism?[63] Michael Hawn shares an impressive example from a Christmas pageant composed by the Argentinian theologian and musician Pablo Sosa. Sosa created it as an invitation to the entire congregation to join in the angels' *Gloria* in the nativity drama:

> He chose the *cueca,* a lively partner dance/song between a man and a woman, as the stylistic basis for this song. The *cueca* is the national dance of Chile, which is also popular in Bolivia and parts of Argentina. The musical characteristics include a lively three-fourths versus six-eights cross-rhythm. . . . "*Gloria*" was written during the Pinochet regime in Chile, when as in Argentina, the government institutionalized violence against its own people, resulting in *los desaparecidos.* As a form of protest, Chilean women whose husbands or sons had disappeared would gather in a public plaza and dance this seemingly joyful dance alone, with their missing partner only in their imagination. Sosa has composed a piano accompaniment that captures more fully the fiesta flavor of the *cueca.*[64]

These women's dance, as well as the transformation of the *cueca* into the angels' *Gloria,* is an act of eschatological imagination par excellence. The dance expresses resistance against the violent body politics of the state by pointing in subversive ways to the absence of those who had disappeared. Sosa brings this ritual from the streets into the center of the narrative that speaks about the Incarnation as a threatened and most dangerous space. This act of eschatological imagination uses the sounds, movements, and words of joy: the *cueca* and the *Gloria* juxtapose in sharp ways the praise of God with the violent realities of torture. This example, although drawn from a Christmas pageant, expresses our attempt to offer a Eucharistic theology that embraces eschatological imagination with regard to fragile bodies and lives.

Moving from interpreting the words about a "body given for you" and "blood shed for you," in what follows we want to address the issue of "sacrificial" language in the New Testament traditions of the Eucharist and in the liturgy.

"My Body—Given for You": Eucharist and the Language of Sacrifice

Feminist criticism of sacrificial christology has caused the corresponding statements in the Eucharistic texts and in the New Testament to be regarded in a more differentiated manner today—among biblical scholars also—than was the case twenty years ago. It is accepted that there is no unified sacrificial christology in the New Testament and that the New Testament formulations may not be read through the lenses of an often unspoken hermeneutical presupposition regarding such a christology of sacrifice. The narrowing of the words at the Last Supper and other corresponding texts to make them solely an interpretation of Jesus' death is being subjected to increasing criticism.[65] Words used to interpret the Eucharist such as *blood, handing over, atoning sacrifice/sacrifice for sins*, and the very word *sacrifice* must be reconsidered as to what they may have meant and whether they are at all appropriate to the content of the New Testament Eucharistic traditions.

In our depiction of covenant theology,[66] it has already become obvious how crucial the Jewish history of martyrdom is for an understanding of the Eucharistic words. That tradition does *not* justify violence or the execution of Jesus and others. The brutality of oppressive rulers who torture and murder people is there, as in the New Testament, neither something willed by God nor necessary for salvation. The suffering and death of the countless martyrs does not signify the victory of such brutality. The theology of martyrdom, indeed, contests any sort of legitimacy for such behavior. That theology makes violence visible and calls it by name. It transforms the victim of unjust violence into the seed of life for the whole people.

The person who tortures and murders, the one who orders torture and murder, desires not merely the death of this *one* person. The prayers of the sisters and brothers who recognize the victims as martyrs rise in opposition to this death. The texts of martyrdom theology speak from the perspective of the community that remembers and that struggles for life. Martyrdom does *not* mean becoming a victim, but rather giving witness (*martyrion*) to the victory of life, willed by God. The New Testament nowhere says that Jesus, through his death, became the victim of violence. Instead, Jesus' death made life possible for "the many"—the people, humanity (see pp. 62–65), because he was recognized as a martyr, one among many sisters and brothers. The isolation of Christ from his sisters and brothers in some christological constructs from later centuries makes the early Christian tradition unrecognizable.

At the present time we need to consider a second level of possible misunderstanding. The "suicide" bombers in contemporary wars are also called "martyrs." But they are fundamentally different from the martyrs of ancient history described here, because they desire and accomplish death and suffering for many. They are a form of violence, not of victory over violence.

The cultic offerings in the First Testament are best understood in the sense of gifts to God. The Greek word *thysia* (sacrifice) encompasses many forms of offering and is also used metaphorically, as in Rom. 12:1. At that time, followers of Jesus Messiah continued to participate in the Temple cult in Jerusalem as usual. Their critique of sacrifices was no different from that of Hosea: Hos. 6:6 is quoted in Matt. 9:13; 12:7, and elsewhere. But neither the critique of sacrifice nor the metaphorical use of words from the context of cultic offerings is a rejection of Jewish sacrificial practice itself.

Paul writes in Rom. 3:25: "God put [him] forward as a *hilasterion* (place of [God's] forgiveness) by his blood, effective through faith (*pistis*)." In the Hebrew Bible, *hilasterion* (Heb. *kapporet*) refers to a kind of golden "plate" beneath the cherubim in the Jewish sanctuary, a place from which forgiveness emanates (Lev. 16:13-16; cf. Heb. 9:5). In Rom. 3:25, the word is applied to Christ in a transferred sense. It does not refer to the (animal) sin offering, nor does it indicate any other cultic rites of atonement.[67] However, by the same token the word *blood* is also denied a significance in the theology of atonement offerings. It is a matter of the blood of the martyrs, not of atoning sacrificial blood in the tradition of animal offerings.

Likewise in 4 Maccabees 17, a text akin to Rom. 3:25, the death of martyrdom is not given a cultic interpretation. This text is especially useful for an understanding of the Jewish tradition of martyrdom in the New Testament.

The tractate was written sometime in the first century CE, probably before 70. It is Hellenistic in style and is intended to give a philosophical presentation of the history of martyrdom as the story of the triumph of virtue. Here is an elaborate narrative of the gruesome and bloody martyrdom of the elderly priest Eleazar and of a mother's seven sons, followed by a great song of praise of the mother and her steadfastness. Her own martyrdom is not described in so much detail: it is said that she threw herself into the flames "so that no one might touch her body" (4 Macc. 17:1). The tyrant who orders these tortures and murders is Antiochus IV Epiphanes (ruled 175–164 CE), but implicitly the text has present tyranny in view, namely, the Roman empire. Martyrdom means the destruction of the violent power of the tyrant (4 Macc. 1:11; 11:24; 17:2; cf. 9:30) and the rescue of the threatened nation (4 Macc. 1:11; 6:28, 29; 9:24; 17:10, 20-22). The nation is being threatened by tyranny because it has sinned (17:21; implicitly also in 6:28, 29). Thus, because it has not obeyed its God, its enemies have power over it (17:20). That power is broken by martyrdom. The event is called "cleansing" or "purification" (1:11; 6:28, 29; 17:21) and signifies the forgiveness of the nation's sins. God's forgiveness of sins emanates from the blood of the martyrs; their blood is *hilasterion* (17:22). The tractate intends, through the model of the martyrs, to give the people courage (13:10; 16:22-23) to overcome the violent power of tyranny through steadfastness (*hypomonē*) and fidelity to the Torah. It is the language of Jesus' interpretive words at the Last Supper and of the New Testament interpretations of his Passion that we encounter here, and it can help us to understand those New Testament traditions. This language does not refer to cultic sacrifices or to self-"sacrifice" or becoming a "victim." "Blood" represents the precious life of the martyr, which is wrongly and violently shed, and yet overcomes the violence perpetrated.

In the words of the Eucharist, Jesus' death is regarded as the death of a martyr, not as that of a "victim" or as an "atoning death."[68] The crucial words are:

> The body "for us" (1 Cor. 11:24; Luke 22:19 precedes these words with "given," without changing the sense).

> The cup "... in my blood" (1 Cor. 11:25; Luke 22:20) or: The blood "... poured out for many" (Mark 14:22); Matt. 26:28 adds "for the forgiveness of sins"; Luke 22:20 has "... for you."

All these formulations, whether the short version or the several variations and additions, express the same thing: The initiative of Jesus' life and death deliver the people, before God, from their violations of the Torah. The substance of this idea, although with variations in its formulation, appears frequently: see especially 1 Cor. 15:3; Gal. 1:4; 1 Pet. 3:18. Isaiah 53:5, 6, 8, 11, 12 also refers to the suffering, torture, and death of the Servant of God for the sake of the people, who had gone astray and are freed from sin through the Servant's life, suffering, and death. The idea behind this interpretation of martyrdom is not one of "sacrifice" that legitimizes violence. The enemies' power is a consequence of the people's sin, and that power is broken by the courageous endurance and death of the martyr. That endurance, the courage and suffering of the person tortured and murdered by the "tyrant" (4 Maccabees) is stronger in its nonviolence than any and all weapons and instruments of torture. It is inappropriate to speak of a representative suffering and death in the traditional sense, as if a human insult to God could only be expiated by suffering and death. Such an interpretation inserts a foreign idea into the notion of God found in these and similar texts. According to this idea, God is only capable of forgiving when his wrath is appeased, as if God demanded suffering as reparation. Such a view of God loses sight of the truth that these texts—like the New Testament's Eucharistic words—are based on the reality of human life. The enemies have power over the people. God loves the people and has mercy on them, despite their sin. Martyrdom destroys the violent power of tyranny. The life of the martyr becomes a gift (*antipsychon* [exchange for life]; 4 Macc. 6:29; 17:21) for the life of the many.

Likewise, no variant of the idea of "self-sacrifice" or cultic sacrifice furnishes a starting point for martyrdom theology. That is why we have cited the formulations from 4 Maccabees outlined above. They bring together the interpretation of martyrdom found in the same or similar words in texts like Isaiah 53, 4 Maccabees, numerous postbiblical interpretations of the martyrs Isaac, Daniel, and the three young men in the fiery furnace.[69]

We will first quote the words of 4 Maccabees 6 about the death of Eleazar:

26   When he was now burned to his very bones and about to expire, he lifted up his eyes to God and said,

27   "You know, O God, that though I might have saved myself, I am dying in burning torments for the sake of the law.

28   Be merciful to your people, and let our punishment suffice for them.[70]

29   Make my blood their purification, and take my life in exchange for theirs."

| 30 | After he said this, the holy man died nobly in his tortures; even in the tortures of death he resisted, by virtue of reason, for the sake of the law. |

We add a summary evaluation of martyrdom from 4 Maccabees 17:

17	The tyrant himself and all his council marveled at their endurance,
18	because of which they now stand before the divine throne and live the life of eternal blessedness.
19	For Moses says, "All who are consecrated are under your hands."
20	These, then, who have been consecrated for the sake of God, are honored, not only with this honor, but also by the fact that because of them our enemies did not rule over our nation,
21	the tyrant was punished, and the homeland purified—they having become, as it were, a gift [NRSV: ransom] for the sin of our nation.
22	And through the blood of those devout ones and their death, which became the place of divine forgiveness of sins [NRSV: as an atoning sacrifice], divine Providence preserved Israel that previously had been mistreated.

The Prayer of Azariah cited above (p. 60) includes a comparison drawn from the context of ritual sacrifice.[71] But that comparison is clearly discernible as an added interpretive element and not the interpretive basis. In the New Testament, we find the idea that the whole life of the faithful is a gift or offering/*thysia* for God (Rom. 12:1), which may include martyrdom. But "thysia" always means a gift for God, namely, life and not death.[72]

In Rom. 8:32, Paul says that God gave up/handed over his son (*paradidonai*)[73] and did not withhold him. Here also, as in our critique of the idea that God requires satisfaction, the interpretation becomes problematic when real experiences of violence and the perspective of the text are set aside. Jesus, like many martyrs, was handed over to the judgment of tyrants. God has turned the aim of the violent earthly power—to bring about death and the rule of violence—on its head. God makes the dead to live (Rom. 4:17; 8:32b). Since the verb *hand over* is burdened by the history of interpretation and its influence, we should seek—in liturgical language, at least—for another word to replace it, one that brings life rather than taking it away. Those who speak here are people who stand before the catastrophe of the humanly caused suffering of Jesus and his countless sisters and brothers. If they see God's hand in suffering, it is because God brings life. Inextricably united with this—subsequent—interpretation of suffering is the praxis of those who behold God in Christ's suffering. They bind themselves to God's covenant, keep the Torah, and fight for the life willed by God. Their perspective on christology is that of sisters and brothers whom God has led into the way of life. They do not surrender the field to violent power. Sometimes they have also told stories about the repentance of executioners and tyrants (Mark 15:39 par.). *Paradidonai* need not be interpreted particularly in terms of Jesus' being handed over; it can also, corresponding to the broader meaning of the word, be read as surrender (of Jesus by God). In the literary context, we should think of Jesus' way of life, its perils, and its acts of resistance, including the courage to face death, and then death itself. His followers will take the same path. Paul quotes Ps. 43:20, "For your sake we are being killed all day long; we are accounted as sheep to be slaughtered" (Rom. 8:36). This psalm verse is constantly quoted in Jewish martyrdom texts.[74] Paul's "we" joins the community and himself to Christ's life and death. The difficulty created by Rom. 8:32 for a reading today is in the idea that God has "given" Christ up, has sent him on the way that ends in death. That sounds as if God were imposing death and suffering. We find the same difficulty in the divine "necessity" (*dei*). The feminist critique that God thus appears as the murderer of his own child is justified, because this idea is strongly suggested by the christology of sacrificial atonement, which Sigrid Brandt calls "misplaced."[75] The only question is whether such an interpretation is historically justified. We believe it is not. In the New Testament, as in Judaism, everything that happens, no matter how dreadful, is regularly attributed to God's will. But this idea does not serve to legitimize—certainly not to glorify—suffering and a submission to fate, nor does it cover up who the murderers and perpetrators of violence are. The thought itself comes from people who call violence by name and exercise resistance against it. They, too, know themselves to be safe in God's hands; even in danger and death God is on their side. True power is with God, not with the powers that exploit, rape, torture, and seek to kill other people.

To translate this tradition into today's language is not an easy task. Through God's action, humanly perpetrated deeds of violence are transformed into the power of life for the whole nation. Death's victory cannot endure. This difficulty cannot be solved by talking about Jesus' surrender.[76] It is only possible to speak out of one's own life and struggles, as Paul does in Rom. 8:31-39. The way of Jesus, the firstborn among many sisters and brothers (Rom. 8:29), was right and willed by God. It was harsh and difficult; God did not withhold suffering from him. The persecution his followers, including Paul, had to withstand came from the same sources as Jesus' experience of hatred and persecution. When Paul says that God gave Jesus up (or handed him over), he is assuring himself and his sisters and brothers of God's love in their own lives. They go their way to fight for the life God desires. In the Roman Empire, such a life required courage and endurance. Their own bodies were endangered because the body was the only place where testimony to God's justice could be made real and truthful.

Thanks to the centuries of intensive Christian initiation into a christology of sacrifice and the image of God as the almighty One who required Jesus' death for his own satisfaction, it is very difficult to read New Testament christology anew and still to make use of the word *sacrifice*. The New Testament's Eucharistic words are crucial for its christology and for today's Eucharistic practice. In the last twenty to thirty years, the protests of the feminist movement have led to a broadened discussion of the christology of atoning sacrifice and to attempts to change our Eucharistic liturgies. There are frequent confrontations between incensed representatives of the institutional church who insistently defend a traditional translation of the "words of institution," on the one hand, and people, both men and women, who can no longer endure the language of sacrificial atonement, on the other. These latter hear simultaneously, when these words are spoken, both the sadistic God-image that legitimates violence through the healing power of a violent death and the individualistic interpretation of the forgiveness of sins. Historical explanations, like those presented in this section, that this christology of sacrificial atonement is a misinterpretation of the New Testament, are difficult to translate into liturgical practice. Here remains a thus far unfulfilled task for communities that individuals cannot accomplish. We want to say something here about our experiences with this process of translation, which means more than merely translating texts. Contextualization is highly important. It must become clear that Jesus' death served the ruling interests of the Roman Empire, and that his life and resurrection were acts of resistance, the resistance of Jesus and those who were his own, even after his death. This contextualization can help us to recognize the Eucharistic words as language of resurrection.

That Christ's body was given "for us" then means that people willed his death, but God did not leave his child in their hands. The most vicious oppression and even murder become powerless because God is on the side of life. "For us" is the message of resurrection, not the theology of the cross. The same is true of the words over the cup, which sing of the new covenant with God. Christ's "blood" is not a sign of his expiring life, but of his new life.[77]

The contextualization of Jesus' death must be accompanied by the contextualization of the Eucharistic communities of today: Jesus was not a victim, but a martyr. Martyrs fight with *hypomonē* (endurance), the nonviolent power of hope. When people remember martyrs like Christ, they themselves are transformed from death into life. This remembrance of the martyrs and on God's justice, to which they witnessed with their lives, is a source of hope even today. At that time the Roman Empire, by means of its propaganda and its violence, created the impression that it possessed an invincible power over the whole world. Jesus contradicted that. Every meal celebrated by his own, during the time of his life and after his death, has brought to new life this power of hope, with *hypomonē* (endurance). It is not true that only the constant refinement and production of more and more expensive weapons can protect life on earth. It is not true that the nations of humanity will remain incapable of heading off a catastrophe of global climate change. Even if our work for a life that is celebrated in the Eucharist, and begun anew there, will not necessarily bring us martyrdom, it is nowhere to be had on the cheap. We can and must change something about our christology of atoning sacrifice, and we need to think anew about the meaning of the cross of Christ. The same is true of the idea of representation.

The idea of representative suffering, if it is divorced from misunderstandings such as a sadistic image of God, can indicate the solidarity that became reality in Jesus' Passion. Jesus stood for the liberation of the poor and those politically deprived of their rights in the Roman Empire. That was the reason why the Roman government had him executed. In Eucharistic celebrations today, we remember Jesus' solidary life and the death it brought him, and in doing so we remember the victims of violence in our own time. People who are violently deprived of the very bases of their existence are, in the Eucharist, set in the midst of the congregation. They become visible in the body of Christ, and they transform the congregation into a solidary community of action.

In the New Testament, as in the Hebrew Bible, we find language reflecting that of the temple cult, but used for different activities and ethical attitudes. In the early church, sacrificial language was continually used and modified.[78] One usage of the term *sacrifice* focuses on praise and thanksgiving and their consequences for the life of the faithful. The sacrifice of praise and thanksgiving is already mentioned in Heb. 13:15-16: "Through him, let us continually offer up a sacrifice of praise to God, that is the fruit of lips that confess his name. Do not neglect to do good and to share what you have, for such sacrifices are pleasing God." It is striking to see that the act of praising God interpreted as sacrifice is intimately intertwined with the ethical demand to do good and to share what one has. Prayer and social life are intertwined.

In the second and third centuries all prayers, not just the Eucharistic prayers, were understood as constituting a sacrifice of praise offered to God. Tertullian spoke of prayer as a spiritual oblation that has abolished the former sacrifices. Here we can already recognize an anti-Jewish polemic. The *Didache* instructs Christians to come together on Sunday,

> break bread, and give thanks, having first confessed your transgressions, that your sacrifice may be pure. Those who have quarreled must also be reconciled to one another before joining in the celebration that your sacrifice may not be defiled.[79]

Justin the Martyr states that prayers of thanksgiving made by worthy men are the only sacrifices that are perfect and well-pleasing to God. The Strasbourg Papyri stress the thanksgiving of the Eucharist as the reasonable sacrifice and bloodless service.

The offering of bread and wine has been interpreted as sacrifice as well. In his dialogue with Trypho, Justin the Martyr states that the offered bread and the cup of thanksgiving constitute the fulfillment of the material oblations of the Hebrew Bible. He describes the bread and wine brought from home as the substance of the sacrifice.[80] In Irenaeus, the Eucharistic oblation of bread and wine is understood as a symbolic offering of the firstfruits of creation. The *Apostolic Tradition* speaks of the bread and the cup that are offered.

Paul Bradshaw names as the third use of sacrificial language the remembering of Christ's sacrifice. In Justin's *Dialogue with Trypho,* again we find the idea of the "bread of the thanksgiving which our Lord Jesus Christ handed down to us, to do for the remembrance of his suffering which he suffered for those who are cleansed in their souls from all wickedness of men so that we might give thanks to God." Many Eucharistic prayers contain multilayered meanings of sacrifice. For instance, the *Apostolic Constitution* refers to the memorial of Christ's death and to the offering of bread and cup.[81] We have suggested interpreting Jesus' words over the bread and wine in the context of the Jewish martyrdom tradition in which the life and death of the martyr have been understood as an event that releases hope in the future of God's people.

The final dimension that should be mentioned is the propitiatory sacrifice. In this case the prayers ask for the forgiveness of sins and the remission of debts. The petitions hope that God will be propitiated through the

Eucharistic celebration. We conclude that the usage of sacrificial language in Eucharistic liturgies is multilayered: it can refer to the sacrifice of life and praise, the sacrifice of gifts, the remembrance of Christ's death, and the propitiatory sacrifice for the forgiveness of sins.

Chapter 5
ESCHATOLOGICAL REMEMBRANCE (ANAMNESIS)

What does it mean to remember?
To weave together the disparate pieces:
day and night, past and present,
one redemptive possibility and another.
To weave together but always to distinguish—
to note, as God did from the first,
the dignity of sacred separation.
It means to stay up late
thinking about the stories that make us who we are.
It means telling tales of redemption
even when the night is dark or the dawn yet gray.
It means not only to take note of the past,
but to own it as the day when YOU came forth.
It is to stand between redemptions.
It means to live in time and beyond time,
because it is our task—Jews and Christians—
to hold the vision of wholeness so near
that we succeed finally—in remembering the future.[1]

OUR FINAL CHAPTER DEALS WITH eschatological anamnesis. The Greek word *anamnesis* means "remembrance." It is used in Jesus' command, "Do this in remembrance of me." Remembrance is at the heart of Eucharistic practice. By delving into biblical and liturgical perspectives about anamnesis and Eucharist, we seek to explore what it means to remember Jesus' life, ministry, and death in the horizon of resurrection faith. We will meditate on what it means to remember God's future while living in this particular place—between redemptions. As David E. Stern notes (see the epigraph above), this is a task that Jews and Christians share, although we have different ways of expressing it theologically.[2]

Since we are interested in sacramental permeability, we will also ask what memory as a neurophysiological, social, and cultural phenomenon is about. We want to sketch out the practice of remembering in its complexity and how it might inform our reflections on Eucharistic theology. In this chapter, we again expand our deliberations into the Eucharistic life beyond actual liturgical practices.

We begin, however, with the notion of anamnesis. Paul Bradshaw offers a helpful research survey of the modern debate among biblical scholars and liturgiologists on the meaning of anamnesis in Eucharistic prayers. He identifies three basic questions: Who is doing the remembering? What is to be remembered? What is being done in the act of remembrance? Bradshaw recognizes three trajectories that scholars have chosen to answer the question about the subject of remembrance: (a) God is the subject of remembrance; (b) the church is the one who remembers; (c) both remember in a mutual process. In terms of what is being remembered, the opinions range from (a) the death of Jesus Christ exclusively to (b) the death and resurrection to (c) the entire Christ event from conception to ascension. With regard to the question of *what is being done* in the act of remembrance, Bradshaw realizes there is no consensus among scholars:

> While these statements have tended to interpret biblical *anamnesis* as meaning something akin to the classic Catholic view of a sacramental act, in which the performance of the ritual is thought to effect some sort of change at the very moment of the liturgical celebration and also within that same spatial location, scripture scholars themselves have been by no means as united over the meaning that the concept had in Israelite tradition. They have been divided over both *what* it was that memory actualized—salvation, or something else, (although seemingly agreed that remembrance did not make a person present, as Thurian and others have claimed)—and also *how* that actualization occurred—whether it was through the cult or in some other way.[3]

First we turn to some further biblical reflections.

The Act of Remembering

In the biblical tradition, remembering is an expression of the experience of liberation given by God. People remember men and women in the history of the nation, and they remember God. Such remembering is directed to past events of the most varied sort that have one thing in common: that they are distinguished by a particular relevance. The memory has to do with this relevance: It seeks the past not for its own sake, but because of current interest. Remembering takes place for the sake of understanding the present, but usually in regard to a particular action that is measured by and acquires its motive from the memory.[4]

God requires of Israel that they remember the Exodus (see only Exod. 12:14). The annual Passover festival served to recall the people's departure from slavery and the consequences of that history for the present. Willy Schottroff characterized this memory of the Passover in Exod. 12:14 as follows:

> Thus *sikaron* here expresses the relationship of a later generation to events that are in the past but are nevertheless fundamental to the salvation and well-being of those who came later. The actions undertaken in the cult make clear to each individual among them that he or she is also included in these events, touched by them; part of their meaning. The dramatic components "make the Exodus event present" not in reality, but in regard to the scope of its significance and relevance.[5]

The great degree to which the memory of the Exodus shaped the daily life of the people of Israel can be seen from the numerous allusions to the Exodus in the New Testament, not least the allusions to the Exodus in the accounts of the Last Supper and Jesus' Passion. Either Jesus' Last Supper is depicted as a Passover meal, or Jesus is portrayed as the Paschal lamb (John 1:29, 36; 19:14, 33, 36; Acts 8:32); the thought is not so much of the slaughter of the lamb as of its defenselessness, in which is recognized the resisting endurance of the martyr (cf. Rom. 8:36 and Ps. 43:23).[6]

The Eucharist, with its remembrance of Jesus Christ, can thus be located within the remembrance of the liberation of the people from slavery. The explicit application of this memorial link appears twice in the New Testament: in the Eucharistic traditions and in the story of the anointing at Bethany in the Gospels of Mark and Matthew.

Mark 14:9 and Matt. 26:13 tell of Jesus' anointing by a nameless woman. In the parallel story in Luke 7:36-50, she is called a "a woman in the city, who was a sinner" (7:37). But the scene is told in such a way in every version that the hearers could know that this nameless woman is a prostitute: She somehow enters from outside into a meal where guests are present and does something unusual, anointing one of the guests, Jesus, with oil.

The erotic overtones are unmistakable.[7] Mark 14:1-9 tells how a name-less woman—to the great irritation of some of the other guests—anointed Jesus' head with an extremely luxurious oil. Jesus dismissed the anger of his fellow guests and made a little speech about the woman's action: "She has anointed my body (*sōma*) beforehand for its burial." She has done something good for him. Then Jesus concludes, emphatically and solemnly, "Truly I tell you: wherever the good news is proclaimed in the whole world, what she has done will be told in remembrance of her" (14:9). In saying this, Jesus places her within the continuity of the history of Israel with its God. She is to be one of those whom the people of God throughout the world remember. Perhaps we can say that the Christian iconographic tradition that dresses Mary Magdalene[8] as a prostitute and places her beneath the cross has become something like what Jesus announces here: Telling the story in memory of the nameless woman who anointed Jesus. What was it that those who told the story in Mark 14:1-9, in these or similar words, wanted to communicate? What was their current interest? It was, as the narrative makes clear, that this woman showed love and reverence for Jesus and his body, which was going to torture and death, and that Jesus needed that love. This story was told by people who awarded Jesus and the women who lived as prostitutes the human dignity that the society denied them (see Luke 7:39 and all versions of the story of Jesus' Passion). It is tragic that later Christian tradition, and some feminist interpretations as well, do not want to acknowledge that this woman is portrayed as a prostitute and that the people of God are to remember her as such.[9] The memory of her combines and intensifies, as if under a magnifying glass, Jesus' practice of solidarity with those who are used, exploited, and made invisible. There is no basis for thinking that the people who transmitted this story took Jesus' command to remember this nameless woman less seriously than his com-mand to remember him in the community meal.

The command to remember him at the meal appears twice in 1 Corin-thians 11 (at vv. 24 and 25) and in Luke 22:19: "Do this in remembrance of me."[10] But the other meal narratives also presume the repetition of the meal and the ongoing speaking of Jesus' words of interpretation and remember-ing Jesus' life, death, and resurrection. Here the remembering is joined to a community meal. "Do this in remembrance of me"—the practice of the community meal as a whole accomplishes the remembering. By so remem-bering, the community—as Paul comments—is to proclaim Jesus' death (1 Cor. 11:26): an act of resistance in the Roman Empire, one that makes visible the end of violence (see above, pp. 56–58). It is clear already that the Eucharist is misunderstood when it is referred, in isolation, to the death of

Jesus. It is a meal of resistance, of resurrection, and of assurance of God's justice in a world of violence. What was the current interest and practice that was linked to this remembering, an act that stands within the Jewish tradition of remembering? The forgiveness of sins comes from Jesus' death, as all versions of the Eucharistic words proclaim. Given "for you" means: for your liberation from slavery to sin (see above, pp. 146–55). The theology of martyrdom in all its versions has this for its purpose: Through the memory of the martyrs, the people can recognize that violence has not conquered. It can be disrupted. In the Christian tradition, especially in the Eucharist as traditionally celebrated, the forgiveness of sins is all too often restricted to the forgiveness of individual sins: The plural "we/us" and "your/our" sins in the New Testament becomes a singular "I" and "my" sins.

Another difficulty arises from contemporary Christian theology, namely, that sin is often regarded as an essential character, even an essential, unchangeable feature of human existence. Paul spoke in great detail about the slavery that sin lays upon human beings, and the Gospels also presume a comparable understanding of sin. Paul writes in general terms about sin, but he understands it concretely. Sin arises through violation of Torah, but the non-Jewish world also acts deliberately against God's will. People participate in violence and falsehood; they do harm to others. All are participants in this deadly network, as perpetrators and accomplices; "there is no one who is righteous" (Rom. 3:10).

God has intervened in this universal structure of death and sin. Christ's death and resurrection free us to be able to live according to the Torah. The violence of sin and death is not thus magically abolished; what is eliminated is self-submission to its inevitability. It is not difficult to apply the analysis of structural sin that Paul has given us to today's world. Nothing is so obvious as powerlessness and subjection to the inevitability of deadly structures. People see themselves compelled to believe in the necessity of wars, the destruction of the earth's natural resources, and poverty. The Eucharist was formerly the community meal of those who had been transformed by the remembrance of Jesus:[11] capable of recognizing the sin in which they are entangled and of seeking together the path of righteousness. The counter-force of death is omnipresent, and yet it is possible to find the path of righteousness. Every Eucharist witnesses to setting out on that path. Every retelling of Jesus' Passion and every Eucharist, with its words about God's forgiveness, is such an act of remembrance out of which grows the strength to labor for life.

What We Remember

Eschatological anamnesis in the context of the Eucharist means practicing resurrection hope by connecting the remembrance of God's saving works, in Israel's history and in the Christ event, with our lives.[12] It is about diving into the Paschal Mystery and, in so doing, discovering the threads to our present lives and to the future in the horizon of the Eucharistic life. We define eschatological anamnesis as a praxis based on empathy, on embodiment, and on reciprocity between God and human beings; it is a praxis of remembering painful memories and dealing with them in a courageous and life-giving way. It is a praxis that does not shy away from the stories of suffering; it rather delves into it by perceiving conrete faces, bodies, and places.[13]

At the center of this praxis is the *memoria passionis et resurrectionis Iesu* and the anamnetic empathy it releases. Eschatological anamnesis does not focus exclusively on Jesus' death. It is equally related "to his person and practice. It includes the memory of his proclamation and practice of God's reign, his proclamation of God as a liberating and saving reality, his prophetic signs, his outreach to the marginalized and excluded, and his communal meals with the devout and the despised."[14] Anamnesis imagines Jesus' ministry and his suffering; it lifts up the love of God as Father and Creator who calls Jesus forth from the power of death into resurrection life.

This broad understanding of anamnesis derives from our reading of the Gospels, which invites us not to focus narrowly on the death of Jesus. We see the command to "do this in remembrance of me" in the Eucharistic account[15] embedded in the larger context of the whole narrative that speaks of the life, ministry, suffering, death, and resurrection of Jesus Christ. The Eucharistic narratives according to the Synoptic Gospels, which talk about Jesus' Last Supper with his disciples, should be understood from the perspectives of readers who already have the resurrection narrative in mind. Paul's understanding of anamnesis includes resurrection, hope for Christ's coming, and a praxis of solidarity.[16]

In addition, our more all-encompassing understanding of anamnesis is nurtured by liturgical traditions that embrace the Christ event in a more inclusive way. The *United Methodist Book of Worship*, for example, offers an expanded understanding of anamnesis in the Great Thanksgiving. In the anamnetic part that refers to Jesus Christ it says:

> Holy are you, and blessed is your son Jesus Christ.
> *Your Spirit anointed him*
> to preach good news to the poor,
> to proclaim release to the captives

and recovering of sight to the blind,
to set at liberty those who are oppressed,
and to announce that the time had come
when you would save your people.
He healed the sick, fed the hungry, and ate with sinners.
By the baptism of his suffering, death, and resurrection
you gave birth to your Church,
delivered us from slavery to sin and death. . . .[17]

The christological anamnesis of this Eucharistic prayer alludes to Jesus' ministry to the poor and the sick. Following Luke 4:18-20, Christ's saving solidarity with the poor, with the oppressed, and with sinners is seen as being initiated by the anointing of the Holy Spirit. His proclamation of good news to the poor,[18] his service of healing and feeding are stressed and juxtaposed with "the baptism of his suffering, death, and resurrection." The latter are interpreted as the events that make Christ's ministry relevant for us today; through his suffering, death, and resurrection our current slavery to sin and death is interrupted. Remembering Christ's ministry to the poor and marginalized is not a nostalgia with no connection to the present; it can rather inspire us to become aware of how Christ's saving and healing presence is at work today and how we can participate in it.[19]

The expansion of what we remember in the Eucharistic liturgy applies not only to Christ's life and ministry. It also affects our notion of the body of Christ. We have stressed the necessity to delve deeply into the meaning of the statement that *we are the body of Christ.*[20] With regard to eschatological anamnesis this means that we become more specific about the company of heaven who sing the unending hymn. Feminist theologians and liturgiologists challenge the churches to expand anamnetic practice not only in its christological dimension but also with regard to the work of God's people in the world, since this is the way the body of Christ is present today. Marjorie Procter-Smith suggests that something crucial is missing if we do not include in our anamnetic practice the work of those who are voiceless and invisible.[21]

Janet Morley gives an example for such an inclusive anamnetic practice in a Eucharistic Prayer for Good Friday. She concludes her remembrance of Jesus' suffering and death in her introduction to the *Sanctus* as follows:

Therefore, with those who are detained without justice,
abandoned or betrayed by friends,
whose bodies are violated or in pain;

with those who have died alone
without dignity, comfort or hope;
and with all the company of saints
who have carried you in their wounds
that they may be bodied forth with life,
we praise you, saying:
Holy, holy, holy, vulnerable God. . . .[22]

The company of heaven here envisioned are people who have suffered in ways similar to Jesus' own sufferings. Those who have experienced tremendous violence and those who died alone await the promise that their bodies will be resurrected. Morley uses the beautiful phrase "that they may be bodied forth with life." They are worthy to sing God's unending praise: "Holy, holy, holy."

The body of Christ wears many faces. It consists of the company of heaven, the dead, and the living. We understand eschatological anamnesis as an invitation to become more specific in terms of names and faces we really do remember. We have had the interesting experience in our classes that when students are asked to identify the "saints," they first come forward with the names of Dr. Martin Luther King and Dietrich Bonhoeffer. Engaging in anamnetic inclusivity means that we envision other names as well.[23] People who are publicly known could come to mind as well as those who are local figures, who belong to local communities and to our families. Their names could emerge in and from our Eucharistic Prayers as well.[24] Calling forth concrete names is essential for a lively practice of anamnetic solidarity.

Anamnetic solidarity can be embodied in a variety of ways. An intriguing and controversial example of modern iconography that embodies an expansive anamnetic spirit is the "Dancing Saints" artwork in St. Gregory of Nyssa Episcopal Church in San Francisco. When celebrating communion the congregation is surrounded in its rotunda by the grand icon of eighty saints who embody faith and the yearning for social justice through the centuries.[25] Donald Shell writes about these dancing saints:

> In addition to our primary goal of showing an image of God's many and diverse ways of working in people's lives, we aimed to achieve a reasonable representation of men and women (and a few children) from different historical periods, life roles and kinds of work. Whenever we heard or felt "of course, we have to include . . ." we paused and gave that

person an extra-skeptical scrutiny, trying to push our list beyond a self-evident "hall of fame" and further, beyond mainstream church consensus, stretching our thinking and enlarging our gratitude for grace overflowing in so many startling and different lives. We were aware of our particular place and time and tried to honor its gift and see past its limitation. Sometimes in a choice between two worthy people, we gave preference to the local figure, emphasizing God's

Fig. 3. *Dancing Saints. Fresco by Mark Dukes. St. Gregory of Nyssa Episcopal Church, San Francisco. Photo: Werner Fritsch.*

work here among us. We represented important events of our historical moment, late 20th-century America—the U.S. Civil Rights movement and World War II—but we also stretched to include other kinds of 20th-century people and to create a balance with other historical periods. If we have done our work well, a hundred years from now the congregation of St. Gregory's and its visitors will recognize a voice from 1997, undoubtedly sensing some of our historical prejudice and also, we hope, seeing us stretch beyond it to show a sweeping, universal vision of God shining through human life.[26]

Celebrating the Eucharist in this space immediately stretches one's eschatological imagination. These dancing saints, with their visual power, draw the worship participants who gather at the table to share bread and wine into the space of eschatological imagination, which holds many surprises.

This, then, is eschatological anamnesis: we remember God's works in creation and God's liberating acts in the history of Israel, Christ's life, ministry, death, and resurrection, as well as the faces and names of the body of Christ who sustains the church and the world. Eschatological anamnesis has its place as well in the celebration of Eucharistic liturgies, and last but not least in our social and political activities that resist at least in fragmentary ways the amnesia that comes with the immense and overwhelming victimization and suffering of people all over the globe. This is the terrain that anamnetic eschatological practices inhabit.

How We Remember

In this section we want to sketch out three dimensions of eschatological anamnesis as *practice*. Those dimensions are anamnesis as reciprocal activity, anamnetic empathy, and anamnesis as embodied practice. These three aspects are important to our project of a Eucharistic theology that holds eschatological imagination in the midst of people's suffering.

Reciprocal Activity

Eschatological anamnetic practice is not meant to be a mere recalling of the Christ event as it is handed down to us through the New Testament and the liturgical traditions of the church. If it was a mere recalling it would be nostalgic or fetishistic memory, disconnected from the promise of resurrection. It would transform neither our present nor our future. Rather, eschatological anamnesis is an expression of our relationship with God. It is a reciprocal activity in which God remembers us and we remember God's saving and healing activity in the world. Retelling these stories happens in the existential trust and experiential faith that by doing so we participate in God's saving activity in the world as it is expressed in creation, in God's covenant with Israel, and in the Christ story. In this sense we can speak of anamnesis as re-actualization. Anamnesis is based on God's encounter with us and our response to God's activity in history, in the world today, and in our lives. Thus it is important for us to speak not only of divine presence but of mutual relationality.

Anamnesis has a Trinitarian dimension. God's relating to us as creating, redeeming, and sustaining force in the Eucharist is God's way of remembering us. We respond with our remembering through our prayers. As Protestants, we are used to focusing on Christ's presence in the Eucharist.[27] However, we find it equally important to point to the works of the creator that reflect the value of the material world: the real bread, the real wine and, as a consequence, the real productivity of people that is represented in the gifts we receive. We remember God the creator when we realize that real bodies consume these precious gifts and that it is by means of the bodily activity of eating and drinking that we have communion with Christ through the Spirit. By giving thanks to God the creator in the Eucharist we have the opportunity to recognize the fragility and beauty of the ecological system that brings forth the fruits of the earth and sustains our bodies. In this sense we remember God's creating work in the world and acknowledge our participation in the continuing process of creation. The reciprocity between God the creator and us as created human beings leads us to acknowledge that we are in constant exchange with and dependence on our environment. As Avery Dulles states,

We are all too inclined to take creation for granted; we need to be reminded that the light and the nourishment we daily receive, and indeed our life itself, are freely bestowed upon us by a loving creator, to whom we render thanks for all the benefits of nature and grace. In the Gloria we thank and praise God not only for his gifts but also for being what he is: "we give thanks to you and to your great glory."[28]

Anamnetic Empathy

We have described eschatological imagination as an artful practice of disruptive perception.[29] It is about discovering hope in the midst of despair and turmoil. This way of imagining and of "seeing as" is a particular way of perceiving reality. It is grounded in a practice of anamnetic empathy.

Anamnetic empathy stretches the eschatological imagination of worshiping communities. Interceding might be thought of as a practice in which our imagination is pushed beyond the dimensions of superficial charity and sympathy. Gordon Lathrop speaks of intercessory prayers as a concrete exercise in the "sacrophilic worldview" of the liturgy that belongs to a community that loves and honors "flesh," the conditions of the created world within which it lives.[30]

The Eucharistic narrative points to the body of Jesus: "This is my body." Christ's body, imagined as a body in pain and as the resurrected body, is related to our own body memories that hold pain and humiliation as well as desire and transcendent imagination. The "body conversation" that emerges pushes toward the question: In which sense can we be empathetic to the pain of others? More, it provokes this question: How we can discover traces of resurrection by imagining the tortured body, the body in pain? This is a core question of eschatological anamnesis.

Anamnesis, being more than a mere distant recollection of an event, has a relational and existential quality. The existential dimension draws us into the Eucharistic narrative in a transformative way. We are no longer distant listeners to a story, but involved participants. This way of remembering has to do with empathy. Empathy can be understood as a process in which we as observers are drawn into the vicarious experiencing of an emotion, a physical state, or the insight of another person. Empathy has been defined as the capacity for participating in, or a vicarious experiencing of, another's feelings, volitions, or ideas.[31] Empathy has cognitive as well as emotional aspects. The cognitive dimension is expressed in the effort to comprehend another person's experience. This happens by engaging imaginative and mimetic faculties.[32] Imagination and mimicry are based on symbolic association, "that is, the association between cues that symbolically indicate another's feelings and the observer's own past distresses. For example, hearing a description of another in distress may evoke empathy by means of association. This mode of empathy requires the ability to interpret symbols, which is, of course, a cognitive skill."[33] Another cognitive aspect of empathy is the ability to take on the perspective of the stranger, which means the ability to identify with another person's intents and feelings. This, however, does not necessarily lead to compassion as a genuine act of solidarity.

Empathy is also about the sharing of affects. Emotions arise in the act of symbolic association, and we relate these to the person, the group, or the cause with which we are empathizing. It is not only about comprehending another person's perspective but also about "feeling oneself into it" by projecting one's own feelings arising out of comparable experiences.

Theodore Reik's model for describing various aspects of the process of empathetic behavior is a classic for understanding how emotional and cognitive aspects intertwine.[34] Reik describes the following aspects of empathy in the context of psychotherapy:

1. *Identification:* paying attention to another and allowing oneself to become absorbed in contemplation of that person.
2. *Incorporation:* making the other's experience one's own via internalizing the other.
3. *Reverberation:* experiencing the other's experience while simultaneously attending to one's own cognitive and affective associations to that experience.
4. *Detachment:* moving back from the merged inner relationship to a position of separate identity, which permits a response to be made that reflects both understanding of others as well as separateness from them.[35]

Although there are distinct differences between psychotherapeutic settings in which empathy occurs and the setting of Eucharistic liturgies, it is helpful to reflect on movements of identification, incorporation, reverberation, and detachment in the ritual setting. The movement toward and the move away from the one we are invited to remember is crucial. In celebrating communion we are invited to draw closer to the mystery of incarnation, which encompasses our memory of the crucified and risen Christ. The incorporation of Christ's presence into our bodies happens in the Holy Meal. This is about communion as oneness and intimacy. The prayers of thanksgiving and the dismissal at the end the liturgy can be interpreted as rites of detachment: from the experience of oneness flows the act of sending forth: "Now go forth in peace."

Can we relate this expression of mystical union to the phenomenon of empathy, which speaks about identification and incorporation as well? The empathy generated in the Eucharist is mediated through ritual practices and our imaginative activity, in which our *images* of Christ's ministry, death, and suffering are pencilled into our memory. This frames our ways of remembering and empathizing. Pondering empathetic remembering in ritual practice should lead also to the crucial debate about the limits of empathy. Elaine Scarry in her groundbreaking book *The Body in Pain*[36] points to the limits of empathy, particularly when we relate to the body in pain. Pain imprisons a person in the boundaries of his or her body. It cannot be communicated in adequate ways, nor can it be shared authentically. Physical pain has no voice. Immediate pain destroys the ability to speak and thus the ability to communicate.[37] This is especially true for people who have experienced torture, who go through profound experiences of speechlessness and disconnect from their environment.

Scarry's work emphasizes not unmediated empathy but the inability to empathize, to be with the pain of another person in the abyss of speechlessness. There is no way of immediate connection or of unmediated reactualization of the Last Supper and Jesus' suffering. Scarry makes the point that our inability to be empathetic with the body in pain in a deep sense can only be addressed through the gift of human imagination in the creation of artifacts. Examples of such artifacts can take the form of narratives, oral or written, poetry, music, or the visual arts.[38] These respond to our inability to be empathetic in an immediate sense and to remember empathetically. I want to suggest that liturgical practice might function as such an artifact insofar as it offers some kind of bridge over the abyss of speechlessness.

It is thus very appropriate to interpret the dominical command "Do this in remembrance of me" as the invitation to craft such a ritual artifact by entering into the ritual realm in which the prayers of thanksgiving and remembrance are spoken, Jesus' story is retold, bread and wine are shared. The artifact is created in the actual performance of the ritual in which a particular relationship between body memory and text memory is created.[39] This is the way of remembering. There is no direct, unmediated way of entering empathetically into the Paschal Mystery. The place that remains is the liturgy.

Dirk Lange offers an intriguing interpretation of the absence of the words of institution in early documents, such as the *Didache*, that reflect holy meal practices and the impossibility of remembering Jesus' death in an immediate way:

The *Didachē* witnesses to the impossibility of "remembering," even to the impossibility of remembering or capturing the meaning of the horrific execution of Jesus by crucifixion. For the community of the *Didachē*, Jesus could not be remembered by this cruel mode of execution. Instead his "presence" as the one who overcame this death was enacted through a meal in which he continually disseminates traditional knowledge, faith and life. The meal was the iteration of something that the disciples, the first community, could not grasp; the iteration of something inaccessible in the event.[40]

Bringing this interpretation into conversation with Elaine Scarry's reflection, we might want to say that the meal practice itself serves as an artifact that bridges the abyss of speechlessness.

Embodied Practice

Anamnetic empathy happens through listening, praying, eating, and drinking. It is an embodied practice. It is not merely initiated by listening to the words that tell the stories of salvation; rather, it embraces all our senses. We bring to the table our actual bodies, which contain a myriad of memories, and there we drink the wine and eat the bread. Through this real eating and drinking we may taste, see, and smell in fragmentary ways what the *basileia* is about: a joyful feast that nourishes everyone and in which we do not need to hide the stories of our lives and our bodies.[41]

We remember a Eucharist in which the assembly was invited to pause, to take a deep breath and smell the goodness of God in the delicious home-baked bread that was distributed. The awareness of how bread smells is intimately interwoven with our appreciation that it tastes good. The same is true for the wine or juice we drink.

Eucharistic celebrations that deprive people of this sensual experience, for instance, by using tasteless wafers, lose their holistic dimension. Smelling and tasting, as well as mental visual images, are crucial to the sensual dimension of memory in worship and in our daily lives. Many people probably know this phenomenon because it is also how we connect with our childhood memories. The reciprocity of anamnetic practices takes seriously the sensual and physical dimension of anamnesis. It takes seriously how memory in general is inscribed into our bodies.

Understanding eschatological anamnesis as embodied practice leads us to the questions: How do our actual bodies, as neurophysiological entities, remember? And how is memory inscribed in our bodies?[42] Neuroscientists say that the visual details, sounds, smells, and touch dimensions of a particular memory, for instance, are each stored in their own locations in the brain and pulled together to reconstruct a representation of the event. The hippocampus, that region entrusted with coordinating the storage of long-term memories, appears also to reunite those separate dimensions of memory during recall and create their sense of coherence.[43]

What we hear, see, and smell is crucial for our way of remembering Christ in the Eucharist. Our sensual faculties hold the very narrative itself. In a similar vein, Marcia McFee notes of the connection between memory and sensory stimuli:

> The more sensory stimuli created around an image, the more neural connections are created in various parts of the brain, the more likely the image will be recalled when associations to the various stimuli are evoked in experiences outside the ritual event. For example, consider a ritual event that utilizes the image of water and its connection to Psalm Twenty-three ("he leads me beside still waters"), a popular psalm already connected in communal memory to the need for comfort in its repeated use at funeral rituals. The more sensory stimuli used in the proclamation of this psalm, the greater the possibility that the same sensory stimuli, when encountered outside of the ritual, will reproduce the emotions evoked during the ritual. So, if the psalm is not only read, but is surrounded by music which mimics the feel of a quiet stream (the kinesthetic sense of the *Hang* dynamic) or accompanied by the recorded sounds of an actual stream itself, the more likely it is that the same sounds (aural stimuli) experienced on a trip to an actual stream will bring to mind the Psalm and reproduce the kinesthetic patterns of *Hang* itself.[44]

If we take seriously that memory is inscribed into our bodies not only through words but through a variety of sensual stimuli, we might want to consider how we can be more intentional about this dimension. We have, for instance, a vivid memory of a Eucharistic liturgy celebrated in the context of a worship service that commemorated the *Reichspogromnacht* (earlier called by the euphemistic term *Kristallnacht* or "Night of Broken Glass"), the night in which hundreds of Jewish synagogues where demolished, burned, and destroyed by the Nazis in Germany in 1939. In this service the preacher struggled with the issue that these atrocities were not prevented or at least criticized by the majority of Christians at that time and how this has affected

Christian identity until today. In that service we listened for a short moment to the recorded sounds of smashed glass projected through the speakers that surrounded the sanctuary. These sounds filled the room immediately before the liturgist spoke the words "In the night when Jesus was betrayed. . . ." The worship leaders had decided to recontextualize Jesus' interpretive words by using these aural stimuli. Although there was the danger of "overdramatizing," we felt that this was a powerful way of fusing the Eucharistic horizon with the collective memory of the *Reichspogromnacht*.

Mapping Sites of Anamnesis

In this section, we are attentive to three major sites in which remembering takes place and eschatological imagination might unfold: body memory, cultural memory, and place memory. Sketching links between bodies, cultures, and places, we seek to integrate a more systemic perspective in which individual body memory is situated in its larger historical, social, and political context.[45]

We ask, in what sense do bodies hold memories, and what does that mean for celebrating the Eucharist and for living the Eucharistic life as a whole? Second, we take into consideration that what is remembered is always cultural memory expressed in narratives and rituals. How we remember and tell our life stories is part of a larger narrative. This means that memory is always cultural memory. This is definitely true for the Eucharistic memory of the church as well. The "institution" narratives in 1 Corinthians, in the Gospels, and in the early Eucharistic prayers have shaped the cultural memory of the church until today. We will thus ask again: What does it mean to be attentive to the space of resonance created by the cultural memory of the Eucharist and our diverse and shifting cultural memories? The third thread we will unfold is the concept of place memory as it relates to eschatological anamnesis. We conclude by conceptualizing eschatological anamnesis as dangerous memory. We reflect on a Eucharistic life that holds up body memory and is sensitive to the ambiguity of cultural memory as it is embodied in narrative as well as in place memory.

Body Memory

Eschatological anamnesis as a practice that embraces empathy, reciprocity, and embodiment is grounded in the human ability to remember. To remember means to be capable of forming meaningful narrative sequences. Remembering is an activity that takes place with a concern for the interpretation of the present by producing links to what is perceived as having happened in the past. Remembering encompasses *re-cognition* of things that happened in the past; it is a *re-constructive* process in which individuals deduce events that have occurred in the past in order to interpret both their present and their future. Remembering is a selective process. Forgetting and suppressing are aspects of this reconstructive activity.[46]

Memory is thus to a certain extent a matter of construction more than a reproduction of things that happened in the past:

> It is the construction of a "schema," a coding which enables us to distinguish and therefore to recall. Three major dimensions of mnemonic coding are known to experimental psychologists today. The semantic code is the dominant dimension; like a library code, it is organized hierarchically by topic and integrated into a single system according to an overall view of the world and the logical relationships perceived in it. The verbal code is the second dimension; it contains all the information and programmes that allow the preparation of a verbal expression. The visual code is the third dimension; concrete items easily translated into images are much better retained than abstract items because such concrete items undergo a double encoding in terms of visual coding as well as verbal expression.[47]

The production of memory in these three dimensions of mnemonic coding happens via cognitive processes as well as through habitual and ritual practices. The semantic, verbal, and visual codes are all operating when we celebrate the Eucharist.

The production of memory through these three ways of coding is lodged in the body, in the textures of cultural memory and place memory. These three aspects are the strands with which we weave the fabric of eschatological anamnesis. Anamnesis is a complex process in which we bring our body memories, our cultural memory, and our place memory to the table. An unconscious/conscious conversation with the narrative of creation, the exodus, and the Christ event unfolds from there. The complexity of remembering makes clear that it is impossible to speak of a fixed, static "content" the celebrants ought to remember. Meaning, as it is generated from the performance itself, is always meaning *to* someone; it depends on personal life stories and the larger sociopolitical context one finds oneself in. Anamnesis is a mutual process in which we respond to God with our whole existence. The ritual performance of the Eucharist opens up a space of resonance that has the potential to make room for an intermingling of these various dimensions. There need to be further places in the lives of the celebrants in which issues around body memory and cultural memory can be articulated. Connecting this articulation with our faith traditions is a task embraced by the Eucharistic life. Those spaces can be opened up by artists who give a visual or musical expression of the distorting and healing aspects of cultural and body memory; it can be initiated by religious educators who assist communities of faith in retrieving events, stories, and images that have hovered in the zones of taboo and forgetfulness.

We have described eschatological anamnesis as an embodied practice. We remember with our bodies. Our bodies remember. And we are called to remember a particular "body story." We are invited to embrace Christ's body and the disciples' bodies as they shared the Last Supper. We visualize a "body broken for us." We delve into the imagination of the resurrection of our bodies.[48]

In the following paragraphs, we further spell out what it means that our bodies remember both as a social and as a neurophysiological phenomenon. We ask what it means that we participate in the meal as remembering bodies. We may say that our bodies "are seen into existence" by our environment. This external social perception shapes our body memory in essential ways. The gaze directed at my body reminds me that I am a middle-aged and middle-class, white, female body. My body is a site of power struggles. This is how I come to the table; this is how the stranger next to me comes to the table. Myriad memories are generated from the external gaze and stored in our bodies. We come with those memories that inhabit the landscape of cultural memory on a larger scale. Our body memory is thus shaped by social constructions that are much more effective than our own individual will and perception. They are so powerful that they seem natural: our race is seen into existence, seemingly attached to our skin color; our gender is interpreted by others through the perception of the shapes of our bodies. The socially constructed gaze upon our body forms our body memory; we may say that this gaze always produces alienation as well as a sense of identity. It is, however, also connected to the experience of domination for the less privileged groups. Our body memory separates us from others; it produces a stratified society shaped by racism, classism, and patriarchal structures. In that structural sense we can say that our bodies live in social sin; they are inseparably connected with the evil that derives from the gazes we direct at each other's bodies.

By immersing ourselves in the Christ narrative in the Eucharist, we become one in Christ. This is an eschatological statement. This faith in the unity of the body of Christ is transformed into radical eschatological imagination when we share the meal together without suppressing the painful experiences and memories of exclusion and privilege. We bring our bodies to the table, and with them our suppressed and distorted memories. We dare to come and encounter the living God because we live from the promise that the holes, the stammering, and the disruptions in our narratives, everything that is forgotten and cannot be remembered, is also held by God's grace and is not lost. God will remember.

So far we have reflected on memories inscribed in our bodies through the gaze of others. Let us take a brief look at two aspects of how our body produces, constructs, and modifies memories and what that means for our worship practices. The human brain exercises a variety of distinct functions that enable it to store and retrieve information over a period of time.[49] Neuroscientists distinguish a variety of types of memory located in different parts of the brain. *Working memory*, also known as short-term memory, is located in an area in the brain called the "medial, temporal cortex, the layer of cortical tissue that lies 'inside' each hemisphere."[50] Working memory enables us to recall approximately seven discrete bits of information at any one time and holds that information for only a few minutes. It is the *long-term memory* that enables us to retain information over time. The capacity for long-term storage of information is spread out all over the neocortex, with distinct places in the brain for information about words, visual images, motor skills, etc. Working and long-term memory are constantly exchanging data. For example, working memory recognizes information by comparing it with long-term data.

> We rely on still other dimensions of memory. *Semantic memory* refers to the knowledge of concepts and facts, regardless of whether we have directly experienced them and whether we can recall any personal stories associated with learning them. Psychologists generally include broad information about the world in this category. *Procedural memory* involves the development of skills and habits, such as playing the piano or reciting multiplication tables or the Lord's Prayer. *Autobiographical memory*, or what psychologist Endel Tulving called *episodic memory*, describes the recall of explicit personal incidents that help shape our lives.[51]

It is clear, therefore, that memory is not a single, isolated function of the brain; rather, it is multifaceted. We engage not only socially but also physiologically in a process of reconstruction when we remember. That is why it is crucial for us to reflect on anamnesis in an embodied and holistic way that takes into account all these various dimensions of memory. Likewise, our memory practice in worship also encompasses all these dimensions: the cognition of facts and concepts, our acquired ritual knowledge, as well as the personal biographical memories we put together in memory sequences. Because all these dimensions are present when we worship, we must ask whether we engage them purposefully in our ritual practices.

We invite you, the reader, to consider the extent to which episodic memory, which is held in individual bodies, can be shared in Eucharistic liturgy. Putting into practice our claim that anamnesis is a practice that engages reciprocity, empathy, and embodied knowing, we envision artful disruptions of our Eucharistic prayers in which people make the body of Christ visible through their embodied actions, for instance, through dance, contact improvisation, or sculpturing. Liturgical dancers such as Sylvia Miller-Mutia or Carla DeSola help congregations envision how to dance the Eucharistic life.[52]

Bruce Saunkeah's Story: "I Find Myself Buying a Suit"

Salvation comes in a "drug holiday."[53]

Another kind of liturgical disruption could be narratives reflecting particular body experiences that are significant for the body of Christ. What about listening to Bruce Saunkeah's story before we join together in the *Sanctus* on a Sunday morning that may be focused on the observance of World AIDS Day? What about joining the angels and archangels in their unending hymn with the resonance this particular body story unfolds in us? The testimony presented here holds eschatological imagination within the struggle for authentic life and enduring health. It reflects life Eucharistic.

So Over Coming Out

I am so over coming out.

I
No one ever told me that coming out
Was something you do over and over again
Like a snake sloughing away last year's skin.

Who would want to relive the dizzying moment
Year after year
Of taking that terrifying, exhilarating first step;
Facing the world, no turning back,
Running the risk of
Being seen in a new light
By those who thought they'd known you best,
Being defined by who or what you do in bed?

The first time I came out was to myself,
After a few of years of therapy
To counteract the effects of an evangelical upbringing
That was loving . . . but narrow and misguided nonetheless.

With my family it was a matter
Not so much of coming out as an *oozing* out. . . .
Slowly, over a period of years,
After the same "roommate" showed up
at Christmas and Thanksgiving.
Their questions about girlfriends and marriage trickled to a halt
Until, finally, the family gave a collective and knowing "Oohhhh!"
And realized I had, in fact, already married and settled down.

II
The emergency room doctor says, "You have four choices:
Hetero, Homo, bi, or asexual."
But the only thought intense enough to penetrate
The fevered delirium and the creeping,
Blissful fog of morphine is: "A sexual *what?*"

Then the searing pain of the shingles erupting
Up and down my arm and across my back
Becomes the one inescapable reality the senses register
before the mind goes blank and slips
into blessed unconsciousness.

Eight days in a hospital bed
And one fateful blood test later,
I am out again: this time HIV-positive
In the hysterical, Homophobic rage

Of the mid-1980s
In the buckle of the Bible Belt.
And I am *really* so over coming out.

III
Fast forward to the year 2000. . . .
After a decade or more of relative success
With combination therapy—one nonstop,
15-year-long antiretroviral cocktail party.
The toxins accumulate, the side effects worsen;
Nauseated, bloated, wasted away,
I find myself buying a suit
In which my partner and I both know I will be buried.

Not long after, a Sunday morning epiphany:
Jesus in a sermon walks on water and holds out a hand
And I am Peter, bereft of everything but shaky faith . . .
Which is all God knows to ask of me.
Salvation comes in a "drug holiday":
I stop poisoning myself, I give my body a chance to heal
And by so doing I am resurrected in this lifetime.

It's been over three years now:
Amazing years of health restored, of faith renewed,
Of living on the razor's edge of grace.

So I come out now just a little bit more each day:
As a born-again believer in the miracle of life,
As one who trusts more in the healing power of God
Than in science—so call me a skeptic;
As one who embraces the inexplicable
Yet undeniable experience of
Everyday life, death, and transformation—so call me a mystic;
As one who knows that God *does* move, speak, and act in this world,
And that there is, indeed, a time and a purpose to everything under
heaven.[54]

Cultural Memory

I died in Vietnam.[55]

Scholars who explore the neuroscientific phenomenon of how the mind-brain codes, stores, and retrieves memory distinguish three aspects: "the mental *capacity* to retrieve stored information and to perform learned mental operations, such as long division; the semantic, imagistic, or sensory *content* of recollections; and the *location* where these recollections are stored."[56] Studies of the phenomenon of cultural memory proceed on the assumption that remembering is also an inter- and intra-cultural phenomenon that happens not only within isolated individual bodies. Remembering is rather something people do together. Our body memory cannot be separated from the larger environment. Our body memory is embedded in cultural memory. Individual expressions of body memory are embedded in cultural expressions that are mediated through language and thus through narrative, rituals, and artifacts or objects that have representational power.

Maurice Halbwachs, in his classic *On Collective Memory*, emphasized the collective and social dimensions of memory.[57] Halbwachs was determined to identify individual memory as a function of social memory. He was convinced that there was no isolated repository in the human psyche that could exist without connection to the environment. Since remembering was for Halbwachs a discursive activity, it had to be socially grounded.[58]

Today Halbwachs's notion of collective memory has been superseded by the concept of cultural memory,[59] whereby the social and individual dimensions of memory are not seen as being in antagonistic opposition to each other or as placed in a hierarchical relationship. Rather, Jan Assmann describes cultural memory as a shared mental space in which a particular group refers to fixed points in the past that receive a symbolic quality. Shared narratives evolve around those points of reference, which then generate new memories. The narratives that constitute cultural memory are in many cases driven by the urge to identify oneself with a story one did not necessarily participate in as a contemporary: "Such an ability is manifested in the Polynesian use of the first-person pronoun when narrating one's ancestral history as well as in statements like 'I smelt iron in Nubia' or 'I built Timbuctoo' used to express a Barbadian poet's distinctly African memories."[60]

In a similar sense we can speak of liturgical storytelling that generates cultural memory. Jews at Passover say, "*We* were slaves to the Pharaoh in Egypt and God liberated *us* from slavery," and Christians proclaim at Easter: "Christ is risen"; by this they always mean "*for us*," This kind of liturgical storytelling is rooted in the power of mnemonic synchronization.[61] It is an existential fusion of one's own life story with a larger narrative, a narrative that is simultaneously ritualized by people who share the same space of cultural memory.[62]

However, it is important to recognize that this space of cultural memory is in many contexts not a peaceful and Homogenous space. It is rather highly contested. Especially crucial is the question of *how* histories of violent conflicts, genocide, and enduring structural violence are remembered.[63] The space of cultural memory is contested and fluid. Stories emerge that have been suppressed or forgotten; marginalized groups articulate their perspectives on what kind of cultural memories are relevant.[64] What is supposed to be remembered becomes a locus of struggle.[65]

> Neither remnant, document, nor relic of the past, nor floating in a present cut off from the past, cultural memory, for better or worse links the past to the present and future. . . . The memorial presence of the past takes many forms and serves many purposes, ranging from conscious recall to unreflected reemergence, from nostalgic longing for what is lost to polemical use of the past to reshape the present. The interaction between present and past that is the stuff of cultural memory is, however, the product of collective agency rather than the result of psychic or historical accident.[66]

This collective agency is expressed not only in written form but also in cultural performances such as everyday habits, collective rituals of remembrance, art works, memorial sites, etc.[67] Cultural memory is transmitted through writing, but also through bodily practices and commemorative performances.

Mieke Bal suggests that we distinguish three dimensions of cultural memory as practice that weave together individual and collective aspects: habitual memory, narrative memory, and traumatic memory. *Habitual memory* refers to things we do almost automatically. It encompasses practices we have learned, things we do not so much by conscious choice but rather because we have an embodied sense of how to do these things. In some cases they are strongly routine-based and enforced by discipline. With regard to rituals, we might say that habitual memory is inscribed into the bodies of worshipers. People engage in embodied knowing of how to bow the head or how to close the eyes, to interlace fingers or hold their hands open with palms up. People know in their bodies how to come to the altar, how to receive bread, wine, or juice.[68] Even those who may no longer attend church regularly will have a vague sense of what to do during communion. People who grew up with a ritual routine have the habitual memories inscribed "deeply into their bones."[69]

The second dimension of cultural memory Bal mentions is that of *narrative memories*:

> Narrative memories, even of unimportant events, differ from routine or habitual memories in that they are affectively colored, surrounded by an emotional aura that, precisely, makes them memorable. Often, the string of events that composes a narrative (and narratable) memory offers high and low accents, foreground and background, preparatory and climactic events.[70]

With regard to ritual practice it probably does not make much sense to draw a clear line of distinction between these two dimensions of cultural memory. We also would oppose Bal's claim that habitual memory is less affectively colored. Habitual as well as narrative memories are integral to the celebration of the Eucharistic liturgy. Our body memories hold it all: movement, sounds, smells, words, and larger narrative sequences of the ritual, all work together to shape its meaning in the larger fabric of cultural memory.

The third category is *traumatic memory*. Traumatic experiences occupy the present of those who have to deal with them. Traumatic memory resists being transformed into narrated memory.[71] What is remembered leaves the realm of actual trauma, since traumas encompass events that are not yet framed into fragments of narrative. Thus traumatic memory refers back to those events as individuals or groups search for ways of articulating memory through narratives or rituals. Trauma leads individuals and groups into the realm of speechlessness; it is accompanied either by repression or dissociation.

> In narratological terms, repression results in ellipsis—the omission of important elements in the narrative—whereas dissociation doubles the strand of the narrative series of events by splitting off a sideline. . . . In other words, repression interrupts the flow of narratives that shapes memory; dissociation splits off material that cannot then be reincorporated into the main narrative.[72]

Many scholars and therapists are convinced that healing can only happen when the traumatic event can be framed in a story. This requires a witnessing listener who gives the diffuse and dispersed energy of trauma a direction.

It is helpful to distinguish between individual traumatic experiences and cultural trauma. "Cultural trauma occurs when members of a collectivity feel they have been subjected to a horrendous event that leaves indelible marks upon their group consciousness, marking their memories forever and changing their future identity in fundamental and irrevocable ways."[73] Jonathan Shay, a therapist who works with Vietnam veterans, reports that many of his clients express their sense of loss of self in the traumatic war experience through the sentence "I died in Vietnam." This sentence perfectly expresses what traumatic experiences encompass: a severe disruption of memory, a dissolving of past from present, and inability to envision a future that is worth living.

Cultural trauma that is rooted in particular events can also affect subsequent generations that have not been directly involved as participants in those events. Those generations have to deal with things that are untold and suppressed, things that find expression in unhealthy forms of communication.[74] Or, if trauma was transformed into narrative and thus into cultural memory, they have to cope with the effects of those stories on their current lives.

Is it possible that Eucharistic liturgies that embrace the possibilities and constraints of anamnetic empathy[75] can be a place of witness and listening? One way this might be accomplished would be to disrupt the familiar Prayers of Thanksgiving by inserting significant stories that hold body and place memories, stories like those of Bruce Saunkeah and Richetta and Ra Amen (see below), which emerge from the depths of the body of Christ. We suggest framing the celebration of the Eucharist as a practice in which the narrative that witnesses to the violence of body politics, to the trauma of torture and violent death might surface. Juxtaposing the people's stories with God's story as it has come to us in God's creating, sustaining, and redeeming work might create the windows that free our eschatological imagination.

When we join in the memorial acclamation "Christ has died, Christ is risen, Christ will come (again)," we can give witness to the potential of divine transformation in the midst of death while celebrating communion with the risen Christ whose resurrected body, according to the Gospels, was marked by the traces of torture. The resurrection hope opens a space in which neither dissolution nor suppression of painful memories need be a strategy of survival. There are things that can be remembered. The Eucharistic liturgy understood as a gestalt of traumatic memory formed into narrative illuminates also what cannot be remembered. We can only trust that the gaps of speechlessness[76] in the narrative that our celebrations reveal will be held in God's grace. We are charged to remember something we are not able to remember authentically: the tortured body of Christ and the love of God that reaches into the depth of that experience of immensurable suffering. In the Eucharist, however, we encounter the God who will not forget and who embraces our amnesia.

Practicing that faith in the larger realm of the Eucharistic life could inspire us to engage the fabric of cultural memory in which we work on narrative and ritual representations that search for the redemption of traumatic memories. The following narrative shows how cultural memory and trauma are related.

Richetta and Ra Amen's Journey: Memories of Captivity[77]

Some things you can forget. Other things you never do.[78]

Richetta and Ra Amen's report of their journey to Cape Coast Castle in Ghana is a powerful testimony to the horrific depth of cultural trauma, to what is lost, to what is remembered, and to the struggle of finding a voice and forming a narrative. They give witness to how the pervasive experience of racism in the present is inextricably intertwined with the traumatic memory of the slave trade, the middle passage, Christianity as slaveholder religion, and the history of slavery in the Americas. This memory attacks bodies, minds, and spirits; this memory is the invasive grounding that shapes African American collective identity and memory until today. However, this narrative also offers glimpses of hope that can be found in the African history of Christianity predating the era of the slave trade; it can be found in the witness, theology, and life of Ghanaian Christians today who profess a life in Christ in its fullness.

> As our tour group from America approached Cape Coast Castle on the Gulf of Guinea in the country of Ghana, West Africa, I looked with amazement at the colorfully adorned women who were able to effortlessly balance and carry baskets on their heads containing vegetables, fruits, clothes, or wood. This was a part of my lost heritage that was stolen from me when my ancestors were taken as captives during the bustling slave trade. The tour guide explained that all of Europe was implicated in the slave trade: the Portuguese were the first Europeans to

come to Ghana in the 1600s. The Dutch, Swedes, and Danes followed. The British defeated all of them in the latter part of the sixteenth century. The British then built Cape Coast Castle with materials imported from England. These materials included cannons and sixty-pound cannon balls that were needed to protect the valuable human captives of the British. Cape Coast Castle was to be the last dwelling place on African soil for millions of men, women, and children.

As we walked through the sunlit courtyard where, according to the tour guide, one "never had to see the captives being conveyed," he pointed out to us the place in Cape Coast Castle that held the first English church in Ghana. Worship services were conducted there just above the dungeon where the captives were being held. We were astounded that it was a Christian church, the Anglican Church, that is, the Church of England. It was ironic to me that these slaveholders believed in a religion whose main rite of worship, the Eucharist, commemorates and celebrates the life, crucifixion, and resurrection of one who, like the captives, was also poor and oppressed.

As we headed to the stairs leading to the dungeon where the slaves were once held, we stopped to read the placard posted outside the door. It read:

> In Everlasting Memory
> Of the anguish of our ancestors
> May those who died rest in peace
> May those who return find their roots
> May humanity never again perpetrate
> Such injustice against humanity
> We the living vow to uphold this.

Next to the above placard is a sign that reads: "Male Slave Dungeon (circa 1792)." The tour guide informed us that 1792 was the peak era of the slave trade, when more labor was needed on the plantations throughout the Americas.

Just before we entered the dungeon, the tour guide's expression indicated that he was carrying a heavy load. I called out to my husband Ra because I was afraid of what I would see, hear, and feel in the dungeons. Or was I afraid that I too might be taken captive? As we entered the dark, slippery stairway, Ra and I both started speaking in hushed tones. In the dungeon, it was incredibly dark. There was very little ventilation. We were standing on floors made of bricks that had been covered by human feces that sometimes went as high as two feet. The captives were required to live in this space for six to twelve weeks without any human comforts. We in the tour group listened to the tour guide's descriptions of the horrors endured by the captives. Our hearts were heavy as we asked questions and some even attempted to make light-hearted banter. It was almost impossible to comprehend the inhumanity of it all. We felt the pain of our ancestors that day, but we drew inspiration to survive this so that we could express our humanity to the fullest as a resistance to that unmatched inhumane effort to deny African people their humanity.

In the dungeon, a shrine was built to block off the exit that has been called the "Door of No Return." When the captives had gone through this door they were never to return to the shores of Africa again. Although over sixty to two hundred million captives were lost during the middle passage, those who survived were to enter into a life of perpetual slavery, a slavery that has been defined by Orlando Patterson, the noted Harvard sociologist, as "the permanent, violent domination of natally alienated and generally dishonored persons."[79] Toni Morrison puts it in everyday practical terms: "that anybody white could take your whole self for anything that came to mind. Not just work, kill, or maim you, but dirty you. Dirty you so bad you couldn't like yourself anymore. Dirty you so bad you forgot who you were and couldn't think it up."[80] An African-American man, a former slave, equated slavery with nonhuman existence when he stated, "Before I'd be a slave again, I'd take a gun and end it all. Because you're nothing but a dog. Nothing but a dog."[81]

Escaping the oppressive atmosphere of the dungeon, we went upstairs to the museum where on display were fabulous photos detailing the history of Ghana and of African people in the Diaspora. There we watched a video that focused at first on traditional African culture and then showed how Africans and African Americans today still perform some of the same rituals.

After the video, I was overcome with a feeling of sickness that seemed to penetrate my soul. My aching head starts throbbing and I could not stop the tears. The dungeons are a poisoned space. They still carry the pain of all their ill-fated inhabitants. That pain had penetrated my soul. As a Baptist preacher can work a congregation into a crying and moaning fervor as they share in the pain of Jesus' crucifixion, so too do the spaces within the slave castles work the visitors into a fervor as they remember and share in the pain of their ancestors.

Eschatological Remembrance (Anamnesis) 185

Ten years later, as Ra and I prepared to view our own video made during our visit to Cape Coast Castle, we felt a sense of dread as if we were going to the funeral of a dearly loved family member. Ra became sick and weak, vomiting up his dinner. I could not stop my tears as we entered the dungeons again in the video. It was as Toni Morrison declared in *Beloved*, "Some things you can forget. Other things you never do."[82]

This painful act of remembrance, as well as other bouts with racism, for a period of my life shaped my identity as a Christian. When I was a child growing up in Detroit, everyone in my family and in my neighborhood attended church and Sunday school every Sunday. During church services the congregation always recited the 100th Psalm. Every morning my parents would have each of my eleven brothers and sisters and myself say a Bible verse to bless our breakfast. The very young would say the shortest verse in the Bible, John 11:35, "Jesus wept." I remember how excited my brother Charles was when he discovered the slick and rhythmical sounding John 1:1, "In the beginning was the word and the word was with G-O-D and the word was G-O-D." Additionally, my father made sure that all of his children memorized the Lord's Prayer and the 23rd Psalm. However, once I moved away to California to attend Stanford University, I not only neglected to attend church regularly but I also failed to require my children to attend church, because I believed, like many other African Americans, that Christianity historically was solely a European religion and Europeans were responsible for the gross mistreatment of people of African descent. But after our return from Ghana and the visit to the slave castle our family returned to the church. One of the reasons for our return was because in Ghana we saw Africans practicing Christianity as a complete and full way of life. Religion was not a separate entity. I also began to learn that Jesus Christ and Christianity originated in lands where people of color lived.

Additionally, this past November I attended the 2005 International Conference on the Bible and its African Roots in Addis Ababa, Ethiopia, organized by Dr. Ephraim Isaac, the first chair of the African Studies department at Harvard University. There in Ethiopia we visited a museum where a replica of Lucy, one of the original African mothers of all humanity, a three-and-a-half-million-year-old skeleton found in Ethiopia, is located. In Lalibela, Ethiopia, I saw beautiful twelfth-century rock-hewn churches that were carved out of mountains. I saw St. Mary's church, believed to be the home of the Ark of the Covenant, and ancient twelfth- and thirteenth-century biblical manuscripts. I also saw seventeenth-century castles where not slaves but Ethiopian royalty lived. Outside the main cities in Ethiopia one sees shepherds herding sheep and cattle and horse-drawn carts. One actually feels that one has been transported into the time of Jesus. I know now that African Americans' first introduction to Jesus Christ and Christianity was many centuries before our slave castle experiences. So, although my body remembers the pain of the captives who had to endure the horrors of enslavement, my faith in G-O-D and Jesus Christ is still strong and my understanding about anamnesis in the Eucharist anticipating the promised and liberating future of the oppressed remains steadfast.[83]

Richetta and Ra's testimony show the powerful connection between place and memory. The memories that the dungeons of the slave castle hold are overwhelming destructive energies. Cape Coast Castle today is not a mere memorial in which the events of the past are documented. The place memory that is evoked here is different.

Place Memory

A most important element in place as a human construct is memory
or, more precisely, multiple memories.
Eucharistic place is very much a landscape of memory—
not least of ambiguous and conflicting memories.
Beyond the immediate participants,
there are wider and deeper narrative currents
in any Eucharistic celebration.[84]

Our cultural memory is embedded in place memory. The spoken and the silenced narratives of suffering and hope that we carry with us are connected with actual places. Those places are not simply geographical locations; they gain meaning through human narratives that are attached to them. Stories we tell, the resonance of sounded word in music and in silence, the bodies and the walls that create space, faces, touches, smells we remember and rituals we perform give shape to what we see in particular places. Our place memory is shaped by all these things. Memory and place are inextricably interwoven: "Place is space that has the capacity to be remembered and to evoke what is most precious."[85]

In conscious or unconscious ways we bring our body memories and our cultural memory to the Eucharistic celebration as it is contextualized in actual experiences of place. When we celebrate the Lord's Supper we create space with our bodies. The way we gather for communion creates Eucharistic space. The energy with which we move forward to the table, the attentiveness with which we relate to the celebrants and to our neighbors in the pews creates space. It matters if and how we pass the plate with the bread and the chalice with wine or juice to our neighbor while we sit in the pews, or if we form a circle around the altar, or if we line up kneeling and head bowing in front of the altar rail. It matters if we move in a spiral dance around the altar so that we create a space, fluid and graceful. The way our bodies move and how we relate to one another matters—we create Eucharistic spaces with our bodies that affect our memories of actual Eucharistic celebrations.[86]

The Eucharistic narratives in their larger contexts evoke many places: Jerusalem as the city in which the Last Supper was held, the upper room where the disciples gathered with Jesus, Golgotha as the place of torture and of death, the garden, the empty tomb as the place of resurrection, the road to Emmaus that leads to a transitional place where the fearful disciples share a meal with the resurrected Christ.

What is true of the biblical narrative can be said in many cases of the understanding of place that Christians have developed over time. The pilgrimage itinerary of the "holy places" visited by Jesus and his friends is significant because of the events that happened there and not so much because of the sites as such.[87] This, at least, is what the Gospels convey. Places become sacred because "holy people" are related to them. Often the transitional aspect is lifted up. Early Christians understood themselves as travelers who were yearning for the heavenly home.

In his theology of space, Philip Sheldrake describes the Eucharist as an eschatological space in which the transformation of death is celebrated. He portrays the Eucharist as

> a "space" of *transitus*—where there is a passing over between worlds. Eucharistic symbolism is founded on death and rebirth. The breaking and sharing of bread is symbolic of a sharing in the power of Jesus' death that opens the doors to new life. However, practicing the Eucharist also, by association, points the members of the community towards their entry *now* into a painful death—the death of a bounded way of being and a selective way of being social. To practice the Eucharist entails the risk of reshaping the place where we stand. [88]

Understanding the Eucharist as an eschatological space leads us beyond the liturgical celebration. It inspires us to sharpen our sensibilities with regard to the shaping of places that hold memories of suffering and the potential for fragmentary transformation as the foretaste of resurrection. The Eucharistic life as we try to describe it is attentive to places in which human bodies are or were humiliated and destroyed. We not only remember the night in which Jesus was delivered and we not only imagine the places in which the Eucharistic narrative is embedded. We rather ask: Where is Golgotha today? And where do we find the witnesses who tell us about the garden of resurrection?[89]

In what follows we invite our readers to discover with us a place that holds memories of painful ambiguities. We are eager to learn what are the transformative practices people engage in by which places of terror are imbued with fragments of hope. We are following the traces of the Holy Spirit, who redeems our memories in the hard work toward reconciliation. Memories that redeem will neither suppress the stories of the victims nor will they try to regenerate hatred. They acknowledge the irrevocable violence and the desperation connected to its remembrance. Memories that redeem will call for justice, but not for revenge and retribution. Memories that redeem will hold possibilities of encounter between enemies; they will open spaces for healing. "'Redeeming memories' refers to the process of both memory retrieval and redemption through remembering."[90]

Here we offer an example in which we see eschatological anamnesis practiced as people engage in place memory. This example leads us to Germany, to the Chapel of Reconciliation in the Bernauer Straße in Berlin.

Bernauer Straße, Berlin: Chapel of Reconciliation[91]

> . . . "healing earth"
> on the wounds of the location,
> which should not be "sealed."[92]

On a cloudy Sunday morning I exited the streetcar at the Nordbahnhof stop in order to visit the Chapel of Reconciliation at the Bernauer Straße in Berlin. It was a couple of minutes before ten o'clock, when the powerful noise of bells flooded into the streets of the still-sleeping Wedding neighborhood, calling people to worship. The sonorous notes of the bells made me expect a glorious cathedral in all its vastness. Instead I discovered an open-air space and, surrounded by wildflowers, the Chapel of Reconciliation, a light, modern rammed-earth building with translucent wood lamellas as its outer skin. This sacred space built in an oval shape struck me as rather fragile. It became for me a Eucharistic space, since I could sense the way its walls and its people tell the story of this particular location without clinging revengefully to its past. The Chapel of Reconciliation[93] holds painful place-memories about the once-divided city. At the same time, it embodies faith that Christ's presence transforms this place of death into a space that holds experiences of resurrection, however fragmented they might seem.

Fig. 4. *The exterior of the Chapel of Reconciliation (Versöhnungs-kapelle), Berlin. Photo: Christian Jungeblodt, courtesy the Archives of the Versöhnungs-gemeinde, Berlin. Special thanks to Rainer Just.*

A brief journey into the history that this place holds: The Church of Reconciliation, a large neo-gothic brick cathedral with a seventy-five-meter tower, was built in the late nineteenth century. It was consecrated by Empress Augusta Victoria herself on August 28, 1894. Located in the blue-collar district of Wedding, from the very beginning its mission was defined by outreach to the economically and socially disenfranchised. The establishment of affordable housing and accompanying programs for youth and unemployed workers shaped the mission and life of the congregation.

During the Nazi regime the Church of Reconciliation was divided: two of the pastors belonged to the Confessing Church, while the third pastor was a member of the Deutsche Christen (so-called German Christians). During a severe air raid in November 1943, the church building and the parish hall were struck by several bombs and severely damaged. The congregation mourned more than two hundred dead; another three hundred people became homeless as a result of the bombing.

The end of World War II brought the division of the city of Berlin. This division had tremendous impact on the congregation as well. The church, the parsonage, one of the parish halls, and more than a hundred members were now located in the Soviet sector of the city, while over ninety percent of the congregation lived in the French sector. Although the bombed church was rebuilt and reconsecrated in 1950, the everyday life of the parish became increasingly difficult due to increasing border controls and the introduction of two different currencies for East and West Germany. The situation became worse when the government of the German Democratic Republic began to build the Wall on August 13, 1961:

> The border separated the entire street lengthwise—it ran directly along the facades of the East Berlin side. The buildings belonged to the Eastern part of the city—but if the residents stepped outside their front doors they would be standing in Wedding—in the West. As several people continued to cross into the West from this location, the government of East Berlin had the doors and windows of the ground floor apartments bricked up within the span of a few weeks. . . . During the subsequent weeks people fled the East by jumping from windows or lowering themselves into the West with ropes.[94]

Deeply engraved in German cultural memory are the images of people throwing their furniture out of the windows of houses on the Bernauer Straße as a desperate attempt to save at least some of their belongings; then, more chilling, the images of people jumping out of their windows into the Western part of the street.[95] Some people died in the attempt to leap to freedom. Neighbors, friends, and families were divided by the wall. All of a sudden the Church of Reconciliation became inaccessible to people from the East as well as from the West. It was now located in the forbidden zone. Over the years this zone was called the death strip. For a while the border police used the steeple of the church as a watchtower to observe and catch people who were trying to escape to West Berlin.

Fig. 5. Inside the exterior "shell" of wooden lamellas, the Chapel walls were built with materials including rubble from the Church of Reconciliation (Versöhnungskirche) that stood in the same location until its destruction in 1985. Photos: Huber & Huber (Samuel Huber) Architekturfotografie, courtesy of the Archives of the Versöhnungsgemeinde, Berlin; special thanks to Rainer Just.

In 1985 another great tragic event happened:

> The Church of Reconciliation was blown up—to increase the "safety, order, and cleanliness at the border to West Berlin," according to the official explanation. The church had long been a thorn in the eye of the GDR regime, a symbol of the separation of Germany. On January 22nd the nave was detonated, followed by the church steeple six days later. The images of the crumbling steeple were broadcast around the world. One year later the congregation in Bernauer Straße said farewell to the church with a three-day funeral service entitled "Wall Jump."[96]

Probably nobody had seriously expected that the Wall would fall only a few years later. From that time on, the congregation dedicated its work to the question of what it means to remember the tragic history of this place. At the same time they wanted to create a space of hope and reconciliation that makes room for meditation, prayer, and self-exploration in the restless city of Berlin. The congregation became engaged in the initiative "*Gedenkstätte Berlin*," which lobbied for a memorial and documentation center focusing on the history of the Wall in Berlin.

Simultaneously, discussions about the rebuilding of a sacred space began. The congregation made some interesting choices that, in my opinion, embody what eschatological anamnesis might mean in the realm of architecture for sacred spaces. They decided (1) not to imitate what was lost and (2) not to rebuild the old church. After the fall of the Wall and the end of the Cold War neither a triumphalist nor a nostalgic attitude toward the memory of this particular location seemed appropriate. The place was supposed to be timely, responsive to ecological needs, energy efficient and not as tall as the old church, since the membership of the church had decreased significantly over the years. The congregation decided to build a chapel, not a church, since chapels in the Christian tradition were sites of special remembrance. A chapel, not a multifunctional space, was envisioned. However, it was decided that traces

Fig. 6. A single tower remains of the Versöhnungs-kirche during its demolition in 1985. Photo collage: Archives of the Versöhnungsgemeinde, Berlin.

of the past should be integrated into the new construction. Pastor Manfred Fischer commented on the significant connection between the idea of remembrance and architecture:

> We tried to avoid what happens all over Berlin nowadays: that the traditional has to disappear in favor of the new, or that the new is nothing but an imitation of the old. We pictured a construction that would respect the traces without making the effort to reconstruct what was lost.[97]

And little by little, objects from the old church were returned: first the communion vessels and the baptismal font, later the altar Bible. The objects that symbolize the Protestant foundation of liturgical practice—word and sacraments—were shortly accompanied by the return of the bells, which were rediscovered in the St. Bartholomew Church in Berlin Friedrichshain.

Fig. 7. The altar area in the interior of the old Versöhnungskirche. Photo: Versöhnungsgemeinde, Berlin.

The congregation chose clay as the basic building material. In the nineteenth century clay was the most common construction material. But it was not merely because of its historical significance that they chose to build with clay. Rather, the congregation perceived its deeper meaning:

Fig. 8. The interior of the new Chapel. Photo: Britta Krehl.

Clay is a natural, living construction material and consequently more easily damaged. The fragility of the structure testifies to the vulnerability of peace and reconciliation. Clay also signifies "healing earth" on the wounds of the place, which should not be "sealed." Accordingly, the liveliness of the material also symbolizes the possibility for transformation and triumph over the place's tragic history.[98]

What impressed me most was that the clay was mixed with rubble from the demolished church, found when the construction work for the chapel started. Those fragments are visible and tangible. Some shimmer in beautiful colors like turquoise through the warm golden-brown of the clay. Walls, as wounds that are not to be sealed, in their fragility and liveliness give shelter to the memory this place contains. Those walls also create a space of imagination.

The inner space of the sanctuary holds a disturbing tension in the way it is shaped by two axes. One axis refers to the middle axis of the old nave. Here we find the niche for the recovered, though damaged, retable, a carving in oak. It depicts the Last Supper. What is most striking is that Jesus' head is cut off. The same is true for the face of the disciple Jesus loved most. Through these traces of destruction, this piece of art—originally probably from an aesthetic point of view not very significant—gains a depth in reference to

what we have called eschatological anamnesis: the Last Supper as well as the current gatherings for the holy meal around the altar do not hide the traces of violence but make them visible when we celebrate communion as the feast of the resurrection of the body.

A view into the depths, much like that in the ambulatory, opens below the altar section in the alcove. The basement steps and the basement door of the old church that was walled in with concrete in 1961 are visible through a glass panel in the floor. An unexploded bomb from World War II discovered during the initial excavation work for the chapel's construction lies on the steps.[99]

Fig. 9. The Last Supper is depicted in an oak retable (shelf), originally installed above the altar when the Versöhnungskirche was built in the 19th century. The church was severely damaged by Allied bombing in World War II, then demolished by the German Democratic Republic. The retable is now part of the Chapel of Reconciliation. Photo: Ines Pohl.

The main axis of the chapel is traditionally east-west oriented. It is geared toward the new compressed-clay altar that stores the baptism and communion vessels. The refectory/mensa of the old church is on the bottom and supports the new altar. A small bronze cross with the body of the crucified Christ who lifts his right hand in a gesture of blessing stands next to the altar.[100]

The Chapel of Reconciliation at the Bernauer Straße in Berlin embodies the memory of its place as eschatological anamnesis. It is sensitive to the traces of destruction the place holds because of World War II and the division of the city of Berlin. The wounds this place bears are not to be covered up, and yet the way it makes visible those traces is not a clinging to the violent past. One can sense the spirit of new creation in this place; the architectural shape holds new opportunities for the people of God to gather around the table and share a meal. The space thus created does not embody Christian triumphalism. It receives its power through its simplicity and its transitional energy. It is open to

Fig. 10. Bronze crucifix, Chapel of Reconciliation, Berlin. Photo: Ines Pohl.

visitors who come to sit and try to comprehend what it means when governments divide cities, territories, landscapes, ethnic groups, congregations, and families by building walls such as this. This chapel is open to visitors who come to pray for reconciliation in a world in which similar walls are continuously being built.

The congregation of the Chapel of Reconciliation is keenly aware of its voice in the public square of the city of Berlin. It was engaged in the struggle of creating *one* place in the city where remnants of the Wall are preserved in order to give future generations at least a sense of what was once going on in the Bernauer Straße in Berlin Wedding after World War II.

Places such as the Bernauer Straße in Berlin can inspire us to leave our churches from time to time and celebrate Holy Communion at places that embody sacramental permeability and Eucharistic life for us, places that do not seal or cover up the wounds of violence and at the same time reveal how God's reconciliation is at work among us.

Anamnesis as Dangerous Memory[101]

The Eucharistic life that flows out of liturgical practice should embrace the practice of remembering in a holistic manner. It should be attentive to body memory, collective memory, and place memory. It should be aware of the ambiguity sustained by practices of remembering. There are distorted memories that produce desire for revenge, and there are things that indeed should not be remembered.

The liturgical practice related to eschatological anamnesis could foster liturgical disruptions through multisensory stimuli, through dance and embodiment, through storytelling and change of place. This demands courage, since many of us have learned not to articulate the memories our bodies hold or to deal with the abyss of violence that scars our collective narratives.

We dream of a Eucharistic practice that gives us courage to engage in both.

NOTES

Introduction

1. Don Saliers, *Worship as Theology: Foretaste of Glory Divine* (Nashville: Abingdon, 1994), 49.

2. "O Come, O Come Emmanuel," *Evangelical Lutheran Worship* (Minneapolis: Augsburg Fortress, 2006), #257, stanzas 1 and 4.

3. Stanley Tookie Williams was an early leader of the Crips, a violent street gang founded in South Central Los Angeles in 1969. He was executed on December 13, 2005, at San Quentin State Prison of California, which was surrounded by thousands of protesters asking for clemency. He was the twelfth person executed by the state since California reinstated the death penalty in 1977. Williams was killed for the murders of Albert Owens, Yen-Yi Yang, Tsai-Shai Lin, and Yee-Chen Lin. He had been on death row since 1979. In the 1990s Williams started writing children's books advocating non-violence and alternatives to gang activism; he also apologized for his role in co-founding the Crips. From the beginning of his sentence, however, he asserted his innocence of the four murders. Williams's story illuminates the prevailing racism of U.S. society that keeps thousands of African American males in prison instead of providing education, work, and a future.

4. "O come, O come, Emmanuel," stanzas 5, 6, 7.

5. "Eucharist" derives from the Greek verb *eucharistein,* which means to give thanks, to render or return thanks. Early on, for example, in *Didache* 9 and 14, to give thanks was equated with celebrating the Lord's Supper. In some liturgical traditions the term Eucharist is used for the entire service of word and sacrament. In this book we use it for the holy meal. The term Communion is often used in Free Church traditions. It refers to the holy meal as providing *koinōnia,* that is, communion or fellowship. Paul speaks in 1 Cor. 10:16 of a sharing/*koinōnia* in the body of Christ. The term Communion also refers to the Roman Catholic and Orthodox tradition of presanctified liturgies in which consecrated bread and wine are distributed, yet the Eucharist is not celebrated.

6. Teresa Berger, "Breaking Bread in a Broken World. Liturgy and Cartographies of the Real," *SL* 36/1 (2006): 77.

7. Geoffrey Wainwright's early work, *Eucharist and Eschatology*, was one of the first attempts to reshape the discourse in Eucharistic theology along these lines. About the major debates during the era of Reformation he states in his introduction: "The treatises were far less concerned with the eucharist as the common meal of the whole churchly people of God in the last days, and with its relation to the messiah's banquet in the kingdom and the abundant feeding that the bible looked for in the days of the new heavens and the new earth. The ecclesiological and cosmological references of the eucharist found themselves severely curtailed." See Geoffrey Wainwright, *Eucharist and Eschatology* (Akron: OSL Publications, 2002), 2. For an emphasis on the eschatological aspects of the Eucharist from the perspective of political and orthodox theology see Bruce T. Morrill, *Anamnesis as Dangerous Memory: Political and Liturgical Theology in Dialogue* (Collegeville, Minn.: Liturgical, 2000).

8. See in a similar vein also Bruce Morrill's assessment: "The move away from thinking about the sacraments as objects that dispense grace to perceiving them as relational events,

as personal encounters among God and people, has been the hallmark of sacramental theology in the second half of the twentieth century." Bruce T. Morrill, "Initial Consideration: Theory and Practice of the Body in Liturgy Today," in Bruce T. Morrill, ed., *Bodies of Worship. Explorations in Theory and Practice* (Collegeville, Minn.: Liturgical, 1999), 1.

9. See Don Saliers, *The Soul in Paraphrase: Prayer and the Religious Affections* (New York: Seabury, 1980).

10. Kenan Osborne's reflection on sacraments and sacramentality has convinced us to emphasize the event (*Ereignis*) and not so much essence and atemporality. Osborne writes: "Sacramentality cannot be presented in an atemporalized and essentialized way. Whenever this is attempted, sacramentality ceases to be principally and primordially the action of God and becomes a form of intellectual ideology. Every essentialization and objectification of sacramentality has the inner capacity of being manipulated and controlled by finite factors. If, on the other hand, sacramentality is God's action within a thoroughly temporalized and existentialed event (*Ereignis*), then all essentialized, and therefore abstract and generalized presentations of sacramentality, are seen in their hermeneutical impotence." Kenan B. Osborne, *Christian Sacraments in a Postmodern World: A Theology for the Third Millennium* (New York and Mahwah, N.J.: Paulist, 1999), 73–74.

11. Berger, "Breaking Bread," 84.

12. There is good information about Jewish festive meals and the Passover, based on the Mishnah and later rabbinic writings, in Hermann L. Strack and Paul Billerbeck, *Kommentar zum Neuen Testament aus Talmud und Midrasch* (Munich: Beck, 1928; 1961) 4:41–76, 611–39. The most important tractate in the Mishnah on this subject is *Berakoth*. For summary information on Jewish table practices see also Jerome Kodell, *The Eucharist in the New Testament* (Wilmington, Del.: Glazier, 1988), 38–52.

13. Rather, we should ask why later generations were interested in depicting that meal as a Passover supper. On this see especially Jonathan Klawans, "Was Jesus' Last Supper a Seder?" *Bible Review* 17/5 (October 2001): 25–33, 47.

14. For the *birkat ha-mazon* see Billerbeck, *Kommentar* 4:627–34.

15. See *Kommentar*, 4:69, 72–73.

16. The sources for designating a meal as *agape* are primarily Tertullian, *Apol.* 39:16–18; Hippolytus, *Ap. Trad.* 25–30; Justin, *Apol. 1*, 67.1–7.

17. Quentin Quesnell, "The Women at Luke's Supper," in Richard J. Cassidy and Philip J. Scharper, eds., *Political Issues in Luke-Acts* (Maryknoll, N.Y.: Orbis, 1983), 59–79, has shown in the case of Luke's Gospel how the text presumes the participation of women as a matter of course. In light of the feminist work done in the period 1970–2000, there can scarcely be any basis today for a hermeneutics that assumes that women and children did not participate in community meals.

18. The word *eschatology* has been in use since the seventeenth century (see pp. 18–23). It first applied to the dogma of the "last things." The word *apocalyptic*, as a designation for Jewish and early Christian mythology of future things, goes back to Rev. 1:1: "The revelation [*apokalypsis*] of Jesus Christ, which God gave him to show his slaves what must soon take place." The word group "apocalypse, apocalyptic" has acquired a popular meaning today that does not correspond to its original content: Nowadays it refers to a catastrophe, the end of the world. That derives from the horrifying images in the Revelation of John, such as the "Four Horsemen of the Apocalypse," although in the Revelation of John such things are not the goal of divine action. Rather, they are mythic interpretations of the humanly created crisis that God means to bring to an end. There have been attempts to refer the concepts of "eschatology" and "apocalyptic" to various ancient sources, and in this way, and with anti-Jewish intent, to differentiate Christian eschatology from Jewish apocalyptic. But early Christian apocalyptic/eschatology is rooted in Judaism. The word *messianism* is also applied to this Jewish and early Christian

tradition, since messianic figures frequently appear in it. It may be appropriate to adopt this term in current church usage, which has no positive term for eschatology.

Chapter 1

1. The following description reflects Andrea Bieler's participation in a World Communion Sunday celebration.

2. "Let Us Now Go to the Banquet," *Evangelical Lutheran Worship* (Minneapolis: Augsburg Fortress, 2006), #523, refrain.

3. *Evangelical Lutheran Worship*, #523, stanza 1.

4. *Global Praise 1: Songs for Worship and Witness*, S. T. Kimbrough, gen. ed., Carlton R. Young, mus. ed. (New York: General Board of Global Ministries, The United Methodist Church, GBG Music, 1995), #36. The places listed are very poor and very rich communities in El Salvador.

5. *Evangelical Lutheran Worship*, #523, stanza 2.

6. Jorge A. Lockward, *Tenemos Esperanza, Temos Esperança: We Have Hope* (New York: The General Board of Global Ministries, The United Methodist Church: GBG Music, 1995), 24.

7. Kwok Pui-lan, *Postcolonial Imagination and Feminist Theology* (Louisville: Westminster John Knox, 2005), 38.

8. See the excellent introduction by Jürgen Ebach, "Eschatologie/Apokalyptik," in *Neues Handbuch Theologischer Grundbegriffe*, ed. Peter Eichler (Munich: Kösel, 2005) 1:260–72. We follow Ebach here in hesitating to distinguish in general between eschatological and apocalyptic thinking.

9. See Gerhard Sauter, "The Concept and Task of Eschatology: Theological and Philosophical Reflections," *SJT* 41 (1988): 499.

10. Sigurd Hjelde, *Das Eschaton und die Eschata: Eine Studie über Sprachgebrauch und Sprachverwirrung in protestantischer Theologie von der Orthodoxie bis zur Gegenwart*, BEvT 102 (Munich: Kaiser, 1987).

11. Christoph Schwöbel, "Last Things First? The Century of Eschatology in Retrospect," in *The Future as God's Gift: Explorations in Christian Eschatology*, ed. David Fergusson and Marcel Sarot (Edinburgh: T&T Clark, 2000), 226.

12. Schwöbel, "Last Things First?", 226.

13. Schwöbel, "Last Things First?", 226. With regard to Barth's approach we may ask: If the *eschaton* has no relation to our everyday experience, how should we, as Christians, be able to explicate what hope is about? The dualistic approach implied here seems to be problematic because it focuses exclusively on the aspect of discontinuity by stressing the aspects of crisis and critique.

14. Ibid.

15. World War I was a crucial event for the further development of eschatological thinking in Western Europe. Facing the brutality of this war and the failure to prevent it, many theologians broke with the modern understanding of progress that had shaped theological and philosophical discourse. The development of eschatological thinking as the grounding hermeneutical perspective of the theological enterprise can be interpreted as a loud protest against the marriage of the Enlightenment's notion of future and progress with Christian eschatological imagination. Theologians such as Barth, Bultmann, and Tillich defined the *eschaton* as the qualification of the present in which the eternal confronts our current experience of life. "For Barth the eternal must be defined in Christological terms, the resurrection becomes the model for the confrontation of time through the eternal. For Tillich it is the breakthrough of the unconditioned in the conditionalities of history, a *kairos* that relativizes all other claims to ultimate meaning within history. For Bultmann it is the challenge, offered in the *kerygma* of Christ, to discover the authentic meaning of existence by being

liberated from the world and its past, and to find orientation in the present through the eschatological moment of decision. From the shared perspective of the dialectic of eternity and time, they concentrated on different fields of eschatological explication. For Barth the infinite qualitative difference between time and eternity is the 'theme of the bible and the sum of philosophy in one.' For Tillich it is the understanding of history as disclosed in the *kairos,* for Bultmann the historicality of existence." Schwöbel, "Last Things First?", 223.

16. Jürgen Moltmann, *The Coming of God: Christian Eschatology,* trans. Margaret Kohl (Minneapolis: Fortress Press, 1996).

17. Joan M. Martin, "A Sacred Hope and a Social Goal: Womanist Eschatology," in *Liberating Eschatology: Essays in Honor of Letty M. Russell,* ed. Margaret Farley and Serene Jones (Louisville: Westminster John Knox, 1999), 212.

18. "Oh, He is going to wake up the dead, Going to wake up the dead, God is going to wake up the dead. One of these mornings bright and fair, God's going to wake up the dead."

19. Martin, "A Sacred Hope," 221–22.

20. Emily Townes, *In a Blaze of Glory: Womanist Spirituality as Social Witness* (Nashville: Abingdon, 1995), 122.

21. Townes, *In a Blaze of Glory,* 139.

22. Richard Bauckham and Trevor Hart, "The Shape of Time," in *The Future as God's Gift,* ed. Fergusson and Sarot, 49.

23. Luise Schottroff, "Celebrating God's Future: Feminist Reflections on the Eschatology of Jesus," in *Time—Utopia—Eschatology:* Yearbook of the European Society of Theological Research of Women (Leuven: Peeters, 1999), 10.

24. Luzia Sutter Rehmann, *Vom Mut, genau hinzusehen: Feministisch-befreiungstheologische Reflexionen zur Apokalyptik* (Lucerne: Edition Exodus, 1998); Jürgen Ebach, "Apokalypse: Zum Ursprung einer Stimmung," *Einwürfe* 2 (1985) 5–61.

25. Catherine Keller, *Apocalypse Now and Then: A Feminist Guide to the End of the World* (Boston: Beacon, 1996), 126.

26. Karl Barth, *Church Dogmatics* (Edinburgh: T&T Clark, 1962) IV/3:938–39.

27. See Margaret Mary Kelleher, "Ritual Studies and the Eucharist: Paying Attention to Performance," in *Eucharist: Toward the Third Millenium,* ed. Martin F. Connell (Eldridge, Iowa: Liturgy Training, 1997), 57.

28. See further chapter 4, "The Body Politics of Eucharist," and Andrea Bieler, "Real Bodies at the Meal," in *"Dies ist mein Leib": Leibliches, Leibeigenes und Leibhaftiges bei Gott und den Menschen*; Jabboq 6; ed. Jürgen Ebach, Hans-Martin Gutmann, Magdalene L. Frettlöh, and Michael Weinrich (Gütersloh: Gütersloher, 2006), 81–90.

29. With this definition we seek to expand and criticize Immanuel Kant's influential theory. He understood imagination as the human ability to create concepts by forming unified images or notions out of sense impressions: "For example, in my perception of a dog, Kant thought that imagination ordered various sense impressions (for example, the feel of fur, four legs, a trunk, long teeth, etc.) into a single perceptual experience (for example, a unified image of a furry creature), such that I can then recognize it (conceptualize it) as a dog. Understood in this way, imagination would appear to be just the bridge needed between the formal and the material sides of cognition." Mark Johnson, *The Body in the Mind: The Bodily Basis of Meaning, Imagination and Reason* (Chicago and London: Univ. of Chicago Press, 1987), xxix. With the approach to imagination proposed here, we try to avoid the dichotomy between sense impression and conceptual thinking, which we consider to be just another expression of the mind-body dualism.

30. Garrett Green makes this helpful distinction in *Imagining God: Theology and the Religious Imagination* (Grand Rapids: Eerdmans, 1998), 64–65.

31. Green, *Imagining God*, 40.

32. Green, *Imagining God*, 43.

33. Paul Ricoeur, "The Metaphorical Process as Cognition, Imagination and Feeling," *Critical Inquiry* 5 (1978) 143–59. For an adaptation of Ricoeur's theory of imagination to the formulation of criteria for artful liturgy see Joyce Ann Zimmerman, "Beauty and the Beast: Criteria for Artful Liturgy," in *Postmodern Worship and the Arts*, ed. Doug Adams and Michael E. Moynahan (San Jose, Calif.: Resource Publications, 2002) 21–32.

34. Zimmerman, "Beauty and the Beast," 27.

35. Richard Kearney, *The Wake of Imagination: Ideas of Creativity in Western Culture* (London: Hutchinson, 1988), 251–55. He refers to Michel Foucault, Jacques Derrida, and Jacques Lacan, who criticize the classical understanding that human imagination reflects original ideas or symbols.

36. Green, *Imagining God*, 106.

37. See pp. 70–74.

38. See Margaret Mary Kelleher, "Liturgy and the Christian Imagination," *Worship* 66/2 (March 1992): 130.

39. See pp. 74–84.

40. Garrett Green, "Imagining the Future," in *The Future as God's Gift*, ed. Fergusson and Sarot, 81.

41. Green, "Imagining the Future," 79.

42. See Johann Baptist Metz, *Unterbrechungen: Theologisch Politische Perspektiven und Profile* (Gütersloh: Gütersloher, 1981).

43. Bruce T. Morrill, *Anamnesis as Dangerous Memory: Political and Liturgical Theology in Dialogue* (Collegeville, Minn.: Liturgical, 2000), 31. Morrill's book offers an intensive discussion of Metz's political theology and its impulses for liturgical theology.

44. The reflection on eschatological imagination as a disruptive force and as dangerous memory is inspired by modern Jewish thought as found in the later works of Walter Benjamin. See Morrill's reference to Benjamin's "Theses on the Philosophy of History" in idem, *Anamnesis*, 30.

45. Green, "Imagining the Future," 76.

46. For further reflections on social integration and critical otherworldliness see Andrea Bieler, *Die Sehnsucht nach dem verlorenen Himmel: Jüdische und christliche Reflexionen zu Gottesdienstreform und Predigtkultur im 19. Jahrhundert*; Praktische Theologie heute 65 (Stuttgart: Kohlhammer, 2003), 39–42.

47. Green, "Imagining the Future," 79.

48. See chapter 3, "The Bread of Life in Two Economies."

49. *b. Sanh.* 98a. For the dating of the Babylonian Talmud see Hermann L. Strack and Günter Stemberger, *Einleitung in Talmud und Midrasch*; 7th ed. (Munich: Beck, 1982), 190; English translation: *Introduction to the Talmud and Midrash* (Minneapolis: Fortress Press, 1992). A precise dating is not (yet) possible; the text contains traditions from different eras, and the final redaction may have taken place in the seventh century CE or even later.

50. This interpretation of the present aspect of eschatology is related to Rudolf Bultmann's view of eschatology. Bultmann emphasizes the aspect of "decision" (see pp. 18–23, and Rudolf Bultmann, *Neues Testament und Mythologie* [Munich: Kaiser, 1941, new ed. 1988; English translation, *The New Testament and Mythology* (Philadelphia: Fortress Press, 1984)], 36: "For believers, the time of salvation [has] already begun; the future life is already present.") However, we understand this decision as contextualized: It has consequences for our praxis of life in society.

51. The notion of a "messianic movement" is also useful for clarifying the relationship of the Jesus movement to other Jewish messianic movements of the time. On this, and on the Jesus movement as a whole, see Richard A. Horsley, with John S. Hanson, *Bandits,*

Prophets, and Messiahs: Popular Movements in the Time of Jesus (San Francisco: Harper and Row, 1988), and Luise Schottroff, *Lydia's Impatient Sisters: A Feminist Social History of Early Christianity,* trans. Barbara and Martin Rumscheidt (Louisville: Westminster John Knox, 1995), 3–11.

52. The concept of the "kingdom" or "reign" of God, the *basileia tou theou,* is central to Jesus' eschatology, according to the Synoptic Gospels. It arises from the notion in the First Testament and postbiblical Jewish literature of God as king. On this see Luise Schottroff, *The Parables of Jesus* (Minneapolis: Fortress Press, 2005), 38–48, on Matt. 22:1-14.

53. We are not drawing distinctions between Jesus traditions going back to the "Jesus of history" and Jesus traditions from later Christian generations (the Christ of faith). The Gospels do not permit such a distinction, because they do not depict the Jesus of history but rather Jesus Messiah, whom many people followed—in his own lifetime and in the contemporary time when the Gospels were written down. On the one hand this point of view signifies skepticism of historical reconstructions of the Jesus of history; on the other hand it represents optimism regarding the historical evaluation of the Synoptic Gospels. The image of Jesus they present is relatively congruent and may not be as distorted as some exegetical projects suppose.

54. See David E. Aune's helpful brief overview of this model of Jesus' eschatology and other models that were applied to the Synoptic Gospels in the twentieth century in "Early Christian Eschatology," *ABD* (1992): 2:599–600.

55. For the history of this concept and its theological implications see Schottroff, *Lydia's Impatient Sisters,* 3–11.

56. See the extended treatment in Schottroff, *Lydia's Impatient Sisters,* 121–35.

57. An early document of this ecclesiological interpretation of the new covenant is Justin, *Dial.* 11.2–4.

58. This vision is univeralist; it includes all peoples. Universalism and particularism should not be associated with a contrast between Christianity (univeralist) and Judaism (particularist). Universalism is anchored in the First Testament and postbiblical Judaism. On this see Eung Chun Park, *Either Jew or Gentile: Paul's Unfolding Theology of Inclusivity* (Louisville and London: Westminster John Knox, 2003), 11–20. The concept put forward in the Acts of the Apostles should not be interpreted as a "history of the early church" but as the development of the consequences of the vision of the new covenant for Christian communities' self-understanding. See, for example, Acts 8:27 in connection with Isa. 56:3-8, or the Pentecost story in Acts 2 as expression of a Jewish vision of universalism in which all peoples maintain their differences and their own languages and yet understand one another, because they are becoming nations of prophets.

59. Josephus, *J.W.,* 6.310–315.

60. When Jesus speaks of himself as the Son of Man, there is no evident reference to the figure of the Son of Man who is to come. Jesus, in describing himself as "Son of Man," is using a circumlocution for "I" (e.g., Matt. 8:20) and speaking of himself as one among many (Matt. 9:6, 8; cf. Mark 2:28 par., which, according to its sense, is the equivalent of Mark 2:27).

61. Since "Son of Man" is not a royal or sovereign title, but is deliberately applied to a human being, we translate "Human One" here.

62. For the ancient notion of patriarchy see Schottroff, *Lydia's Impatient Sisters,* 22–33.

63. It is unknown what means for combating fire and water the people here have in mind. But the sense is clear: They intend to protect themselves with these technological means instead of doing penance.

64. Schottroff, *Lydia's Impatient Sisters,* 128.

65. For this see, for example, Marcus Borg, *Jesus in Contemporary Scholarship* (Valley Forge, Pa.: Trinity Press International, 1994), 47–96.

66. *Palin parousia* in Justin, *Apol. 1*, 52.3, and frequently elsewhere.

67. As we see from the internal context of 1 Cor. 11:26; 16:22; *Did.* 10.6. For *maranatha* see pp. 56–58.

68. For example, Marcus Borg (see above) and the Jesus Seminar.

69. Tim LaHaye and Jerry Jenkins, *Left Behind: A Novel of Earth's Last Days*; vol. 1 of the Left Behind series (Wheaton, Ill.: Tyndale, 1996).

70. A whole lucrative end-times industry has evolved around the series: two movies (to date), children's books, a Web site, and a board game. See Barbara R. Rossing, *The Rapture Exposed: The Message of Hope in the Book of Revelation* (Boulder, Colo.: Westview, 2004), x.

71. Rossing, *The Rapture Exposed*, 1–10.

72. Quoted in Stephen J. Klein, "American Millennial Visions: Towards the Construction of a New Architectonic of American Apocalypticism," in *Imagining the End: Visions of Apocalypse from the Ancient Middle East to Modern America*, ed. Abbas Amanat and Magnus Bernhardson (London and New York: Tauris, 2002), 193.

73. See Andrea Bieler, "Die Rede von Gott im Krieg gegen den Terrorismus," in *Das Imperium kehrt zurück. Das Imperium in der Bibel und als Herausforderung für die Ökumene heute*, ed. Luise Schottroff, Gerard Minnard, Ruth Gütter, Klara Butting, and Andrea Bieler (Wittingen: Erev-Rav, 2006).

74. Klein, "American Millenial Visions," 196.

75. Keller, *Apocalypse Now and Then*, 141–42.

76. Kwok Pui-lan, *Postcolonial Imagination*, 14.

77. Bieler, *Die Sehnsucht*, 21–25.

78. Schwöbel, "Last Things," 218.

79. Bieler, *Die Sehnsucht*, 25–26. This experience of transition represented a serious challenge for all religious traditions that were founded on reciprocity with regard to past and future. It affected especially the anamnetic practices of Jewish and Christian worship. Since the Enlightenment, the Jewish-Christian traditions find themselves in conflict with this modern sense of time. In these traditions the experience of time is structured through the rhythm of the Christian church year or the Jewish festival cycle, which focus on repetition and reflection on the past. Both the Jewish and the Christian cycles present a complex structure of celebrations that, in the interplay of diverse cycles of time, construct a sequence of time that relates to natural, cosmic-vegetative alternation and its cultic-religious interpretation. In addition, festivals are connected with historically understood events in Israel's history of salvation or with the history of Jesus Christ and the church. When, for example, Jews at Passover recall the acts of God at the exodus from Egypt they qualify the present by evoking the memory of the past in such a way that God's saving activity is seen to be effective in the present and related to God's as-yet-unfulfilled future with God's people. In this sense the Jewish-Christian tradition's understanding of the present is always defined both with an eye to the past and "eschatologically." This double orientation creates a conflict with modernity's consciousness of the present described above, the "spirit of eternal revision."

80. At least in the Western ideology of division of labor, those activities are interpreted as predominantly female.

81. See Debra Dean Murphy, "Bread, Wine, and the 'Pledge of Heaven': A (Wesleyan) Feminist Perspective on Eucharist and Eschatology," *QR* 14 (1994/1995): 401.

82. Ute E. Eisen analyzes how, in the early church, the more liturgical celebrations lost their connections with meal practices the more women lost their status in the life of their communities. See Ute E. Eisen, *Women Officeholders in Early Christianity: Epigraphical and Literary Studies*; trans. Linda M. Maloney (Collegeville, Minn.: Liturgical, 2000).

83. Rosemary Radford Ruether, *Sexism and God Talk: Toward a Feminist Theology* (Boston: Beacon, 1983), 250; Ruether, "Eschatology and Feminism," in *Lift Every Voice: Constructing Christian Theologies from the Underside*, ed. Susan B. Thistlethwaite and Mary Potter Engels (Maryknoll, N.Y.: Orbis, 1998), 111–24; Debra Dean Murphy, "Bread, Wine, and the 'Pledge of Heaven,'" 401–12.

84. Keller, *Apocalypse Now and Then*, 30.

85. Schwöbel, "Last Things," 239.

86. June Christine Goudey, *Reimaging Communion: The Feast of Our Lives* (Cleveland: Pilgrim, 2002), 40.

87. We speak deliberately of *formal* features in order to avoid the contention that particular theological interpretations inevitably produce a colonized imagination.

88. See Goudey, *Reimaging Communion*, 137.

89. Goudey, *Reimaging Communion*, 41. In chap. 4, "The Body Politics of Eucharist," we take a deeper look at how torture and Eucharist are related.

Chapter 2

1. *Did.* 10.6.

2. See also on this topic Martha L. Moore-Keish, "Eucharist and Eschatology," in *A More Profound Alleluia: Theology and Worship in Harmony*, ed. Leanne van Dyk (Grand Rapids and Cambridge: Eerdmans, 2005), 109–32.

3. See already Geoffrey Wainwright's assessment in *Eucharist and Eschatology* (Akron: OSL, 2002), 2–3. Wainwright's work, which was first published in 1971, was crucial for the attempt of liturgical theologians and historians to reflect on the topic.

4. Interestingly, John Zizioulas sees a similar narrowing of focus at work in Eastern Orthodox theologies of the Eucharist: "Thus the question which has for centuries dominated the dispute between Roman Catholics and Protestants in the West is whether or not the Eucharist is a repetition of the sacrifice of Golgotha, not whether it is an image of the last times. Orthodox theology also became embroiled in the same question, particularly from the seventeenth century onwards (the Orthodox *Confessions* of Peter of Mogila, Cyril of Loukaris, Dositheus of Jerusalem, and so forth), with the result that the connection of the Eucharist with the last times, with the Kingdom of God, was overlooked." John Zizioulas, "The Eucharist and the Kingdom of God," *Sourozh* 58 (November 1994): 2.

5. The anaphora of the *Apostolic Constitutions*, chap. 8: "You proclaim my death until I come. . .," or in the Syriac *St. James* "ye do proclaim my death and confess my resurrection until I come." In the liturgy of St. Basil: "You announce my death until I come." See Wainwright, *Eucharist and Eschatology*, 60–73.

6. *Did.* 10:6.

7. See Wainwright, *Eucharist and Eschatology*, 70–71. Wainwright compares in detail where the Benedictus was placed in various Eucharistic prayers.

8. Wainwright points out that the *Benedictus* needs to be understood in the context of the midrashic messianic exegesis of Ps. 118:26a (*Eucharist and Eschatology*, 71).

9. *Did.* 9.

10. *The United Methodist Book of Worship* (Nashville: United Methodist Publishing House, 1992), 79.

11. See pp. 53–56.

12. "The Anaphora of the Twelve Apostles," in *Prayers of the Eucharist: Early and Reformed*, ed. R. C. D. Jasper and G. J. Cuming; 3rd rev. ed. (Collegeville, Minn.: Liturgical, 1990), 127.

13. "The Anaphora," 126.

14. *Ap. Trad.* 4:7, in *Prayers of the Eucharist: Early and Reformed*, 35. The *Apostolic Tradition* has traditionally been attributed to Hippolytus, ca. 215 CE

15. *Testamentum Domini*, in *Prayers of the Eucharist: Early and Reformed*, 140.

16. See J. Denny Weaver, *The Nonviolent Atonement* (Grand Rapids and Cambridge: Eerdmans, 2001). The *Christus Victor* narrative occurs in the Gospels as well: in the Magnificat in Luke 2, the temptation narrative in Luke 4:1-13, in exorcisms and healing stories that picture Jesus' acts as expressions of the reign of God that overcomes the spiritual and physical forces that enslave the individual, including the exorcism at Capernaum in Luke 4:31-37 and the healing of Peter's mother-in-law at Luke 4:38-39. See especially 1 Cor. 15:23-28 and pp. 38–41.

17. Mark 15:40-41 reveals the androcentric character of the language used to describe discipleship in Mark. The same is true for all the Gospels. The group of "disciples" consisted, from its beginnings in Galilee, of female and male followers of Jesus. See Luise Schottroff, *Let the Oppressed Go Free: Feminist Perspectives on the New Testament*; trans. Annemarie S. Kidder (Louisville: Westminster John Knox, 1993), 91–105. For exegetical arguments in favor of the presumed presence of women at Jesus' Last Supper according to Luke, see Quentin Quesnell, "The Women at Luke's Supper," in *Political Issues in Luke-Acts*, ed. Richard J. Cassidy and Philip J. Scharper (Maryknoll, N.Y.: Orbis, 1983), 59–79.

18. Mark may serve as an example: In Mark 4:1-2 Jesus speaks to a large crowd, and in Mark 4:10 only to his disciples. In 4:33 it is presumed that the preceding speech was public. Is Jesus, then, in public from 4:21 onward? This seems to be presupposed as a matter of course, as is the idea that the content of the subsequent explanation for the group of disciples corresponds to that in the public speech, because Mark 4:13-20 does not differ in content from Mark 4:3-9.

19. This appears to be the oldest reading in the manuscripts.

20. The dispute over rank in 22:24-27 shows that the group being addressed cannot be restricted to the Twelve.

21. For the eschatological judgment, see below. At this point, however, we want to emphasize again that the eschatological judgment cannot be anticipated by human beings in order to declare parßticular groups to be "the outsiders."

22. See the materials in George F. Moore, *Judaism in the First Centuries of the Christian Era: The Age of the Tannaim* (Cambridge, Mass.: Harvard Univ. Press, 1954), 2:364–65, and John Priest, "A Note on the Messianic Banquet," in *The Messiah: Developments in Earliest Judaism and Christianity*, ed. James H. Charlesworth (Minneapolis: Fortress Press, 1992), 222–38.

23. See the historical material in Gustaf Dalman, *Arbeit und Sitte in Palästina* (Gütersloh: Bertelsmann, 1935; repr. Hildesheim: Olms, 1964), 4:388–89, 397–98.

24. The concepts of an "institution narrative" or "words of institution" presuppose an institution, the church, in which the Eucharist is part of the institution's identity. At the time of the New Testament a church, as institution, was not anything the participants had in mind. But the accounts of Jesus' last meal in the Synoptic Gospels presuppose a meal praxis like that described in 1 Cor. 11:17-34. To that extent the distinction one frequently encounters between the "Last Supper" and the "Lord's Supper" is inappropriate.

25. This statement is sometimes interpreted to mean that Jesus himself ate and drank nothing ßat the Last Supper. Other interpretations propose that in the period between his resurrection and ascension he ate with groups of disciples; therefore his hope was fulfilled very quickly. See the material on the history of interpretation in Geoffrey Wainwright, *Eucharist and Eschatology* (Akron: OSL, 2002), 46, 48. But the text clearly refers to the reign of God and presupposes that Jesus eats in community, both now and in the reign of God. Suppositions that he did not eat with the community here, or that the meals taken after his resurrection were the fulfillment of his hope, are not supported by the text. The reign of God is future in the sense of early Christian eschatology.

26. A few manuscripts omit Luke 22:19b-20 in order to accommodate the account of the meal to the meal praxis using only one cup of wine. However, the "long version,"

with a cup of wine at the beginning and at the end of the meal, should be regarded as the original Lukan version.

27. Cf. Matt. 19:28. This is about the hope for the restoration of the dignity of their own Jewish people, not about the superiority of the church, which will judge the Jewish people—a traditional anti-Jewish model of interpretation.

28. Wainwright, *Eucharist and Eschatology*, 77–78.

29. Nicola Wendebourg, *Der Tag des Herrn: Zur Gerichtserwartung im Neuen Testament auf ihrem alttestamentlichen und frühjüdischen Hintergrund* (Neukirchen: Neukirchener, 2003), 266 n. 260; 212–13. The reason for this is not a divinization of Jesus that would have contradicted monotheism, but a reticence in the portrayal of eschatological events.

30. Not the "return" or "second coming of Christ"—see 38–41.

31. In light of *Did.* 10:6 and Rev. 22:20, the imperative translation, "Our Lord, come!" is to be preferred to the statement, "Our Lord has come." Add to this that the simple statement does not fit the context of early Christian eschatology.

32. See 38–41.

33. Gerd Theißen and Annette Merz, *Der historische Jesus: Ein Lehrbuch*; 2nd ed. (Göttingen: Vandenhoeck & Ruprecht, 1997), 13.2.42; see the English translation, *The Historical Jesus: A Comprehensive Guide*; translated by John Bowden (Minneapolis: Fortress Press, 1998).

34. The charge that human flesh is eaten in the Eucharist is found, for example, in Theophilus, *Ad Autolycum*, 3.14–15. The accusation of drinking human blood is mentioned, for example, by Justin, *2 Apol.*, 12.

35. Joachim Gnilka, *Das Evangelium nach Markus* (Zürich: Benziger; Neukirchen: Neukirchener, 1979), 2:245. Arguments for the interpretation we propose can also be found, for example, in Ulrich Luz, *Matthew 21–28*; Hermeneia (Minneapolis: Fortress Press, 2005), 381.

36. The "many" (Mark 14:24; Matt. 26:28) is traditionally associated by most with Isa. 53:11-12; 52:14-15, and is often interpreted to refer to the nations. It is clear that there is a hope for the nations in the text of the First Testament. But the decision about whether the Last Supper traditions refer to Israel, or to Israel and the nations, must rest primarily on the context in the particular Gospel. The covenant is that with Israel, but it has significance for the nations. To that extent, even if "the many" refers primarily to the twelve who are participants at the meal (like "for you" in Luke 22:20), the nations are still in view; see what was said above about the group of "the Twelve."

37. The (new) covenant, like the reassembly of the twelve tribes of Israel, are things hoped for to heal the sufferings of the people of Israel. Even if the (new) covenant is not a covenant with the nations or with the church, hope for Israel is united with hope for the healing of all nations and of creation (see n. 3.3). On this question see especially Frank Crüsemann, "Der Neue Bund im Neuen Testament. Erwägungen zum Verständnis des Christusbundes in der Abendmahlstradition und im Hebräerbrief," in idem, *Kanon und Sozialgeschichte* (Gütersloh: Kaiser/Gütersloher, 2003), 295–303. Crüsemann rightly emphasizes that the covenant is not an ecclesiological concept in any sense. For the covenant in post-biblical Judaism see E. P. Sanders, *Paul and Palestinian Judaism: A Comparison of Patterns of Religion* (Philadelphia: Fortress Press, 1977).

38. The prayer is inserted after Dan. 3:23 in the Masoretic text. It is difficult to date it, but it appears to refer (at 3:38) to the religious edict of Antiochus IV (167–164 BCE).

39. NRSV.

40. Leonhard Rost, *Einleitung in die alttestamentlichen Apokryphen und Pseudepigraphen einschliesslich der grossen Qumranschriften* (Heidelberg: Quelle und Meyer, 1971), 67.

41. Ulrike Mitmann-Richert, "Historische und legendarische Erzählungen," in *Supplementa: Einführungen zu den Jüdischen Schriften aus hellenistisch-römischer Zeit*, ed.

Hermann Lichtenberger and Gerbern S. Oegeme (Gütersloh: Gütersloher, 2000), 119–33, reveals how the "furnace of fire," as "an image of the primitive threat to Israel in Egypt," portrays the threat to the people from Antiochus IV (p. 121). But in the later use of the book of Daniel this in turn became the primeval situation of threat to Israel, which for some people meant death by martyrdom as the price for confessing the God of Israel.

42. Since the prayer here speaks of individuals' surrender of their lives, the prayer cannot be a collective lament, according to Mittmann-Richert, "Historische und legendarische Erzählungen," 132. It must be read as an individual, contextualized text. But this thesis fails to recognize that the sacrifice of the martyrs arises from the people's situation of suffering and leads to the people's being healed by God. Even though it is individuals who die, this sacrifice is a collective act. For the question of sacrificial language in the tradition of martyrdom see pp. 146–55.

43. For this interpretation of the new covenant in Jer. 31:31-34 and the Last Supper tradition, see Crüsemann, *Kanon und Sozialgeschichte*, 297–99.

44. This has been the case since Justin, *Dial.* 11.2–4, and Irenaeus. On this see Hans von Campenhausen, *Die Entstehung der christlichen Bibel* (Tübingen: Mohr, 1968), 303ff. (English trans.: *The Formation of the Christian Bible*, trans. J. A. Baker [Philadelphia: Fortress Press, 1977].) The term New Testament for the NT part of the canon, which thus assumed primacy over the "Old Testament," grew out of this ecclesiological covenant theology and anti-Judaism in the ancient church (see pp. 33–34).

45. We are aware that we are here presuming a new paradigm for interpreting the New Testament and especially Paul, according to whom the Torah is valid without restriction—even for so-called Gentile Christians. For this interpretation of Paul see Luise Schottroff, "Gesetzesfreies Heidenchristentum," in *Von der Wurzel getragen: Christlich-feministische Exegese in Auseinandersetzung mit Antijudaismus*, ed. Luise Schottroff and Marie-Theres Wacker (Leiden, New York, and Cologne: Brill, 1996), 227–45.

46. Krister Stendahl, *Paul among Jews and Christians and other Essays* (Philadelphia: Fortress Press, 1976), 37.

47. John Koenig, *The Feast of the World's Redemption: Eucharistic Origins and Christian Mission* (Harrisburg: Trinity Press International, 2000), 225.

48. Willibald Bösen, *Jesusmahl, Eucharistisches Mahl, Endzeitmahl* (Stuttgart: Katholisches Bibelwerk, 1980), 58.

49. See the examples in Geoffrey Wainwright, *Eucharist and Eschatology*, 109, 138–39.

50. On this see Renate Kirchhoff, *Die Sünde gegen den eigenen Leib: Studien zu pornē und porneia in 1 Kor 6,12-20 und dem sozio-kulturellen Kontext der paulinischen Adressaten* (Göttingen: Vandenhoeck & Ruprecht, 1994), and pp. 137–42.

51. In 1 Cor. 6:14, the verb *exegeirein* is found in the manuscripts in the future, the present, and in the aorist. The *lectio difficilior* is the present tense, which explains the origin of the future. In early Christianity, resurrection as a present experience very quickly came to be seen as a heretical teaching, and consequently the present was replaced by the future. The meaning of the aorist corresponds to the present.

52. On this see especially Claudia Janssen, *Anders ist die Schönheit der Körper: Paulus und die Auferstehung in 1 Kor 15* (Gütersloh: Gütersloher Verlagshaus, 2005). Martin Luther and Irenaeus emphasize the significance of the Eucharist for bodily resurrection: see Jeffrey Bingham, "Eucharist and Incarnation: The Second Century and Luther," in *Rediscovering the Eucharist: Ecumenical Conversations*, ed. Roch A. Kereszty (New York and Mahwah, N.J.: Paulist Press, 2003), 138–39.

53. Janssen, *Anders ist die Schönheit der Körper*, 186–203, at 197.

54. On this see especially Frank Crüsemann, "Schrift und Auferstehung: Beobachtungen zur Wahrnehmung des auferstandenen Jesus bei Lukas und Paulus und zum Verhältnis der Testamente," in Crüsemann, *Kanon und Sozialgeschichte*, 306–18, at 315.

55. Antoinette C. Wire, *Holy Lives, Holy Deaths: A Close Hearing of Early Jewish Storytellers* (Leiden, Boston, and Cologne: Brill, 2002), offers a selection of postbiblical Jewish sources that document this aspect of martyrdom theology.

56. *Shemoneh Esrei, Gevurot,* translation from Web site "Hebrew for Christians," http://www.hebrew4christians.com/index.html (accessed April 24, 2007).

57. *Did.* 6:2, "the whole yoke of the Lord," is the Torah, which if possible is to be kept entire; however, the non-Jewish environment of the addressees makes this difficult. Therefore some detailed exceptions are allowed, for example, as regards food laws, but in any case sacrificial meats from non-Jewish worship are not to be eaten. For this interpretation see Klaus Wengst, *Didaché (Apostellehre), Barnabasbrief, zweiter Klemensbrief, Schrift an Diognet* (Darmstadt: Wissenschaftliche Buchgesellschaft, 1984), 95, 96. See also Kurt Niederwimmer, *The Didache: A Commentary,* trans. Linda M. Maloney; ed. Harold W. Attridge; Hermeneia (Minneapolis: Fortress Press, 1998), 121. For Jewish discussion of the details of the extent to which proselytes or God-fearers must keep the Torah in their concrete situations, see Luise Schottroff, "Gesetzesfreies Heidenchristentum," in *Von der Wurzel getragen,* ed. Schottroff and Wacker, 227–45.

58. The polemic against "hypocrites" who fast on Mondays and Thursdays (8:1) does not refer to a practice typical of Judaism at that period. The subsequent polemic against those who are "hypocritical" in prayer (8:2) refers to Matt. 6:7-8 and thus more probably to non-Jewish prayer practices than to Jewish praxis. Here we evaluate the findings differently from Wengst, *Didaché,* 34, 96.

59. Krister Stendahl, *Paul among Jews and Christians,* p. 5 and passim.

Chapter 3

1. We borrow the term *economy of grace* from Kathryn Tanner, *Economy of Grace* (Minneapolis: Fortress Press, 2005).

2. The term *dieting America* is inspired by Patrick T. McCormick, "How Could We Break the Lord's Bread in a Foreign Land? The Eucharist in 'Diet America,'" *Horizons* 25 (1998) 43–57.

3. Jacques Pepin, quoted in Michelle Stacey, *Consumed: Why Americans Love, Hate, and Fear Food* (New York: Simon & Schuster, 1994), 10.

4. Mayra Hornbacher, *Wasted: A Memoir of Anorexia and Bulimia* (New York: Harper-Flamingo, 1998).

5. McCormick, "How Could We Break the Lord's Bread," 45.

6. L. Shannon Jung, *Food for Life: The Spirituality and Ethics of Eating* (Minneapolis: Fortress Press, 2004), 45.

7. Monika K. Hellwig, *The Eucharist and the Hunger of the World,* 2nd rev. and expanded ed. (Franklin, Wisc.: Sheed & Ward, 1999), 5.

8. See Andrea Bieler, "Eucharist as Gift Exchange. Liturgical Theology and Ritual Studies in Dialog," in *Dem Tod nicht glauben: Sozialgeschichte der Bibel; Festschrift für Luise Schottroff zum 70. Geburtstag,* ed. Frank Crüsemann, Marlene Crüsemann, Claudia Janssen, Rainer Kessler, and Beate Wehn (Gütersloh: Gütersloher, 2004), 127–40.

9. Michelle Mary Lelwica, *Starving for Salvation: The Spiritual Dimensions of Eating Problems among American Girls and Women* (Oxford: Oxford Univ. Press, 2002), 5.

10. See Lelwica, *Starving for Salvation,* 39–66.

11. In addition to dieting and fitness as means of body formation and control, Susan Bordo points to the tremendous increase of plastic surgery for cosmetic reasons in the United States. She notes that in 2001, 8.5 million listed surgical procedures were performed; in 1989 the statistic was 681,000. See Susan Bordo, *Unbearable Weight: Feminism, Western Culture and the Body* (Berkeley: Univ. of California Press, 1993), xvii.

12. Lelwica, *Starving for Salvation,* 93.

13. See R. Marie Griffith, *God's Daughters: Evangelical Women and the Power of Submission* (Berkeley: Univ. of California Press, 1997), 139–50.

14. Lelwica, *Starving for Salvation,* 105.

15. Lelwica, *Starving for Salvation,* 77.

16. Jung, *Food for Life,* 84.

17. See David Beckmann and Arthur Simon, *Grace at the Table: Ending Hunger in God's World* (New York and Mahwah, N.J.: Paulist, 1999), 102.

18. See Beckmann and Simon, *Grace at the Table*, 103. Beckmann and Simon refer to Amartya Sen, *Mortality as an Indicator of Economic Success and Failure* (Florence, Italy: UNICEF, 1995), 22–25.

19. Jung, *Food for Life,* 78.

20. Ford Runge et al., *Ending Hunger in our Lifetime: Food Security and Globalization*, published for the International Food Policy Research Institute (Baltimore and London: Johns Hopkins Univ. Press, 2003) 15.

21. Runge, *Ending Hunger in our Lifetime*, 15.

22. On the tradition of the interpretation of this story, see Luise Schottroff, "Der Hunger Jesu," in *Kontexte der Schrift: Festschrift für Wolfgang Stegemann*, ed. Christian Strecker (Stuttgart: Kohlhammer, 2005), 2:150–60.

23. Translation in H. F. D. Sparks, *The Apocryphal Old Testament* (Oxford: Clarendon, 1984), 845–46.

24. On this see Schottroff, "Der Hunger Jesu," 150–60.

25. René Krüger, "Conversion of the Pocketbook: The Economic Project of Luke's Gospel," in *God's Economy: Biblical Studies from Latin America*, ed. Ross Kinsler and Gloria Kinsler (Maryknoll, N.Y.: Orbis, 2005), 169–201, at 179.

26. See pp. 53–56.

27. *Jub.* 17:15–18; *T.Job* 6–8, 16:7; *Mart. Isaiah* 5; *GenR* 56; *Apoc. Abr.* 13.

28. For the details of this parable see Luise Schottroff, *The Parables of Jesus* (Minneapolis: Fortress Press, 2006), 221–24.

29. Josephus, *Ant.* 15.11.5 (412) writes of the south side of the Herodian temple: "this cloister deserves to be mentioned better than any other under the sun; for while the valley was very deep, and its bottom could not be seen, if you looked from above into the depth, this farther vastly high elevation of the cloister stood upon that height, insomuch that if anyone looked down from the top of the battlements, or down both those altitudes, he would be giddy, while his sight could not reach to such an immense depth." *The Works of Josephus*, trans. William Whiston; updated ed. (Peabody, Mass.: Hendrickson, 1987), 425.

30. Rabbi Dr. H. Freedman, *Shabbath*, trans. with notes, glossary, and indices, chapters I–IV, ed. Rabbi Dr. Isidore Epstein, at http://www.come-and-hear.com/shabbath/index.html (accessed April 24, 2007).

31. *Velleius Paterculus, Res Gestae Divi Augusti*; LCL 152 (Cambridge, Mass.: Harvard Univ. Press, 1924).

32. For more detail see Andrea Bieler, "Wenn der *Homo oeconomicus* betet: Über die Symbolisierung des Ökonomischen in der Liturgie," *Junge Kirche* 4 (2004): 16–19.

33. See Luise Schottroff, "Die Befreiung vom Götzendienst der Habgier," in *Wer ist unser Gott? Beiträge zu einer Befreiungstheologie im Kontext der 'ersten' Welt*, ed. Luise Schottroff and Willy Schottroff (Munich: Kaiser, 1986), 137–52.

34. See Ovid, *Metamorphoses*, 11.92–145.

35. See for the following reflections on *pleonexia* Luise Schottroff, "Die Befreiung vom Götzendienst der Habgier," 137–52.

36. Pliny, *Natural History,* 33.1.1–3.

37. Dio Chrysostom, *Or.,* 17, 20.

38. See also Marion Grau's inspiring interpretation of the affluent young man. She focuses on the question of what he is actually lacking and how this lack has been

interpreted. Grau discovers a discourse in antiquity that reveals some sort of masculine hysteria. She makes the claim that this masculine hysteria is still visible in contemporary reflections on economics, redemption, and masculinity. Marion Grau, *Of Divine Economy: Refinancing Redemption* (New York and London: T&T Clark, 2004), 40, 44–47, 83–87. Another example is Luke 12:13-34. In v. 15 Jesus says: "Be on your guard against all kinds of greed; for one's life does not consist in the abundance of possessions." He tells the story of the man who builds bigger barns, then dies. Then he speaks of God providing food and clothing.

39. Modern *Homo oeconomicus* theories are explicated on three levels. The first level can be described as the attempt to develop a science that investigates economic activity on the basis of mathematics as a lawful, organized system. The second tries to understand the *Homo oeconomicus* as an empirical reality. This approach emphasizes that mathematical theories should not be in contradiction with the empirical perception of human behavior. The determination of the relation between both levels has caused many controversies in the theoretical debate about the status of the *Homo oeconomicus*. The third dimension deals with the ethical and political aspects. Here the legitimacy of economic activity is questioned, e.g., in the discussion of criteria for welfare politics and economic exchange that take into consideration the well-being of all people. It is this third dimension that interests us most. See Reiner Manstetten, *Das Menschenbild der Ökonomie: Der* Homo oeconomicus *und die Anthropologie von Adam Smith*; Alber-Reihe Thesen 7 (Freiburg and Munich: Karl Alber, 2002).

40. See Manstetten, *Das Menschenbild*, 261. The neoclassical theory that followed Smith developed a *methodological individualism* that puts the actions of the individual at the center of its worldview. The envisioned economic agent is equipped with instrumental reason, but it is neither a cosmological order, a deity, nor the hierarchy of the visible church that shapes his actions. In that sense, those who developed the economic sciences saw the arena of economics as a self-referential sphere with no need for any allusion to a transcendental perspective. The major intention of the economic agent is to increase his individual benefit; this benefit might be defined as pleasure or happiness. It can also be the readiness to give up or sacrifice parts of one's life. See Friedhelm Hengsbach, s.j., "Marktkonkurrenz auf der Grundlage gesellschaftlicher Kooperation," in *Homo oeconomicus: Der Mensch der Zukunft?* ed. Norbert Brieskorn and Johannes Wallacher; Globale Solidarität: Schritte zu einer neuen Weltkultur 2 (Stuttgart, Berlin, and Cologne: Kohlhammer, 1998), 48.

41. See Adam Smith, *The Theory of Moral Sentiments*, ed. Knud Haakonssen (Cambridge: Cambridge Univ. Press, 2002).

42. "By the imagination, we place ourselves in his situation, we conceive ourselves enduring all the same torments, we enter as it were into his body, and become in some measure the same person with him, and thence, form some idea of his sensations, and even feel something which, though weaker in degree, is not altogether unlike them. His agonies, when they are thus brought home to ourselves, when we have thus adopted and made them our own, begin at last to affect us, and we then tremble and shudder at the thought of what he feels. For as to be in pain or distress of any kind excites the most excessive sorrow, so to conceive or to imagine that we are in it, excites some degree of the same emotion, in proportion to the vivacity or dulness [sic] of the conception." Smith, *Theory of Moral Sentiments*, 11–12.

43. Birger P. Priddat, "Moral Based Rational Man," *Homo oeconomicus: Der Mensch der Zukunft?* 15–16, 26.

44. See Priddat, "Moral Based Rational Man," 24.

45. See Adam Smith, *The Nature and Causes of the Wealth of Nations*; The Works of Adam Smith, reprint of the edition of 1811–1812 (Aalen: Zeller, 1963), Part One; and Manstetten, *Das Menschenbild der Ökonomie*, 265.

46. See Hans-Willy Hohn, *Die Zerstörung der Zeit* (Frankfurt: Fischer, 1984), and Rudolf Wendorff, *Zeit und Kultur: Geschichte des Zeitbewusstseins in Europa*; 3rd ed. (Wiesbaden: Westdeutscher, 1985).

47. See Irmgard Schultz, *Der erregende Mythos vom Geld: Die neue Verbindung von Zeit, Geld und Geschlecht im Ökologiezeitalter* (Frankfurt: Campus, 1994), 154.

48. Schultz, *Der erregende Mythos*, 158.

49. In the second half of the seventeenth century, the first multilateral payment system was created in Amsterdam as the center of the credit business. It established a secured exchange rate system that was guaranteed by various states that followed protectionist politics. See Schultz, *Der erregende Mythos*, 189.

50. Another force that made the myth of infinity powerful was the naturalization of time consciousness as it was introduced by biologists such as Jean-Baptiste Lamarck and Charles Darwin. Lamarck proceeded from the assumption that time exists infinitely in nature. These scientists constructed an understanding of history that put humanity and nature in a hierarchical time perspective by perceiving the appearance of the human species as the climax of the development of nature. The modern understanding that history can be made by human beings was supported by this evolutionary worldview in which history was understood as the history of species. The notions of infinity and human dominance were merged. See Schultz, *Der erregende Mythos*, 168–69.

51. See Smith, *Wealth of Nations*, 2:21.

52. In the eighteenth and nineteenth centuries, it might have been appropriate to focus on the economic agency of the individual. Nowadays we need an approach to economic exchange that takes into consideration the tremendous interconnectedness of economic agents, which makes their subjectivity disappear in the context of globalization.

53. See William W. Goodwin, ed., *Plutarch's Morals* (Boston: Little Brown, 1870), 2:294–305.

54. With regard to the constraints of rational choice theory see Priddat, "Moral Based Rational Man," 15.

55. See Christoph Deutschmann, *Die Verheißung des absoluten Reichtums: Zur religiösen Natur des Kapitalismus*; 2nd ed. (Frankfurt and New York: Campus, 2001).

56. See Karl Marx, "The Fetishism of Commodities and the Secret Thereof," in *Capital: A Critique of Political Economy*, ed. Frederick Engels (New York: International, 1967), 1:71–83.

57. For a deeper analysis of Marx's understanding of the fetish character of goods as the actual critique of religion, see Franz J. Hinkelammert, *The Ideological Weapons of Death: A Theological Critique of Capitalism*, trans. Phillip Berryman (Maryknoll, N.Y.: Orbis, 1986).

58. See Hans-Martin Gutmann, "Der gute und der schlechte Tausch: Das Heilige und das Geld—gegensätzliche ökonomische Beziehungen?" in *"Leget Anmut in das Geben": Zum Verhältnis von Ökonomie und Theologie*; Jabboq 1 (Gütersloh: Gütersloher, 2001), 162–225, at 193.

59. Deutschmann, *Die Verheißung*, 53.

60. See Deutschmann, *Die Verheißung*, 11.

61. 1 Corinthians 4:7.

62. David N. Power, *Sacrament: The Language of God's Giving* (New York: Crossroad, 1999), 85.

63. Marcel Mauss, *The Gift: The Form and Reason for Exchange in Archaic Societies*; trans. W. D. Halls (New York: W.W. Norton, 1990). Published originally as *Essai sur le Don* (Presses Universitaires de France, 1950).

64. Mauss, *The Gift*, 11–13.

65. See also Catherine Bell, *Ritual: Perspectives and Dimensions* (New York: Oxford Univ. Press, 1997), 108–109.

66. See Jacques Derrida, *Given Time I: Counterfeit Money*, trans. Peggy Kamuf (Chicago: Univ. of Chicago Press, 1992).

67. Bernhard Waldenfels, "Das Un-ding der Gabe," in *Einsätze des Denkens: Zur Philosophie von Jacques Derrida*, ed. H. D. Gondek and Bernhard Waldenfels (Frankfurt: Suhrkamp, 1997), 385–407.

68. Hélène Cixous and Catherine Clémont, *The Newly Born Woman: Theory and History of Literature* (Minneapolis: Univ. of Minnesota Press, 1975), 68–87. For a discussion of how the misappropriated stereotype of female giving as total exhaustion can be reclaimed see Grau, *Of Divine Economy*, chap. 3.

69. This question will be discussed on pp. 118–22, "Consecrating Private Property."

70. Louis-Marie Chauvet, *The Sacraments: The Word of God at the Mercy of the Body* (Collegeville, Minn.: Liturgical, 2001), 122.

71. Chauvet, *The Sacraments*, 123–24.

72. Chauvet, *The Sacraments*, 124–25.

73. See Andrea Bieler, "Eucharist as Gift Exchange," 127–40.

74. See *WA* 7, 55.

75. See Hans-Martin Gutmann, *Symbole zwischen Macht und Spiel: Religionspädagogische und liturgische Untersuchungen zum "Opfer"* (Göttingen: Vandenhoeck & Ruprecht, 1996), 260–303.

76. Luke 1:17.

77. Steven C. Rockefeller, "The Earth Charter: Building a Global Culture of Peace," *The Ecozoic Reader* 2 (Fall 2001): 8.

78. John E. Carroll offers suggestions to help put issues of sustainability at the center of the quest for a spiritual life. He introduces examples of faith communities that develop models for sustainable living in his book *Sustainability and Spirituality* (Albany: State Univ. of New York Press, 2004).

79. Alan Durning makes this point in his book on consumer society and sustainability: Consumer-class "people living in the nineties are on average four-and-a-half times richer than their great-grandparents were at the turn of the century, but they are not four-and-a-half times happier. Psychological evidence shows that the relationship between consumption and personal happiness is weak. Worse, two primary sources of human fulfillment—social relations and leisure—appear to have withered or stagnated in the rush to riches." Alan T. Durning, *How Much Is Enough? The Consumer Society and the Future of the Earth* (New York: W.W. Norton, 1992), 23.

80. Carroll, *Sustainability and Spirituality*, 15.

81. Durning, *How Much is Enough?* 51.

82. An example of this perverted understanding of abundance can be found in a Mervyn's Super Sale commercial in which a wife coming home with a Mervyn's shopping bag responds to her husband's question about what she bought: "Oh, just a few things." After she places her bag on the bed, the husband enters the bedroom and pulls item after item out of the bag, which seems to be miraculously bottomless. Heather Moody shared with us this example in her excellent paper, "The Fear of Scarcity, the Power of Abundance, and the Challenge of Sufficiency," unpublished paper, 2004, Graduate Theological Union, Berkeley.

83. Sallie McFague, *Life Abundant: Rethinking Theology and Economy for a Planet in Peril* (Minneapolis: Fortress Press, 2001), 210.

84. Walter Brueggemann, "The Liturgy of Abundance, the Myth of Scarcity," *The Christian Century* (24–31 March 1999): 342.

85. Psalm 104:27,28, trans. Walter Brueggemann in "The Liturgy of Abundance."

86. Brueggemann, "The Liturgy of Abundance," 342.

87. Jesus takes, blesses, and breaks the bread and gives it to the people.

88. See pp. 77–80.

89. Rabbi Leon Klenicki and Myra Cohen Klenicki, *The Passover Celebration: A Haggadah for the Seder*, intro. Gabe Huck (Chicago: Liturgy Training Publications and Anti-Defamation League, 2001), 34–35.

90. See pp. 103–9, Giving thanks.

91. Edward Kilmartin, "The Sacrifice of Thanksgiving and Social Justice," in *Liturgy and Social Justice*, ed. Mark Searle (Collegeville, Minn., Liturgical, 1980), 57. Kilmartin directs our attention to the fact that there were other material gifts besides bread and wine offered at the Eucharist.

92. Kilmartin, "The Sacrifice of Thanksgiving," 60.

93. Kilmartin, "The Sacrifice of Thanksgiving," 61.

94. Justin Martyr, *First Apology* 66.1, in *Prayers of the Eucharist: Early and Reformed*, ed. and trans. R. C. D. Jasper and G. J. Cuming; 3rd ed., rev. and enl. (Collegeville, Minn.: Liturgical, 1990), 29.

95. We do not have the original version of the *birkat ha-mazon*; some scholars, however, have tried to reconstruct a hypothetical general pattern. See, for example, the proposed reconstruction by Louis Finkelstein, "The Birkath Ha-Mazon," *JQR* n.s. 19 (1929): 215–16: "(I) Blessed art Thou, O Lord, our God, King of the Universe, Who feedest the whole world with goodness, with grace and with mercy. Blessed art Thou, O, Lord Who feedest all. (II) We thank Thee, O Lord, our God, that Thou hast caused us to inherit a goodly and pleasant land, the covenant, the Torah, life and food. For all these things we thank Thee and praise Thy name forever and ever. Blessed art Thou, O, Lord, for the land and the food."

96. From Leo Hirsch, *Jüdische Glaubenswelt* (Basel: Victor Goldschmidt, 1978), 63–65.

97. See for a detailed treatment of the topic Thomas J. Talley, "From *Berakah* to *Eucharistia*: A Reopening Question," in *Living Bread, Saving Cup. Readings on the Eucharist*; ed. R. Kevin Seasoltz (Collegeville, Minn.: Liturgical, 1987), 80–101.

98. In 9.1 and 10.1 the following instructions are given: "*About the thanksgiving: give thanks thus: First, about the cup:* We give thanks to you, our Father, for the holy vine of your child David, which you made known to us through your child Jesus; glory to you for evermore. *And about the broken bread:* We give thanks to you, our Father, for the life and knowledge which you made known to us through your child Jesus; glory to you for evermore. . . . 10.1. *And after you have had your fill, give thanks thus:* We give thanks to you, holy Father, for your holy Name which you have enshrined in our hearts and for the knowledge and faith and immortality which you made known to us through your child Jesus." Jasper and Cuming, *Prayers of the Eucharist*, 23.

99. Power, *Sacrament*, 86.

100. Per Harling, "Hymn 803," in *Psalmeri 90-talet* (Stockholm: Verbum Förlag, 1994), quoted in Teresa Berger, ed., *Dissident Daughters: Feminist Liturgies in Global Context* (Louisville and London: Westminster John Knox, 2001), 173–74.

101. *Did.* 10.3, in Jasper and Cuming, *Prayers of the Eucharist*, 23.

102. The term *anaphora* is used for Eucharistic prayers. It derives from the Greek word *anaphorein*, which means to carry up or offer up.

103. "We render thanks to you, O God, through your beloved child, Jesus Christ, whom in the last times you sent to us as a savior and redeemer and angel of your will. . . . And when he was betrayed to voluntary suffering that he might destroy death, and break the bonds of the devil, and tread down hell, and shine upon the righteous, and fix a term, and manifest the resurrection, he took bread and gave thanks to you, saying: 'Take, eat, this is my body, which shall be broken for you.' . . . Remembering therefore his death and resurrection, we offer you the bread and the cup, giving you thanks because you have held us worthy to stand before you and to minister to you." Jasper and Cuming, *Prayers of the Eucharist*, 35.

104. Worship here means liturgical celebration and service in the world.

105. See pp. 49–53.

106. "And when the president has given thanks and all the people have assented, those whom we call deacons give to each of those present a portion of the bread and wine and water over which thanks has been given, and take them to those who are not present." Jasper and Cuming, *Prayers of the Eucharist*, 29.

107. "And the wealthy who so desire give what they wish, as each chooses; and what is collected is deposited with the president. He helps orphans and widows, and those who through sickness or any other cause are in need." Jasper and Cuming, *Prayers of the Eucharist*, 30. For money and gift collections given to the poor see also pp. 118-22.

108. See Martin Luther, *WA* 10/1, 2,61, 2–6

109. Richard R. Gaillardetz uses the word *thingification* in speaking about an "episodic spirituality" that has "the tendency to imagine divine grace as a kind of spiritual fuel, and the church and its ministers as sacramental grace dispensers." He credits this concept of grace to "the peculiar logic of technological devices" that shape our daily lives through the "commodification of goods." Gaillardetz elaborates that this entails "the extraction of a particular good from the context in which it is produced, such that this good can now be quantified and measured, making it subject to economic exchange, manipulation, and control." See Richard R. Gaillardetz, *Transforming Our Days: Spirituality, Community, and Liturgy in a Technological Culture* (New York: Crossroad, 2000), 49–50.

110. Paul F. Camenish, "Gift and Gratitude in Ethics," *JRE* 9 (1981): 1–34, at 26.

111. D. Mark Wilson, "Little Is Never Enough: Sermon on Deuteronomy 26:1-11," Pacific School of Religion, November 2004. We thank Dr. Wilson for putting the unpublished sermon manuscript at our disposal.

112. Gordon Lathrop, "The Bodies on Nevado Ampato: A Further Note on Offering and Offertory," *Worship* 71 (1997): 546–54, at 550.

113. Enrique Dussell, "The Bread of the Eucharistic Celebration as a Sign of Justice in the Community," in *Can We Always Celebrate the Eucharist?* ed. Mary Collins and David Power (New York: Seabury, 1982), 60.

114. Lathrop, "The Bodies on Nevado Ampato," 551.

115. Power, *Sacrament*, 316.

116. Carter Heyward, "All Shall Have Power," in *No Longer Strangers: A Resource for Women and Worship*, ed. Iben Gjerding and Katherine Kinnamon (Geneva: World Council of Churches, 1983).

117. See Joseph A. Jungmann, s.j., *The Mass of the Roman Rite: Its Origins and Development (Missarum Sollemnia)*, trans. Francis A. Brunner (Westminster, Md.: Christian Classics, 1986), 2:1–31; R. P. C. Hanson, *Eucharistic Offering in the Early Church*; Grove Liturgical Study 19 (Bramcote: Grove, 1979); Colin Ogilvie Buchanan, *The End of the Offertory: An Anglican Study*; Grove Liturgical Study 14 (Bramcote: Grove, 1978).

118. See Edward Kilmartin, "The Sacrifice of Thanksgiving and Social Justice," 53–71.

119. "1. Our Apostles also knew through our Lord Jesus Christ that there would be strife for the title of bishop. 2. For this cause, therefore, since they had received perfect foreknowledge, they appointed those who have been already mentioned, and afterwards added the codicil that if they should fall asleep, other approved men should succeed to their ministry. 3. We consider therefore that it is not just to remove from their ministry those who were appointed by them, or later on by other eminent men, with the consent of the whole Church, and have ministered to the flock of Christ without blame, humbly, peaceably, and disinterestedly, and for many years have received a universally favourable testimony. 4. For our sin is not small, if we eject from the episcopate those who have blamelessly and holily offered its sacrifices." *1 Clem.*, 44:1-4, in *The Apostolic*

Fathers, trans. Kirsopp Lake; 2 vols. (Cambridge, Mass.: Harvard Univ. Press; London: Heinemann, 1912), 1:83–85.

120. See Justin, *Apol. 1*, 65.1 and 67.1., in Jasper and Cuming, *Prayers of the Eucharist*, pp. 28–29.

121. "And because we are his members and are nourished by what is created he who makes his sun rise on and rains on whomever he chooses provides us with a created thing from which he causes our blood to flow, to be his blood, and the bread taken from created things, from which he gives growth to our bodies, he affirms to be his body. Therefore when the wine mixed with water and the baked bread receive the Word of God and the eucharist becomes the body of Christ, and the substance of our flesh grows and is sustained from these elements, how can they deny that our flesh is capable of receiving the gift of God, which is eternal life, since it is nourished by the body and blood of Christ and is a member of his?" *Sancti Irenaei Libros quinque Adversus Haereses* 5.2.2,3; trans. R. P. C. Hanson, in *Eucharistic Offering*, 10.

122. These instructions follow the ordination of a bishop: "And when he has been made a bishop, all shall offer the kiss of peace, greeting him because he has been made worthy. Then the deacons shall present the offering to him; and he laying his hands on it with all the presbytery, shall give thanks. . . ." See *Hippolytus: A Text for Students*, trans. and ed. with introduction and commentary by Geoffrey J. Cuming; Grove Liturgical Study 9 (Bramcote: Grove, 1976), 10. See also Cuming's remark about the offerings in the instruction for the conferring of Holy Baptism, *Hippolytus*, 21.

123. Cuming, *Hippolytus*, 31.

124. "5. If anyone offers oil, [the bishop] shall render thanks in the same way as for the offering of bread and wine, not saying it word for word, but to similar effect saying: O God, sanctifier of this oil, as you give health to those who are anointed and receive that with which you anointed kings, priests, and prophets, so may it give strength to all those who taste it, and health to all that are anointed with it.

6. Likewise, if anyone offers cheese and olives, he shall say thus: Sanctify this milk which has been coagulated, coagulating us also to your love. Make this fruit of the olive not to depart from your sweetness, which is an example of your richness which you have poured from the tree of life for those who hope in you." Cuming, *Hippolytus*, 11–12.

125. See Richard Kieckhefer, *Theology in Stone: Church Architecture from Byzantium to Berkeley* (New York: Oxford Univ. Press, 2004), 29. See also Jungmann, *Mass of the Roman Rite*, 10.

126. Jungmann, *Mass of the Roman Rite*, 10.

127. "When a bishop or priest, contrary to the institutions of the Lord about the sacrifice at the altar, offers up something else: honey or milk, or, in place of [the right kind], wine turned to vinegar, or fowl, or any type of beast or vegetable, in opposition to the mandate, he should be deposed. Aside from ears of wheat and grapes in season and oil for the lamps and incense, nothing should be brought to the altar at the time of the sacrifice. All other fruits should (as firstlings) be sent to the bishop or the priests at their homes and not to the altar; it is clear that the bishop and priests distribute these too among the deacons and the other clergy." Jungmann, *Mass of the Roman Rite*, 10.

128. Kieckhefer, *Theology in Stone*, 29.

129. Jungmann, *Mass of the Roman Rite*, 13.

130. See John Everett Millais, *The Parables of our Lord and Saviour Jesus Christ*; intro. Mary Lutyens (New York: Dover, 1975), 6–7.

131. Doug Adams, "Changing Patterns and Interpretations of Parables in Art," in *Arts, Theology and the Church: New Interpretations*, ed. Kimberly J. Vrudny and Wilson Yates (Cleveland: Pilgrim, 2005), 136.

132. On this see the Introduction and pp. 103–9.

133. On this see Ivoni Richter Reimer, *Women in the Acts of the Apostles: A Feminist Liberation Perspective*, trans. Linda M. Maloney (Minneapolis: Fortress Press, 1995), 6–11.

134. Reimer, *Women in the Acts of the Apostles*, 11, with reference to Acts 5:1-11.

135. Lucian, "The Liar," in *The Works of Lucian of Samosata*, trans. H. W. Fowler and F. G. Fowler; 4 vols. (Oxford: Clarendon Press, 1905), 3:240–41.

136. For the justice-praxis of the Jewish communities see the materials collected in Hermann L. Strack and Paul Billerbeck, *Kommentar zum Neuen Testament aus Talmud und Midrasch* (Munich: Beck, 1928, 1961) 4/1, 536–610, which, despite its problematic hermeneutical presuppositions, is still useful.

137. Marjorie Hewett Suchocki, *In God's Presence: Theological Reflections on Prayer* (St. Louis: Chalice, 1996), 47.

138. Suchocki, *In God's Presence*, 52.

139. Dorothee Sölle, "Life without Suffering a Utopia?" in Sölle, *The Strength of the Weak: Toward a Feminist Christian Identity*, trans. Rita and Robert Kimber (Philadelphia: Westminster, 1984), 28.

140. See also Andrea Bieler, "The Language of Prayer between Truth Telling and Mysticism," in *The Theology of Dorothee Sölle*, ed. Sarah Pinnock (Harrisburg, Penn.: Trinity Press International, 2003), 55–70.

141. Ninna Edgardh Beckman, "Lady Wisdom as Hostess for the Lord's Supper: Sofia-mässor in Stockholm, Sweden," in *Dissident Daughters*, ed. Teresa Berger, 172–73.

142. See Don E. Saliers, *Worship as Theology: Foretaste of Glory Divine* (Nashville: Abingdon, 1994), 126–30.

143. Saliers, *Worship as Theology*, 129.

144. Saliers, *Worship as Theology*, 130. Saliers refers here to the work of Leonel Mitchell.

145. The term in Greek means "double-folded."

146. See Robert F. Taft, *The Diptychs*; Orientalia Christiana Analecta 238 (Rome: Pontificum Institutum Studiorum Orientalium, 1991).

147. It is especially remarkable how the diptychs of the dead are related to the remembrance of the patriarchs, to Mary, the mother of Jesus, and to John the Baptist: "We offer you this reasonable service also for those who rest in faith, (forefathers,) Fathers, patriarchs, prophets, apostles, preachers, evangelists, martyrs, confessors, ascetics, and all the righteous (spirits) perfected in faith; (*aloud*) especially our all-holy, immaculate, highly glorious Blessed Lady, Mother of God and ever-Virgin Mary; (*diptychs of the dead*); St John the (prophet), forerunner, and Baptist, and the holy, (glorious), and honored Apostles; and this saint whose memorial we are keeping: and all your saints: at their entreaties, look on us, O God. And remember all those who have fallen asleep in hope and resurrection to eternal life. . . ." See Jasper and Cuming, *Prayers of Eucharist*, 133.

Chapter 4

1. Jonathan Bishop, *Some Bodies: The Eucharist and Its Implications* (Macon, Ga.: Mercer Univ. Press, 1992), 1.

2. Parts of the following section have been published in Andrea Bieler, "Real Bodies at the Meal," in Jürgen Ebach, Hans-Martin Gutmann, Magdalene L. Frettlöh, and Michael Weinrich, eds., *"Dies ist mein Leib": Leibliches, Leibeigenes und Leibhaftiges bei Gott und den Menschen*; Jabboq 6 (Gütersloh: Gütersloher, 2006), 81–90.

3. Lisa Isherwood and Elizabeth Stuart, *Introducing Body Theology*; IFT 2 (Sheffield: Sheffield Academic Press, 1998), 148.

4. Isherwood and Stuart, *Introducing Body Theology*, 148.

5. Rev. Colette Jackson, "Witness God's Welcome: A Communion Liturgy," presentation at the *Witness Our Welcome Conference 2000*; unpublished document, used with permission of the author.

6. For a deeper exploration of corporeality and worship, see Bruce T. Morrill, ed., *Bodies of Worship: Explorations in Theory and Practice* (Collegeville, Minn.: Liturgical, 1999).

7. See pp. 62–65.

8. For the Roman Catholic debate on transubstantiation, see Edward Schillebeeckx, "Transubstantiation, Transfinalization, Transignification," in *Living Bread, Saving Cup: Readings on the Eucharist*, ed. R. Kevin Seasoltz (Collegeville, Minn.: Liturgical, 1987), 175–89.

9. See James F. White, *The Sacraments in Protestant Practice and Faith* (Nashville: Abingdon, 1999), 73–144.

10. D. Jeffrey Bingham, "Eucharist and Incarnation: The Second Century and Luther," in *Rediscovering the Eucharist: Ecumenical Conversations*, ed. Roch A. Kereszty (New York and Mahwah, N.J.: Paulist, 2003), 123. For a thorough discussion of the topic of incarnation and Eucharist during the reformation, see Lee Palmer Wandel, *The Eucharist in the Reformation: Incarnation and Liturgy* (Cambridge: Cambridge Univ. Press, 2006).

11. Quoted in Bingham, "Eucharist and Incarnation," 127.

12. See Bingham, "Eucharist and Incarnation," 134.

13. Martin Luther, in LW, *Word and Sacrament III*, vol. 37, ed. R. H. Fischer (Philadelphia: Fortress Press, 1961), 94. See also Magdalene L. Frettlöh, "'Gott ist im Fleisch . . .': Die Inkarnation Gottes in ihrer leibeigenen Dimension beim Wort genommen," in *"Dies ist mein Leib,"* ed. Ebach et al., 186–229.

14. See LW, *Word and Sacrament III*, 29.

15. See also pp. 166–67 on body memory.

16. Racializing bodies through the U.S. Census Bureau is a major tool of the state's body politics.

17. Michel Foucault has coined the term *normalizing gaze*. He describes how the modern Western human sciences developed standards and norms about identity and corporeality with regard to race, gender, health, and hetero-normativity that let these aspects appear as natural, omnihistorical phenomena and not as social, historically grounded constructions. This gaze did not simply replace religious ideas and convictions about the human person in relation to the divine; it incorporated and modified them. See Michel Foucault's concept of the normalizing gaze in *The Order of Things: An Archaeology of Human Sciences* (1970; repr., New York: Vintage, 1973). For a discussion of Foucault's concept of the gaze, see Iris Marion Young, "The Scaling of Bodies and the Politics of Identity," in her *Justice and the Politics of Difference* (Princeton: Princeton Univ. Press, 1990).

18. See also pp. 170–72.

19. See also Andrea Bieler, "Embodied Knowing: Understanding Religious Experience in Ritual," in *Empirical Theology and Phenomenology of Religious Experience*, ed. Christopher Scholtz and Hans Günter Heimbrock (Göttingen: Vandenhoeck & Ruprecht, 2007).

20. Catherine Bell, *Ritual Theory, Ritual Practice* (New York: Oxford Univ. Press, 1992), 100.

21. Louis-Marie Chauvet, *The Sacraments: The Word of God at the Mercy of the Body* (Collegeville, Minn.: Liturgical, 2001), 114.

22. The following reflections are based on Andrea Bieler's participation in this particular worship service.

23. We are aware that this insight is spelled out in various places, for example, in *Sacrosanctum Concilium* (1963), the Second Vatican Council's Constitution on the Sacred Liturgy. Article 7 explicitly names the liturgical assembly as the place where Christ is present in the Eucharist: "Lastly, he is present when the church prays and sings, for

he has promised 'where two or three are gathered together in my name there am I in the midst of them' (Matt. 18:20)." Austin Flannery, gen. ed., "The Constitution on the Sacred Liturgy," *Vatican Council II: Constitutions, Decrees, Declarations* (Northport, N.Y.: Costello, 1996).

24. Conversation with Reverend Jim Mitulski in Berkeley on May 15, 2005.

25. Chauvet, *The Sacraments,* 114.

26. Maurice Merleau-Ponty reflects on the question of how our embodied knowing and speaking shapes our perception. He lifts up embodied seeing as the source for subjective perception: "If a friend and I are standing before a landscape, and if I attempt to show my friend something which I see and which he does not yet see, we cannot account for the situation by saying that I see something in my own world and that I attempt, by sending verbal messages, to give rise to an analogous perception in the world of my friend. There are not two numerically distinct worlds plus a mediating language which alone would bring us together. There is—and I know it very well if I become impatient with him—a kind of demand that what I see be seen by him also. And at the same time this communication is required by the very thing which I am looking at, by the reflections of sunlight upon it, by its color, by its sensible evidence. The thing opposes itself not as true for every intellect, but as real for every subject who is standing where I am." Maurice Merleau-Ponty, "The Primacy of Perception and its Philosophical Consequences," in Merleau-Ponty, *The Primacy of Perception and other Essays on Phenomenological Psychology, the Philosophy of Art, History and Politics,* ed. and intro. James M. Edie (Evanston: Northwestern Univ. Press, 1964), 17.

27. Gail Ramshaw, *Liturgical Language: Keeping it Metaphoric, Making it Inclusive* (Collegeville, Minn.: Liturgical, 1996), 7.

28. Ramshaw, *Liturgical Language,* 8.

29. Gordon W. Lathrop, *Holy People: A Liturgical Ecclesiology* (Minneapolis: Fortress Press, 1999), 86–87.

30. See Dale Martin, *The Corinthian Body* (New Haven and London: Yale Univ. Press, 1995). This book is an excellent study of how Paul's notion of *sōma*/body in 1 Corinthians responds to the larger body-politics discourse of the time.

31. "that is given for you" is in Luke 22:19, and there is a similar formulation in 1 Cor. 11:24; John 6:51. Mark and Matthew do not have this part of the sentence.

32. *Midrash Lev. Rabba* §34.3. German translation in Paul Fiebig, *Altjüdische Gleichnisse und die Gleichnisse Jesu* (Tübingen and Leipzig: Mohr, 1904), 110–12.

33. For the *tributum capitis* see Werner Stenger, *"Gebt dem Kaiser, was des Kaisers ist. . . ! Eine sozialgeschichtliche Untersuchung zur Besteuerung Palästinas in neutestamentlicher Zeit* (Frankfurt: Athenäum, 1988), 25; W. Schwahn, "Tributum, tributus," Pauly-Wissowa, 12:1–78.

34. See Raphael Taubenschlag, "Das Sklavenrecht im Rechte der Papyri," *ZSSR,* Roman section 50 (1930): 141. For the Septuagint see Eduard Schweizer, *sōma, TDNT* 7:1047–48; see also Rev. 18:13.

35. For the interpretation of Rom. 3:9-20 see also Luise Schottroff, "Die Lieder und das Geschrei der Glaubenden. Rechtfertigung bei Paulus," *EvT* 60 (2000): 332–47; the English translation, "The Songs and the Cries of the Believers. Justification in Paul," is available at www.chora-strangers.org/pdf/Is_Songs_and_Believers.pdf (accessed April 24, 2007).

36. Translations of the Greek word *paradidonai* in 1 Cor. 11:23 are quite often pointed at Judas's betrayal, but the verb does not refer particularly to Judas's act; rather, it points to Jesus' being handed over to judgment by human beings and thus also by God, or more generally to his surrender of his life (Rom. 8:32); see further below in this section.

37. The later ecclesial-dogmatic interest in Jesus' sinlessness often hinders perception of this point. In the Gospels, Jesus is shown in his despair and his guilt. At first he

behaves unjustly toward the Syro-Phoenician woman (Mark 7:24-30; Matt. 15:21-28); in his hunger he destroys a fig tree that might still have borne fruit (see pp. 74–77).

38. In 1 Cor. 12:12-24, 27; Rom. 12:5, the congregation is the body of Christ and is not simply called a "body" in some transferred sense. In 1 Cor. 12:15-26, then, Paul uses a similitude about the body and its members in order to explain the egalitarian community of the body/the congregation. This similitude clearly shifts the level of discourse from what has been said about the body of Christ; Paul is now making a comparison. The similitude stands within the Hellenistic tradition of body parables, which were employed especially in the ideology of the state as a way of justifying hierarchy (for example, Livy, *History*, 2.32).

39. Some manuscripts insert *eis* (into), thus pointing to baptism, while others add *poma* (drink), thus indicating the Eucharist.

40. That people become God's dwelling should not be given an anti-Jewish interpretation, as if this meant that God had withdrawn from the Temple in Jerusalem.

41. On this see pp. 118–22; 1 Cor. 11:29 "without discerning the body" can refer to the distinction between the holy meal (God's property) and private meals (in the sense of private property) and/or to the distinction between the holiness of the congregation and an ordinary gathering of human beings in which all insist on their own rights and property.

42. This is the common interpretation of 1 Cor. 15:36; see the groundbreaking new interpretation by Claudia Janssen, *Anders ist die Schönheit der Körper: Paulus und die Auferstehung in 1 Kor. 15* (Gütersloh: Gütersloher, 2005).

43. Whether by design or inadvertently, the determination that resurrection occurs only "beyond death" made the human body, and therefore life itself, a material sphere outside the love of God; thus Cartesian dualism was interpreted into Paul. See the helpful analysis of dualism in Dale Martin, *The Corinthian Body* (New Haven and London: Yale Univ. Press, 1995).

44. From the *Evangelisches Gesangbuch Kassel* (Evangelisches Medienverband, 1994), 518, following the medieval "*media in vita in morte sumus*."

45. William T. Cavanaugh, *Torture and Eucharist: Theology, Politics, and the Body of Christ* (Malden, Mass. and Oxford: Blackwell, 2000), 12.

46. An ecumenical survey shows that books of worship offer various versions of the so-called words of institution. Interestingly, none of them is a direct quotation from the Gospel of Mark, Luke, or Matthew, or from Paul.

47. See in more detail pp. 167–70 on anamnetic empathy.

48. Countless efforts have been made by artists through the centuries to imagine the tortured body of Christ. See, for instance, Magdalene Frettlöh's interpretation of the Isenheimer Altar or Benita Joswig's theological and aesthetic interpretation of the crucified Christ by contemporary artists in *Erinnern und aufstehen—antworten auf Kreuzestheologien* (Mainz: Matthias-Grünewald, 2000).

49. See also David Power, "Words That Crack: The Uses of Sacrifice in Eucharistic Discourse," in *Living Bread, Saving Cup*, ed. Seasoltz, 157–74.

50. Cf., for example, the lines from a gospel song: "There is power, power, wonderworking power in the blood of the lamb. There is power, power wonder-working power in the precious blood of the lamb." We thank Johari Jabir for this reference. Cf. further, as a womanist voice who seeks to reclaim the power in the blood: JoAnne Marie Terrell, *Power in the Blood? The Cross in the African American Experience* (Maryknoll, N.Y.: Orbis, 1998).

51. Delores S. Williams, *Sisters in the Wilderness: The Challenge of Womanist God-Talk* (Maryknoll, N.Y.: Orbis, 1993).

52. The major issue is the glorification of violence through the idea that violence (killing) could be a means of redemption. The interpretation of Jesus' death within

the Trinitarian drama is challenged: the idea that God the Father sacrifices the Son reflects the intimate divine family relationship as abusive and mirrors experiences of child abuse in intimate relationships. Thus many feminist theologians conclude that it is unacceptable to depict God as a father who demands the sacrificial death of his son in order to restore his offended honor. A further argument against satisfaction atonement is articulated in the area of cultural criticism. Critics state that satisfaction atonement finds its cultural expression in the understanding of retributive justice that is foundational for the American legal system: To do justice means to punish criminal perpetrators according to the logic that the more serious the offense the greater the penalty. Punishment is considered to be a means of achieving justice, and the level of violence in the punishment has to correspond with the level of violence in the criminal act.

53. See, for example, June Christine Goudey, *Reimaging Communion: The Feast of Our Lives* (Cleveland: Pilgrim, 2002).

54. With regard to the Christus Victor motif see pp. 49–53 and J. Denny Weaver, *The Nonviolent Atonement* (Grand Rapids: Eerdmans, 2001).

55. See Cavanaugh, *Torture and Eucharist*, here at 205.

56. Cavanaugh, *Torture and Eucharist*, 206.

57. Cavanaugh, *Torture and Eucharist*, 12.

58. Cavanaugh, *Torture and Eucharist*, 37.

59. Cavanaugh, *Torture and Eucharist*, 35.

60. Cavanaugh reports that in the case of Chile, many torturers or those who indirectly supported the state terror were members of Christian congregations. In these circumstances the question of worthy participation in the Eucharist arose in dramatic ways.

61. Cavanaugh, *Torture and Eucharist*, 280.

62. See chapter 5 on eschatological anamnesis, especially pp. 166–72.

63. For the general question of how to look at pictures that depict the suffering of others see Susan Sontag, *Regarding the Pain of Others* (New York: Farrar, Straus and Giroux, 2003).

64. C. Michael Hawn, *Gather into One: Praying and Singing Globally* (Grand Rapids: Eerdmans, 2003), 45–46.

65. See especially Rudolf Weth, ed., *Das Kreuz Jesu: Gewalt, Opfer, Sühne* (Neukirchen: Neukirchener, 2001); Sigrid Brandt, *Opfer als Gedächtnis: Auf dem Weg zu einer befreienden Rede von Opfer* (Münster: Lit-Verlag, 2001); Bernd Janowski and Michael Welker, eds., *Opfer: Theologische und kulturelle Kontexte* (Frankfurt: Suhrkamp Taschenbuch Wissenschaft, 2000); Christian Eberhart, *Studien zur Bedeutung der Opfer im Alten Testament* (Neukirchen: Neukirchener, 2002).

66. See pp. 62–65.

67. Frank Crüsemann, "*Kipper*, etc.," in *Bibel in gerechter Sprache*, ed. idem et al. (Gütersloh: Gütersloher, 2006), 2366.

68. From a historical point of view, the christology of atoning sacrifice is without any point of reference in the New Testament Eucharistic traditions and christology. For a critique of this false interpretation, see the works cited in n. 65 above. These authors, however, continue to use "sacrificial" language in the sense of life-orientation and self-surrender (corresponding to Rom. 12:1). However, atoning sacrifice should no longer be used in regard to the Eucharistic tradition, because the New Testament does not do so and because it can be misunderstood in the sense of "misplaced Christian notions of sacrifice in theology, church, and society." (See the list of those who accept this perverted christology in Sigrid Brandt, *Opfer als Gedächtnis*, 433–34.) The occasional comparison with sacrifice in the Jewish tradition of martyrdom (see pp. 62–65 and below in this section) is not a basic element.

69. In postbiblical interpretation Isaac is not regarded as a passive victim, but as an active hero according to the model of the martyrdom tradition. On Isaac see, for example, 4 Macc. 16:20-21, and Antoinette Wire, *Holy Lives, Holy Deaths: A Close Hearing of Early Jewish Storytellers* (Atlanta: Society of Biblical Literature, 2002), 281–84. For the Jewish tradition of martyrdom as a whole see Eduard Lohse, *Märtyrer und Gottesknecht* (Göttingen: Vandenhoeck & Ruprecht, 1963); Wire, *Holy Lives*; J. W. van Henten, ed., *Die Entstehung der jüdischen Martyrologie* (Leiden, New York, et al.: Brill, 1989), especially 10–11 and 204–206.

70. Hans-Josef Klauck, *4. Makkabäerbuch*; JSHZ 3/6 (Gütersloh: Mohn, 1989), 671 n. 113, rightly points out that v. 28 is not to be interpreted in the sense of a "satisfaction theory, as though a wrathful deity had to be pacified by human sacrifice." However, he translates 6:29 as "sacrifice of purification" and 17:22 "atoning death," because he interprets the texts as witnesses to the idea of atoning sacrifice. But in fact, nothing is said here about sacrifice. The tradition of translation of 4 Maccabees by Christians is heavily burdened by the idea of a christology of sacrificial atonement.

71. Luther's translation of Isa. 53:10 ("sacrifice for sin") and many interpretations of Isaiah 53 do the same thing, but the appropriateness of the translation is currently disputed: See Bernd Janowski, "'Hingabe' oder 'Opfer,'" in *Das Kreuz Jesu*, ed. Rudolf Weth, 13–43, at 32–36.

72. Newer attempts to overcome the false idea of sacrificial atonement appeal to this idea. Here "surrender" or "offering" of one's whole life as an active work is developed as an alternative to sacrificial christology. See, for example, Sigrid Brandt, *Opfer als Gedächtnis: Auf dem Weg zu einer befreienden Rede von Opfer* (Münster: Lit-Verlag, 2001), and further below.

73. In this context the word *paradidonai* has a spectrum of meaning from handing over a person to the police, officials, and judges (e.g., Mark 13:11; Matt. 27:18) to the surrender of one's own life to God, which includes death but primarily means an active choice of a way of life (see, for example, Eph. 5:25). The translation "betrayal" in the Judas story is inaccurate. For 1 Cor. 11:23, pp. 137–42.

74. See the rabbinic material on the interpretation of Ps. 43:23 in terms of the experience of martyrdom in Billerbeck, at Rom. 8:36.

75. Brandt, *Opfer als Gedächtnis*. Bernd Janowski calls the feminist critique unjustified, branding it, for example, "a false assessment of the biblical view," "'Hingabe' oder 'Opfer,'" 28.

76. Janowski, "'Hingabe' oder 'Opfer,'" 41.

77. Sigrid Brandt, *Opfer als Gedächtnis*, 415, translates the interpretive words without reference to Jesus' death; they are about "communion in Christ's body and life." But it should be added that these are the body and life (*haima*/blood) of a human being who, in his place and time, trod the path of a martyr.

78. See for a thorough treatment of the topic Robert J. Daly, *The Origins of the Christian Doctrine of Sacrifice* (Philadelphia: Fortress Press, 1978). The following reflection is based on Paul Bradshaw, *Early Christian Worship: A Basic Introduction to Ideas and Practice* (Collegeville: Liturgical, 1996), 51–57.

79. *Did.*, 14.

80. *Dial. Trypho*, 41.3; 117.2

81. "Remembering therefore his death and resurrection, we offer to you the bread and the cup." In addition, Bradshaw mentions that in later writings the idea begins to show up that in the Eucharist itself Christ is offered again, thus Cyril of Jerusalem: "we offer Christ who has been slain for our sins" or Gregory Nazinanus: "You sacrifice the Master's body and blood with a bloodless knife." See Bradshaw, *Early Christian Worship*, 55.

Chapter 5

1. David E. Stern, "Remembering and Redemption," in *Rediscovering the Eucharist: Ecumenical Conversations*, ed. Roch A. Kereszty (New York and Mahwah, N.J.: Paulist, 2003), 12.

2. For a critical discussion how the Jewish Pesach remembrance is related to the Eucharist see Andreas Pangritz, "'Solches tut zu meinem Gedächtnis': Eine Kritik der Domestizierung von Erinnerung in der kirchlichen Abendmahlslehre," in *Erinnern: Erkundungen zu einer theologischen Basiskategorie*, ed. Paul Petzel and Norbert Reck (Darmstadt: Wissenschaftliche Buchgesellschaft, 2003), 228–49.

3. Paul Bradshaw, "Anamnesis in Modern Eucharistic Debate," in *Memory and History in Christianity and Judais*, ed. Michael A. Signer (Notre Dame: University of Notre Dame Press, 2001), 79-80.

4. Willy Schottroff, *"Gedenken" im Alten Orient und im Alten Testament* (Neukirchen: Neukirchener, 1967), 117; cf. 339.

5. Schottroff, *"Gedenken,"* 316.

6. For the complexity of the lamb metaphor, see Sigrid Brandt, *Opfer als Gedächtnis: Auf dem Weg zu einer befreienden Rede von Opfer* (Münster: Lit-Verlag, 2001), 225–31; Klaus Wengst, *Das Johannesevangelium;* 2nd ed. (Stuttgart: Kohlhammer, 2000), 1:91–92.

7. On this, see the convincing arguments of Avaren Ipsen, "Sexworker Standpoint and Sacred Text" (diss., Graduate Theological Union, Berkeley, September 2006), 189ff. See also Luise Schottroff, "Through German and Feminist Eyes: A Liberationist Reading of Luke 7:36-50," in *The Feminist Companion to the Hebrew Bible in the New Testament*, ed. Athalya Brenner (Sheffield: Sheffield Academic Press, 1996), 332–41.

8. At this point we can only reference the complex discussion of the identification of this nameless woman with Mary Magdalene. See, for example, Jane Schaberg, *The Resurrection of Mary Magdalene: Legends, Apocrypha, and the Christian Testament* (New York: Continuum, 2003).

9. On this see Avaren Ipsen, *Sexworker Standpoint*, passim.

10. *Eis anamnēsin* in the Eucharistic tradition is, in substance, no different from *eis mnēmosynon* (Mark 14:9; Matt. 26:13). Basic to both formulations is the Hebrew tradition of remembrance, of memory (*sakar*). On this see, for example, Wolfgang Schrage, *Der erste Brief an die Korinther* (Zürich, Düsseldorf, and Neukirchen: Benziger and Neukirchener, 1999), 3:42.

11. In 1 Cor. 11:24, 25; Luke 22:19, the words are "in remembrance of me." Remembering Jesus means remembering not only his death but his whole existence, as Paul tells about it (Phil. 2:5-11) or as the Gospels do.

12. Bradshaw, "Anamnesis in Modern Eucharistic Debate," 79–80.

13. This will be further spelled out on pp. 166–72.

14. Edmund Arens, "Anamnetische Praxis: Erinnern als elementare Handlung des Glaubens," in *Erinnern*, ed. Petzel and Reck, 41–55, at 49.

15. See 1 Cor. 11:25; Luke 22:19.

16. See 1 Cor. 11:17-34; 15:12-19.

17. "The Great Thanksgiving," *The United Methodist Book of Worship* (Nashville: United Methodist Publishing House, 1992), 36–37. "Slavery to sin" is an allusion to Rom. 6:12-23.

18. Luke 4:18-20 stresses this reference to Isa. 61:1-2.

19. The phrase "delivered us from slavery to sin and death" refers to a notion of forgiveness of sin that overcomes a narrow individualistic and moralistic understanding of sin. Speaking of slavery to sin in our current context should support a systemic notion of sin that reflects experiences of violence and of death.

20. See chapter 4, "The Body Politics of Eucharist."

21. Marjorie Procter-Smith, "Something Missing: Memory and Imagination," in Procter-Smith, *In Her Own Rite: Constructing Feminist Liturgical Tradition* (Akron: OSL, [1990], 2000), 25–47, and "Our Bodies, Our Blood: Christian Feminist Eucharistic Praying," in Procter-Smith, *Praying with Our Eyes Open: Engendering Feminist Liturgical Prayer* (Nashville: Abingdon, 1995), 115–42.

22. Janet Morley, ed., *Bread of Tomorrow: Prayers for the Church Year* (Maryknoll, N.Y.: Orbis, 1992), 86.

23. On further reflection, our students suggested Sojourner Truth, Harriet Tubman, Anne Hutchinson, Malcolm X, Harry Moore, Langston Hughes, Jarena Lee, and Lin Siung. This took place in the course "Eucharist as Holy Eating," Pacific School of Religion, Spring 2004, class session on 15 April 2004.

24. On Good Friday it is appropriate to focus on people who endured violent death, but this should not be the focus for every Eucharistic liturgy. We use the term *martyrs* in a broader sense: martyrs are people who give witness to the violence they see, and in doing so testify to God's justice.

25. Donald Shell, "The Dancing Saints," in *God's Friends*, (Regan 1997); see also www.saintgregorys.org. The figures include Aelred of Rievaulx (ca. 1110–1167), English Cistercian monk and Abbot of the monastery of Rievaulx. In contrast to other monastic writers, he regarded deep human friendship as an essential element of spiritual life and closeness to God (January 12). Alexandrian Washerwoman (fourth century), the anonymous woman who prays ceaselessly as she works washing dishes. To the desert fathers, the founders of monasticism in the fourth and fifth centuries, she represents the holiness of all that is ordinary and routine (July 29). Thomas Aquinas (1225–1274), daring to counter the neo-Platonic theology of his age, revived interest in Aristotle, whose ideas had been preserved and developed in the Islamic world and were therefore suspect to Christians. He was convinced of the goodness of all creation and its participation in the goodness of God's own self. His work embodies what one historian has called the essential principle of Western Civilization, namely, that "truth unfolds in time through a communal process." Called "The Angelic Doctor" for his brilliant synthesis of faith and reason, he is among the teachers of the whole church whom Dante saw dancing before God in his final vision in the *Paradiso* (January 28). Barnabas (first century), a Levite Jew, a man of learning and generosity and one of the first post-resurrection apostles. Deeply respected by the disciples, his trust in the authenticity of Paul's conversion led to their acceptance of this former persecutor. He was the first apostle to embrace the evidence of God's grace in the hearts of Gentile converts to the Way (June 11). Black Elk (1872–1957), the Holy Man of the Ogallala Sioux, visionary and mystic. A youthful convert and Episcopalian, his life and teaching showed forth God's radiant and powerfully healing presence in all of nature. William Byrd (1543–1623), composer of music for the Roman Catholic church and also for the early Anglican church. He created a deeply moving tradition of Anglican choral music which continues to inspire composers of religious music at St. Gregory's and elsewhere (July 4). Donaldina Cameron (1869–1968), Scottish Presbyterian social worker who defied Chinese gangs and crime lords, corrupt police and complacent politicians to rescue girls kidnapped from China to San Francisco for sale as prostitutes and slaves. Founder of Cameron House in San Francisco's Chinatown. Cesar Chavez (1927–1993), the son of Mexican migrants to California, devoted his life to organizing farm workers despite the opposition of both employers and powerful union leaders. His movement succeeded in giving migrant workers bargaining power, restoring dignity to this poor and dispossessed population. A man of religious faith and commitment to nonviolence, his vocation embodied his "deepest belief that only by giving life do we find life, that the truest act of courage, the strongest act of manliness is to sacrifice ourselves for others in a totally nonviolent struggle for justice" (April 23). Christine de Pisan (1365–1431), French writer and single mother

whose witty theological polemic tweaking clergy attitudes towards women was the first writing of its kind available to a popular audience. John Coltrane (1926–1967), African-American saxophone player, composer, eminent jazz innovator. Coltrane's faith in God was a powerful healing force in his overcoming addiction to heroin. He testifies to God's omnipotence, our need for God, dependence on God and God's power to remake us on his seminal album *Love Supreme,* and dedicates his music, saying, "Let us sing all songs to God" (July 17). Edited from Donald Shell, "The Dancing Saints," in *God's Friends* 8 (August 1997); see also www. saintgregorys.org.

26. Shell, "The Dancing Saints."

27. Avery Dulles argues in a similar direction from a Roman Catholic perspective: "The repeated reference to the Father in the eucharistic texts is of some importance. It means, for one thing, that the Eucharist does not revolve simply about Christ the Redeemer. Even more fundamentally, it acknowledges God as the Creator of the whole world and thanks him for all the gifts of creation and redemption. As a sacrifice of praise, the Eucharist is offered in the name of all creation. As we read in the third Eucharistic Prayer, 'All creation rightly gives you praise. All life, all holiness comes from you. . . .' The liturgy thus tends to impart a sense of God's transcendence as a source and goal of the whole universe. It reminds us of our total dependence upon the Father as creatures. . . ." "The Eucharist and the Mystery of the Trinity," in *Rediscovering the Eucharist,* ed. Kereszty, 229.

28. Dulles, "The Eucharist," 229.

29. See pp. 25–30.

30. "And pray. Especially recover the praying. Before God who 'knows their sufferings,' on the holy ground. Find, train and appoint leaders in the assembly who are gifted to lead us in prayer with simplicity and directness and honesty. . . . for the poor, the hungry, the homeless, the unemployed, the war torn, the tortured, the raped, the enslaved, the orphaned and widowed, the lonely, the sick, the alienated, the grieving, the refugees, the incurably ill, the dying, the dead; but also for our enemies, for people who see the world differently; for people filled with hate; but also for strangers and sojourners, for judges and magistrates, police and firefighters, political leaders, soldiers, workers for peace; but also for threatened cultures, threatened life-ways of the various peoples of the earth, threatened waterways, polluted landscapes, endangered ecological systems, threatened species, whales, frogs and sea turtles, whooping cranes, and other species, perhaps also ones that are not so beautiful to us. . . . Such a prayer is a concrete exercise of the sacrophilic worldview." Gordon W. Lathrop, *Holy Ground: A Liturgical Cosmology* (Minneapolis: Fortress Press, 2003), 144–45.

31. For a critical engagement of various concepts of empathy that can be found in psychotherapy, developmental psychology, and aesthetics see also *Empathy and Its Development,* ed. Nancy Eisenberg and Janet Strayer (Cambridge and New York: Cambridge Univ. Press, 1987).

32. See Nancy Eisenberg and Janet Strayer, "Critical Issues in the Study of Empathy," in *Empathy and Its Development,* 3–13, at 4.

33. Eisenberg and Strayer, "Critical Issues," 9.

34. Theodore Reik, *Listening with the Third Ear* (New York: Farrar, Straus, 1949).

35. See also James Marcia, "Empathy and Psychotherapy," in *Empathy and its Development,* ed. Eisenberg and Strayer, 81–102, at 83.

36. Elaine Scarry, *The Body in Pain: The Making and Unmaking of the World* (New York: Oxford Univ. Press, 1985).

37. See especially the Introduction, in which Scarry elaborates on the impossibility of finding adequate expressions for bodily pain by discussing the medical language applied to different forms and degrees of pain and by looking at reports from Amnesty International about instances of torture.

38. Scarry points to the multitude of depictions of Jesus' crucifixion in visual art in which the body in pain is imagined in a wide range of ways.

39. In her attempt to flesh out the possibilities of how to speak about the resurrection of the body, Marianne Sawicki refers to Elaine Scarry's reflection on the connection of bodies and artifacts such as texts: "In Scarry's account, the worker fabricates a product in two steps: by first imagining a potential reconfiguration of physical materials in correspondence to a bodily need (that is, by making up a fictional object) and, second, by actualizing that reconfiguration (that is, by making it real, material, nonfictional)." Marianne Sawicki, *Seeing the Lord: Resurrection and Early Christian Practices* (Minneapolis: Fortress Press, 1994), 191. Ritual performances as well as the Gospels or liturgical texts might be interpreted in this sense as acts of reconfiguration and actualization of reconfiguration.

40. Dirk Lange, "In, With and Under: Liturgical Disruption of Theology," diss., Emory University, Atlanta, 2005, 174–75.

41. In a similar way, David E. Stern mentions the multi-sensual dimension of remembering as it occurs in ritual practices such as the Kiddush, the prayer of sanctification that inaugurates the Sabbath and the High Holydays; "we recite the phrases *zekher litsiat mitsrayim* (in remembrance of the Exodus from Egypt) and *zikaron le-ma-aseit vereishit* (in remembrance of the work of creation). The Sabbath and festivals are not simply for us to recall past events, but for us to re-experience them: on the Sabbath, we rest as God rested; on Passover, we taste affliction in the bitter herbs" (Stern, "Remembering and Redemption," in *Rediscovering the Eucharist,* ed. Kereszty, 3). *Zekher* is thus making past things present; it is a "pointer through time."

42. See further the section on body memory.

43. David A. Hogue, *Remembering the Future, Imagining the Past: Story, Ritual and the Human Brain* (Cleveland: Pilgrim, 2003), 60.

44. Marcia McFee, "Primal Patterns: Ritual Dynamics, Ritual Resonance, Polyrhythmic Strategies and the Formation of Christian Disciples," diss., Graduate Theological Union, California, March 2005, 83.

45. Archie Smith Jr. and Ursula Riedel-Pfaefflin offer the following definition of systemic thinking, which is also helpful for our project: "*Systemic thinking* is a way of thinking about multipersonal and reciprocal influences within certain contexts and making connections between our social location, immediate life situation, and the wider world of which we are part." Archie Smith Jr. and Ursula Riedel-Pfaefflin, *Siblings by Choice: Race, Gender, and Violence* (St. Louis: Chalice, 2004), 11.

46. See Christian Stäblein, *Predigten nach dem Holocaust: Das jüdische Gegenüber in der evangelischen Predigtlehre nach 1945;* Arbeiten zur Pastoraltheologie 44 (Göttingen: Vandenhoeck & Ruprecht, 2004), 31–65. See also Freud's classic text on remembering and forgetting: "Remembering, Repeating and Working-Through (Further Recommendations on the Technique of Psycho-Analysis II)," in *The Standard Edition of the Complete Psychological Works of Sigmund Freud* (1911–1913); trans. ed. James Strachey (London: Hogarth, 1958), 12:147–56. For a current debate on the psychoanalytic understanding of memory, see Roger Horrocks, *Freud Revisited: Psychoanalytic Themes in the Postmodern Age* (New York: Palgrave, 2001), 56–70.

47. Paul Connerton, *How Societies Remember; Themes in Social Sciences* (Cambridge: Cambridge Univ. Press, 1989), 27.

48. We discussed these questions in chapter 4, "The Body Politics of Eucharist." See also Andrea Bieler, "Real Bodies at the Meal," in *"Dies ist mein Leib." Leibliches, Leibeigenes und Leibhaftiges bei Gott und den Menschen,* ed. Jürgen Ebach, Hans-Martin Gutmann, Magdalene L. Frettlöh, and Michael Weinrich; Jabboq 6 (Gütersloh: Gütersloher, 2006), 81–90.

49. For the following see Hogue, *Remembering the Future,* and Peter Atkins, *Memory and Liturgy: The Place of Memory in the Composition and Practice of Liturgy* (Aldershot: Ashgate, 2004).

50. Hogue, *Remembering the Future,* 57.

51. Hogue, *Remembering the Future,* 60.

52. See Sylvia Jean Miller-Mutia, "Action, Relationship, and Time: The Contribution of Bodies to a Fuller Eucharistic Anamnesis," MA thesis, Berkeley: Pacific School of Religion, 2002.

53. From Bruce Saunkeah, "So Over Coming Out," reflection given in a chapel service at Pacific School of Religion in October 2004.

54. Saunkeah, "So Over Coming Out."

55. With this sentence, numerous Vietnam veterans struggle to form a narrative that reflects their traumatic war experience. It reflects collective trauma and the loss of self of U.S. soldiers who have survived Vietnam. See Susan, J. Brison, "Trauma Narratives and the Remaking of the Self," in *Acts of Memory. Cultural Recall in the Present,* ed. Mieke Bal, Jonathan Crewe, and Leo Spitzer (Hanover, N.H., and London: Univ. Press of New England, 1999), 39.

56. See Allan Young, *The Harmony of Illusions: Inventing Post-Traumatic Stress Disorder* (Princeton: Princeton Univ. Press, 1995).

57. Maurice Halbwachs, *On Collective Memory* (1941), ed., trans., and intro. Lewis A. Coser (Chicago and London: Univ. of Chicago Press, 1992).

58. "To be sure, everyone has the capacity for memory [mémoire] that is unlike that of anyone else, given the variety of temperaments and life circumstances. But individual memory is nevertheless a part or an aspect of group memory. . . . One cannot in fact think about the events of one's past without discoursing upon them. But to discourse upon something means to connect within a single system of ideas our opinions as well as those of our circle. . . . In this way the framework of collective memory confines our most intimate remembrances to each other." Halbwachs, *On Collective Memory,* 53.

59. See, for example, Jan Assmann's work on cultural memory: Jan Assmann, *Das kulturelle Gedächtnis: Schrift, Erinnerung und politische Identität in frühen Hochkulturen* (Munich: Beck, 1992), 52.

60. Eviatar Zerubavel, *Time Maps: Collective Memory and the Social Shape of the Past* (Chicago and London: Univ. of Chicago Press, 2003), 3.

61. Zerubavel, *Time Maps,* 3.

62. The structuring of liturgical time through the year can have this effect of *mnemonic synchronization.*

63. See David E. Lorey and William H. Beezley, eds., *Genocide, Collective Violence, and Popular Memory: The Politics of Remembrance in the Twentieth Century;* The World's Beat Series 1 (Wilmington, Del.: SR Books, 2002).

64. We learn from the anthropologist Renato Rosaldo how much the search for cultural patterns might be an expression of colonial consciousness about the other. "Although the classic vision of unique cultural patterns has proven merit, it also has serious limitations. It emphasizes shared patterns at the expense of processes of change and internal inconsistencies, conflicts, and contradictions. By defining culture as a set of shared meanings, classic norms of analysis make it difficult to study zones of difference within and between cultures. From the classic perspective, cultural borderlands appear to be annoying exceptions rather than central areas for inquiry." Renato Rosaldo, *Culture and Truth: The Remaking of Social Analysis* (Boston: Beacon, 1993), 27–28.

65. With regard to a variety of countries such as Rwanda or Chile, where massive genocide or state violence was carried out, Lorey and Beezley summarize: "In the aftermath of incidents of genocide and state-sponsored violence, officials, individuals, and a broad array of social groups have attempted to shape the historical consciousness of

societies. Such efforts can last for decades. Major conflicts have arisen as social groups battled for the preeminence of a certain interpretation of what happened, who is to blame, and who should be punished. One of the most troubling realities of the aftermath of genocide and collective violence was the attempt to use history in the service of forgetting; historical memory was sometimes abused in order to provide perpetrators with impunity for their earlier actions. Thus the past became key to interpreting the present and to shaping the future." Lorey and Beezley, *Genocide*, xiv.

66. Mieke Bal, "Introduction," in *Acts of Memory*, ed. Bal, et al., vii–xvii, at vii.

67. See Connerton, *How Societies Remember*, 41–104.

68. See also Andrea Bieler, "Embodied Knowing: Understanding Religious Experience in Ritual," in a volume edited by Christopher Scholtz and Hans-Günter Heimbrock (Göttingen: Vandenhoeck & Ruprecht, 2007).

69. Ronald Grimes talks about how ritual knowledge lodges in the bone. See his *Deeply into the Bone: Reinventing Rites of Passage* (Berkeley: Univ. of California Press, 2000), 7.

70. Bal, "Introduction," viii.

71. See also Petar Ramadanovic, *Forgetting Futures: On Memory, Trauma, and Identity* (Lanham, Md.: Lexington, 2001).

72. Bal, "Introduction," ix.

73. Jeffrey C. Alexander, "Toward a Theory of Cultural Trauma," in *Cultural Trauma and Collective Identity*, ed. Jeffrey C. Alexander, Ron Eyerman, Bernhard Giesen, Niel Smelser, and Pi Sztompka (Berkeley: Univ. of California Press, 2004), 1.

74. See, for example, Flora Keshgegian's narrative of how Armenian refugees who came as refugees to the U.S. suppressed the memory of the genocide they had experienced. Flora A. Keshgegian, *Redeeming Memories: A Theology of Healing and Transformation* (Nashville: Abingdon, 2000).

75. See pp. 167–70.

76. See pp. 167–70.

77. Richetta and Ra Amen, "Memories of Captivity," unpubl. ms., Berkeley 2005. We express our deep respect and gratitude to Richetta Amen for her energy and passion in sharing these memories in class and putting them in writing together with her husband, Ra Amen.

78. Toni Morrison, *Beloved* (New York: Knopf, 1987), 251.

79. Orlando Patterson, *Slavery and Social Death* (Cambridge: Harvard Univ. Press, 1982), 13.

80. Morrison, *Beloved*, 251.

81. *Remembering Slavery: African Americans Talk about Their Personal Experiences of Slavery and Emancipation;* Tapes of Smithsonian Productions' Radio Documentary, 1998.

82. Morrison, *Beloved*, 36.

83. Richetta and Ra Amen, "Memories of Captivity."

84. Philip Sheldrake, *Spaces for the Sacred: Place, Memory, and Identity* (Baltimore: John Hopkins Univ. Press, 2001), 80.

85. Sheldrake, *Spaces for the Sacred*, 1.

86. The ritual theorist Catherine Bell speaks about the "ritualized body environment" and describes how bodily interactions in ritual shape this environment: "Yet a focus on the acts themselves illuminates a critical circularity to the body's interaction with this environment: generating it, it is molded by it in return. By virtue of this circularity space and time are redefined through the physical movements of bodies projecting organizing schemes on the space-time environment on the one hand while absorbing these schemes as the nature of reality on the other." Catherine Bell, *Ritual Theory, Ritual Practice* (New York and Oxford: Oxford Univ. Press, 1992), 99.

87. See Sheldrake, *Spaces*, 37–38.

88. Sheldrake, *Spaces*, 89.

89. Sheldrake formulates a similar challenge for a theology of space in general: "Theological reflections on place can no longer ignore that the world of concrete places is full of exiles, displaced peoples, diaspora struggles by indigenous people and cultural minorities to achieve liberation." Sheldrake, *Spaces*, 22.

90. Flora A. Keshgegian, *Redeeming Memories*, 29.

91. What follows is Andrea Bieler's account. I am grateful to Benita Joswig, who introduced me to this place long before the chapel was built.

92. Ulrike Braun, *Versöhnungskirche. Kapelle der Versöhnung* (Berlin: Evangelische Versöhnungsgemeinde Selbstverlag, 2003), 37.

93. This new building is intentionally called a chapel and not, like its forebears, a church. In a documentation of the history of this congregation, its sacred places, and its social location, the following definition is given: "'Chapel,' the initial name for the shrine in the court of the Franconian kings for the legendary coat, or 'cape' of Saint Martin; later court and palace chapels were part of a building in which relics and other precious objects were stored. The less a chapel had the full legal position of a parish or parochial church under canon law, the more its elementary significance grew as a place of peace, reflection, personal contemplation, and the encounter with central life questions and attempts to answer them. For years in Christian culture 'chapels' have been places of special and spiritual memorial, whether memorializing important people like 'saints' or significant events. Chapels are therefore rarely found in marketplaces or in centers of trade and transit." Braun, *Versöhnungskirche*, 40.

94. Braun, *Versöhnungskirche*, 30.

95. The German artist and theologian Benita Joswig created an installation called "The Return of the Furniture" (*Die Rückkehr der Möbel*) in which she reflected the dramatic event of the division of the Bernauer Straße. See Benita Joswig, "Die Rückkehr der Möbel: Reste im Gehweg: Beitrag zur Archäologie der Gegenwart," http://benita-joswig.de/moebel.htm (accessed April 24, 2007).

96. Braun, *Versöhnungskirche*, 31–32.

97. Manfred Fischer, "Zwischen Glas und Stahl—Lehm," *Reformatio* 3 (2002) 190.

98. Braun, *Versöhnungskirche*, 37.

99. Braun, *Versöhnungskirche*, 36.

100. This cross is the work of the Armenian artist Shavarsh Kachatryan.

101. Bruce Morrill introduced Johann Baptist Metz's notion of dangerous memory to the field of liturgical theology. See Bruce T. Morrill, *Anamnesis as Dangerous Memory: Political and Liturgical Theology in Dialogue* (Collegeville, Minn.: Liturgical, 2000).

BIBLIOGRAPHY

Adams, Doug. "Changing Patterns and Interpretations of Parables in Art." In *Arts, Theology and the Church: New Interpretations.* Edited by Wilson Yates. New York: Pilgrim, 2005.

Alexander, Jeffrey C. "Toward a Theory of Cultural Trauma." In *Cultural Trauma and Collective Identity.* Edited by Jeffrey C. Alexander, Ron Eyerman, Bernhard Giesen, Niel Smelser, and Pi Sztompka. Berkeley: Univ. of California Press, 2004.

Amen, Richetta and Ra Amen. "Memories of Captivity." Unpublished. Berkeley, 2005.

Arens, Edmund. "Anamnetische Praxis: Erinnern als elementare Handlung des Glaubens." In *Erinnern: Erkundungen zu einer theologischen Basiskategorie.* Edited by Paul Petzel and Norbert Reck. Darmstadt: Wissenschaftliche Buchgesellschaft, 2003.

Assmann, Jan. *Das kulturelle Gedächtnis: Schrift, Erinnerung und politische Identität in frühen Hochkulturen.* Munich: C. H. Beck, 1992.

Atkins, Peter. *Memory and Liturgy: The Place of Memory in the Composition and Practice of Liturgy.* Aldershot: Ashgate, 2004.

Augustus. *Meine Taten: Res Gestae Divi Augusti*, Latin-German. Munich: Heimeran, 1975.

Bal, Mieke. "Introduction." In *Acts of Memory: Cultural Recall in the Present.* Edited by Mieke Bal, Jonathan Crewe, and Leo Spitzer. Hanover and London: Univer. Press of New England, 1999.

Barth, Karl. *Church Dogmatics* IV/3. Edinburgh: T&T Clark, 1962.

Bauckham, Richard, and Trevor Hart. "The Shape of Time." In *The Future as God's Gift: Explorations in Christian Eschatology.* Edited by David Fergusson and Marcel Sarot. Edinburgh: T&T Clark, 2000.

Beckman, Ninna Edgardh. "Lady Wisdom as Hostess for the Lord's Supper: Sofia-mässor in Stockholm, Sweden." In *Dissident Daughter: Feminist Liturgies in Global Context.* Edited by Teresa Berger. Louisville and London: Westminster John Knox, 2001.

Beckmann, David and Arthur Simon. *Grace at the Table: Ending Hunger in God's World.* New York/Mahwah: Paulist, 1999.

Bell, Catherine. *Ritual Theory, Ritual Practice.* New York and Oxford: Oxford Univ. Press, 1992.

———. *Ritual: Perspectives and Dimensions.* New York and Oxford: Oxford Univ. Press, 1997.

Berger, Teresa. "Breaking Bread in a Broken World: Liturgy and Cartographies of the Real." In *Studia Liturgica* 36/1 (2006): 74-85.

Bieler, Andrea. "The Language of Prayer between Truth Telling and Mysticism." In *The Theology of Dorothee Sölle.* Edited by Sarah Pinnock. Harrisburg, Pa.: Trinity Press International, 2003.

———. "Die Rede von Gott im Krieg gegen den Terrorismus." In *Die Rückkehr des Imperiums: Das Imperium in der Bibel und als Herausforderung für die Ökumene heute.* Edited by Luise Schottroff, Gerard Minnaard, Ruth Gütter, Klara Butting, Andrea Bieler. Breklum: Erev Rav, 2006.

———. "Embodied Knowing: Understanding Religious Experience in Ritual." In *Empirical Theology and Phenomenology of Religious Experience.* Edited by Christopher Scholtz, and Hans Günter Heimbrock. Göttingen: Vandenhoeck & Ruprecht, 2007.

———. "Eucharist as Gift Exchange: Liturgical Theology and Ritual Studies in Dialog." In *Dem Tod nicht glauben: Sozialgeschichte der Bibel. Festschrift für Luise Schottroff zum 70. Geburtstag.* Edited by Frank Crüsemann, Marlene Crüsemann, Claudia Janssen, Rainer Kessler, and Beate Wehn. Gütersloh: Gütersloher, 2004.

———. "Real Bodies at the Meal." In *"Dies ist mein Leib": Leibliches, Leibeigenes und Leibhaftiges bei Gott und den Menschen.* Jabboq 6. Edited by Jürgen Ebach, Hans-Martin Gutmann, Magdalene L. Frettlöh, and Michael Weinrich. Gütersloh: Gütersloher, 2006.

———. *Die Sehnsucht nach dem verlorenen Himmel: Jüdische und christliche Reflexionen zu Gottesdienstreform und Predigtkultur im 19. Jahrhundert.* Praktische Theologie heute 65. Stuttgart: Kohlhammer, 2003.

———. "Wenn der Homo oeconomicus betet: Über die Symbolisierung des Ökonomischen in der Liturgie." *JK* 4 (2004): 16–19.

Bingham, D. Jeffrey. "Eucharist and Incarnation: The Second Century and Luther." In *Rediscovering the Eucharist: Ecumenical Conversations.* Edited by Roch A. Kereszty. New York & Mahwah, N.J.: Paulist, 2003.

Bishop, Jonathan. *Some Bodies: The Eucharist and Its Implications.* Macon: Mercer Univ. Press, 1992.

Bordo, Susan. *Unbearable Weight: Feminism, Western Culture and the Body.* Berkeley: Univ. of California Press, 1993.

Borg, B. Marcus. *Jesus in Contemporary Scholarship.* Valley Forge: Trinity Press International, 1994.

Bösen, Willibald. *Jesusmahl, Eucharistisches Mahl, Endzeitmahl.* Stuttgart: Katholisches Bibelwerk, 1980.

Bradshaw, Paul. "Anamnesis in Modern Eucharistic Debate." In *Memory and History in Christianity and Judaism.* Edited by Michael A. Signer. Notre Dame, Ind.: Univ. of Notre Dame Press, 2001.

———. *Early Christian Worship: A Basic Introduction to Ideas and Practice.* Collegeville, Minn.: Liturgical, 1996.

Brandt, Sigrid. *Opfer als Gedächtnis: Auf dem Weg zu einer befreienden theologischen Rede vom Opfer.* Münster: Lit.-Verlag, 2001.

Braun, Ulrike. *Versöhnungskirche: Kapelle der Versöhnung.* Berlin: Evangelische Versöhnungsgemeinde Selbstverlag, 2003.

Brison, Susan J. "Trauma Narratives and the Remaking of the Self." In *Acts of Memory: Cultural Recall in the Present.* Edited by Mieke Bal, Jonathan Crewe, and Leo Spitzer. Hanover and London: University Press of New England, 1999.

Brueggemann, Walter. "The Liturgy of Abundance, the Myth of Scarcity." *The Christian Century* (24–31 March 1999): 342–47.

Buchanan, Colin Ogilvie. *The End of the Offertory: An Anglican Study.* Grove Liturgical Study 14. Bramcote: Grove, 1978.

Bultmann, Rudolf. *Neues Testament und Mythologie* 1941. Munich: Kaiser, 1988.

Camenish, Paul F. "Gift and Gratitude in Ethics." *JRE* 9 (1981): 1–34.

Campenhausen, Hans von. *Die Entstehung der christlichen Bibel.* Tübingen: Mohr, 1968.

Carroll, Jon E. *Sustainability and Spirituality.* Albany: State Univ. of New York Press, 2004.

Cavanaugh, William T. *Torture and Eucharist: Theology, Politics, and the Body of Christ.* Malden, Mass.: Oxford: Blackwell, 2000.

Chauvet, Louis-Marie. *The Sacraments: The Word of God at the Mercy of the Body.* Collegeville, Minn.: Liturgical, 2001.

Cixous, Hélène, and Catherine Clémont. *The Newly Born Woman: Theory and History of Literature.* Minneapolis: Univ. of Minnesota Press, 1975.

Clementz, Heinrich. *Des Flavius Josephus Jüdische Altertümer.* Volume 2. Darmstadt: Melzer, 1967.

Connerton, Paul. *How Societies Remember: Themes in Social Sciences.* Cambridge: Cambridge Univ. Press, 1989; tenth printing 2003.

Crüsemann, Frank. "Der Neue Bund im Neuen Testament: Erwägungen zum Verständnis des Christusbundes in der Abendmahlstradition und im Hebräerbrief." In *Kanon und Sozialgeschichte.* Edited by Frank Crüsemann. Gütersloh: Kaiser/Gütersloher, 2003.

———. "Schrift und Auferstehung: Beobachtungen zur Wahrnehmung des auferstandenen Jesus bei Lukas und Paulus und zum Verhältnis der Testamente." In *Kanon und Sozialgeschichte.* Edited by Frank Crüsemann. Gütersloh: Kaiser/Gütersloher, 2003.

———. "*Kipper* etc." In *Bibel in gerechter Sprache.* Edited by Frank Crüsemann et al. Gütersloh: Gütersloher, 2006.

Dalman, Gustaf. *Arbeit und Sitte in Palästina.* Volume 4. Gütersloh 1935; reprint, Hildesheim: Olms, 1964.

Daly, Robert J. *The Origins of the Christian Doctrine of Sacrifice.* Philadelphia: Fortress Press, 1978.

Derrida, Jacques. *Falschgeld: Zeit geben I.* Translated by A. Knop and M. Wetzel. Munich: Fink, 1993.

Deutschmann, Christoph. *Die Verheißung des absoluten Reichtums: Zur religiösen Natur des Kapitalismus.* 2nd ed. Frankfurt & New York: Campus, 2001.

Dulles, Avery. "The Eucharist and the Mystery of the Trinity." In *Rediscovering the Eucharist. Ecumenical Conversations.* Edited by Roch A. Kereszty and O. Cist. New York/Mahwah, N.J.: Paulist, 2003.

Durning, Alan T. *How Much Is Enough? The Consumer Society and the Future of the Earth.* New York: W.W. Norton, 1992.

Dussell, Enrique. "The Bread of the Eucharistic Celebration as a Sign of Justice in the Community." In *Can We Always Celebrate the Eucharist?* Edited by Mary Collins and David Power. New York: Seabury, 1982.

Ebach, Jürgen. "Apokalypse: Zum Ursprung einer Stimmung." *Einwürfe* 2 (1985): 5–61.

———. "Eschatologie/Apokalyptik." In *Neues Handbuch Theologischer Grundbegriffe.* Volume 1. Edited by Peter Eichler. Munich: Kösel, 2005: 260–272.

Eberhart, Christian. *Studien zur Bedeutung der Opfer im Alten Testament.* Neukirchen: Neukirchener, 2002.

Eisen, Ute E. *Women Officeholders in Early Christianity: Epigraphical and Literary Studies*, transl. by Linda Maloney. Collegeville, Minn.: Liturgical, 2000.

Eisenberg, Nancy, and Janet Strayer. "Critical Issues in the Study of Empathy." In *Empathy and its Development*. Edited by Nancy Eisenberg, and Janet Strayer. Cambridge, Mass.: Cambridge Univ. Press, 1987.

Fiebig, Paul. *Altjüdische Gleichnisse und die Gleichnisse Jesu*. Tübingen und Leipzig: Mohr, 1904.

Finkelstein, Louis. "The Birkath Ha-Mazon." *JQR* New Series 19 (1929): 215–216.

Fischer, Manfred. "Zwischen Glas und Stahl: Lehm." *Reformatio* 3 (2002): 190.

Flannery, Austin , general editor. "The Constitution on the Sacred Liturgy." In *Vatican Council II: Constitutions, Decrees, Declarations*. Northport, N.Y.: Costello, 1996.

Foucault, Michel. *The Order of Things: An Archaeology of Human Sciences*. 1970; reprint, New York: Vintage, 1973.

Frettlöh, Magdalene L. "'Gott ist im Fleische...': Die Inkarnation Gottes in ihrer leibeigenen Dimension beim Wort genommen." In *"Dies ist mein Leib:" Leibliches, Leibeigenes und Leibhaftiges bei Gott und den Menschen*. Jabboq 6. Edited by Jürgen Ebach, Hans-Martin Gutmann, Magdalene L. Frettlöh, and Michael Weinrich. Gütersloh: Gütersloher, 2006.

Freud, Sigmund. "Remembering, Repeating and Working-Through: Further Recommendations on the Technique of Psycho-Analysis II." In *The Standard Edition of the Complete Psychological Works of Sigmund Freud*. Volume 12 (1911–1913). Translated from the German under the general editorship of James Strachey. London: Hogarth, 1958.

Gaillardetz, Richard R. *Transforming Our Days: Spirituality, Community, and Liturgy in a Techonological Culture*. New York: Crossroad, 2000.

Gnilka, Joachim. *Das Evangelium nach Markus*. Volume 2. Zürich: Benziger; Neukirchen: Neukirchener, 1979.

Goldschmidt, Lazarus. *Der Babylonische Talmud*. Volume 1. Darmstadt: Wissenschaftliche Buchgesellschaft, Nachdruck 1967.

Goudey, June Christine. *Reimaging Communion: The Feast of Our Lives*. Cleveland: Pilgrim, 2002.

Grau, Marion. *Of Divine Economy: Refinancing Redemption*. New York & London: T&T Clark International, 2004.

Green Garrett. *Imagining God: Theology and the Religious Imagination*. Grand Rapids, Mich.: Eerdmans, 1998.

———. "Imagining the Future." In *The Future as God's Gift: Explorations in Christian Eschatology*. Edited by David Fergusson and Marcel Sarot. Edinburgh: T&T Clark, 2000.

Griffith, R. Marie. *God's Daughters: Evangelical Women and the Power of Submission*. Berkeley: Univ. of California Press, 1997.

Grimes, Ronald. *Deeply into the Bone: Reinventing Rites of Passage*. Berkeley: Univ. of California Press, 2000.

Gutmann, Hans-Martin. "Der gute und der schlechte Tausch: Das Heilige und das Geld—gegensätzliche ökonomische Beziehungen? In *"Leget Anmut" in das Geben Zum Verhältnis von Ökonomie und Theologie*. Jabboq 1. Gütersloh: Gütersloher, 2001.

———. *Symbole zwischen Macht und Spiel: Religionspädagogische und liturgische Untersuchungen zum "Opfer."* Göttingen: Vandenhoeck & Ruprecht, 1996.

Halbwachs, Maurice. *On Collective Memory* (1941). Edited, translated and introduced by Lewis A. Coser. Chicago and London: Univ. of Chicago Press, 1992.

Hanson, R. P. C. *Eucharistic Offering in the Early Church*. Grove Liturgical Study 19. Bramcote: Grove, 1979.

Harling, Per. "Hymn 803." In *Psalmeri 90-talet*. Stockholm: Verbum (1994). Quoted in *Dissident Daughters: Feminist Liturgies in Global Context*. Edited by Teresa Berger. Louisville and London: Westminter John Knox, 2001, 173–74.

Hellwig, Monika K. *The Eucharist and the Hunger of the World*. 2nd edition, revised. Franklin, Wisc.: Sheed & Ward, 1999

Hengsbach, Friedhelm S.J. "Marktkonkurrenz auf der Grundlage gesellschaftlicher Kooperation." In *Homo oeconomicus: Der Mensch der Zukunft? Globale Solidarität— Schritte zu einer neuen Weltkultur*. Volume 2. Edited by Norbert Brieskorn, and Johannes Wallacher. Stuttgart/Berlin/Cologne: Kohlhammer, 1998.

Henten, J.W. van (ed.). *Die Entstehung der jüdischen Martyrologie*. Leiden and New York: Brill, 1989.

Heyward, Carter. "All Shall Have Power." In *No Longer Strangers: A Resource for Women and Worship*. Edited by Iben Gjerding and Katherine Kinnamon. Geneva: World Council of Churches, 1983.

Hinkelammert, Franz J. *The Ideological Weapons of Death: A Theological Critique of Capitalism*. Translated by Phillip Berryman. Maryknoll, N.Y.: Orbis, 1986.

Hirsch, Leo. *Jüdische Glaubenswelt*. Basel: Victor Goldschmidt, 1978.

Hjelde, Sigurd. *Das Eschaton und die Eschata: Eine Studie über Sprachgebrauch und Sprachverwirrung in protestantischer Theologie von der Orthodoxie bis zur Gegenwart*. BEvT 102, Munich: Kaiser, 1987.

Hogue, David A. *Remembering the Future, Imagining the Past: Story, Ritual and the Human Brain*. Cleveland: Pilgrim, 2003.

Hohn, Hans-Willy. *Die Zerstörung der Zeit*. Frankfurt a.M.: Fischer, 1984.

Hornbacher, Mayra. *Wasted: A Memoir of Anorexia and Bulimia*. New York: Harper-Flamingo, 1998.

Horrocks, Roger. *Freud Revisited: Psychoanalytic Themes in the Postmodern Age*. New York: Palgrave, 2001.

Horsley, Richard A. and John S. Hanson. *Bandits, Prophets, and Messiahs: Popular Movements in the Time of Jesus*. San Francisco: Harper, 1988.

Isherwood, Lisa and Elizabeth Stuart. *Introducing Body Theology*. IFT 2. Sheffield: Sheffield Academic Press, 1998.

Jackson, Colette. "Witness God's Welcome. A Communion Liturgy." Unpublished document from the *Witness Our Welcome Conference 2000*.

Janowski, Bernd and Michael Welker (eds.). *Opfer: Theologische und kulturelle Kontexte*. Frankfurt a.M.: Suhrkamp Taschenbuch Wissenschaft, 2000.

Janowski, Bernd. "'Hingabe' oder 'Opfer.'" In *Das Kreuz Jesu*. Edited by Rudolf Weth. Neukirchen: Neukirchener, 2001.

Janssen, Claudia. *Anders ist die Schönheit der Körper: Paulus und die Auferstehung in 1 Kor. 15*. Gütersloh: Gütersloher, 2005.

Johnson, Mark. *The Body in the Mind: The Bodily Basis of Meaning, Imagination and Reason*. Chicago & London: Univ. of Chicago Press, 1987.

Josephus, Flavius, *De bello Judaico*. Greek and German. Three volumes. Darmstadt: Wissenschaftsstadt Buoh Gesellschaft 1959–1969.

Joswig, Benita (ed.). *Erinnern und aufstehen – antworten auf Kreuzestheologien.* Mainz: Matthias-Grünewald, 2000.

Joswig, Benita. "Die Rückkehr der Möbel: Reste im Gehweg. Beitrag zur Archäologie der Gegenwart." Available from www.benita-joswig.de/moebel.htm. Internet; accessed 17 August 2005.

Jung, L. Shannon. *Food for Life: The Spirituality and Ethics of Eating.* Minneapolis: Fortress Press, 2004.

Jungmann, Joseph A., s.j. *The Mass of the Roman Rite: Its Origins and Development (Missarum Sollemnia).* Translated by Francis A. Brunner. Westminster, Md.: Christian Classics, 1986.

Justin Martyr. "First Apology." In *Prayers of the Eucharist: Early and Reformed.* Edited by R. C. D. Jasper and G. J. Cuming. Third edition, Revised. Collegeville, Minn.: Liturgical, 1990.

Kautzsch, Emil. *Die Apokryphen und Pseudepigraphen des Alten Testaments.* Volume 2. Tübingen: Mohr, 1900.

Kearney, Richard. *The Wake of Imagination: Ideas of Creativity in Western Culture.* London: Hutchinson, 1988.

Kelleher, Margaret Mary. "Liturgy and the Christian Imagination." *Worship* 66/2 (March 1992): 125–48.

Kelleher, Margaret Mary. "Ritual Studies and the Eucharist: Paying Attention to Performance." In *Eucharist: Toward the Third Millennium.* Edited by Martin F. Connell. Eldridge, Iowa: Liturgical Training, 1997.

Keller, Catherine. *Apocalypse Now and Then: A Feminist Guide to the End of the World.* Boston: Beacon, 1996.

Keshgegian, Flora A. *Redeeming Memories. A Theology of Healing and Transformation.* Nashville: Abingdon, 2000.

Kieckhefer, Richard. *Theology in Stone: Church Architecture from Byzantium to Berkeley.* New York: Oxford Univ. Press, 2004.

Kilmartin, Edward. "The Sacrifice of Thanksgiving and Social Justice." In *Liturgy and Social Justice.* Edited by Mark Searle. Collegeville, Minn.: Liturgical, 1980.

Kimbrough, S. T. Jr. (gen. ed.) and Carlton R. Young (mus. ed.). *Global Praise 1: Songs for Worship and Witness.* New York: General Board of Global Ministries, The United Methodist Church, 1995.

Kirchhoff, Renate. *Die Sünde gegen den eigenen Leib: Studien zu porne and porneia in 1 Kor 6,12-20 und dem sozio-kulturellen Kontext der paulinischen Adressaten.* Göttingen: Vandenhoeck & Ruprecht, 1994.

Klauck, Hans-Josef. *4. Makkabäerbuch.* JSHZ 3/6. Gütersloh: Mohn, 1989.

Klawans, Jonathan. "Was Jesus' Last Supper a Seder?" *Bible Review* 17/5 (October 2001): 25-33, 47.

Klein, Stephen J. "American Millennial Visions: Towards the Construction of a New Architectonic of American Apocalypticism." In *Imagining the End: Visions of Apocalypse from the Ancient Middle East to Modern America.* Edited by Abbas Amanat, and Magnus Bernhardson. London/New York: Tauris, 2002.

Kodell, Jerome. *The Eucharist in the New Testament.* Wilmington, Del.: Glazier, 1988.

Koenig, John. *The Feast of the World's Redemption: Eucharistic Origins and Christian Mission.* Harrisburg, Pa.: Trinity, 2000.

Krüger, René. "Conversion of the Pocketbook: The Economic Project of Luke's Gospel." In *God's Economy: Biblical Studies from Latin America*. Edited by Ross Kinsler and Gloria Kinsler. Maryknoll, N.Y.: Orbis, 2005.

LaHaye, Tim, and Jerry Jenkins. *Left Behind: A Novel of Earth's Last Day. Left Behind* 1. Wheaton, Ill: Tyndale, 1996.

Lange, Dirk. "In, With and Under: Liturgical Disruption of Theology." Dissertation, Emory University, 2005.

Lathrop, Gordon W. "The Bodies on Nevado Ampato: A Further Note on Offering and Offertory." *Worship* 71/6 (1997): 546–54.

———. *Holy Ground: A Liturgical Cosmology*. Minneapolis: Fortress Press, 2003.

———. *Holy People: A Liturgical Ecclesiology*. Minneapolis: Fortress Press, 1999.

Lelwica, Michelle, Mary. *Starving for Salvation: The Spiritual Dimensions of Eating Problems among American Girls and Women*. Oxford and New York: Oxford Univ. Press, 2002.

Lockward, Jorge A. *Tenemos Esperanza: Temos Esperanca; We Have Hope*. The General Board of Global Ministries, The United Methodist Church, 2002.

Lohse, Eduard. *Märtyrer und Gottesknecht*. Göttingen: Vandenhoeck, 1963.

Lorey, David E., and William H. Beezley (eds.). *Genocide, Collective Violence, and Popular Memory: The Politics of Remembrance in the Twentieth Century*. The World's Beat Series 1. Wilmington, Del.: SR Books, 2002.

Lukian. *Die Hauptwerke*. Edited and translated by Karl Mras. NP: Heimeran, 1954.

Luther's Works. *Word and Sacrament* 3. Volume1 37. Edited by R. H. Fischer. Philadelphia: Fortress Press, 1961.

Luz, Ulrich. *Das Evangelium nach Matthäus* 4. Teilband. Zürich/Neukirchen: Benziger/Neukirchener, 2002. English translation: *Matthew 21–28*. Heremenia. Minneapolis: Fortress Press, 2007.

Manstetten, Reiner. *Das Menschenbild der Ökonomie: Der Homo oeconomicus und die Anthropologie von Adam Smith*. Alber-Reihe Thesen 7. Freiburg and Munich: Karl Alber, 2002.

Marcia, James. "Empathy and Psychotherapy." In *Empathy and Its Development*. Edited by Nancy Eisenberg and Janet Strayer. Cambridge: Cambridge Univ. Press, 1987.

Martin, Dale. *The Corinthian Body*. New Haven and London: Yale Univ. Press, 1995.

Martin, Joan M. "A Sacred Hope and a Social Goal: Womanist Eschatology." In *Liberating Eschatology: Essays in Honor of Letty M. Russell*. Edited by Margaret Farley and Serene Jones. Louisville: Westminster John Knox Press, 1999.

Marx, Karl. "The Fetishism of Commodities and the Secret Thereof." In *Capital: A Critique of Political Economy*. Edited by Frederick Engels. New York: International, 1967.

Mauss, Marcel. *The Gift: The Form and Reason for Exchange in Archaic Societies*. Translated by W. D. Halls. New York: Norton, 1990. Published originally as *Essai sur le Don*. Presses Universitaires de France, 1950.

McCormick, Patrick T. "How Could We Break the Lord's Bread in a Foreign Land? The Eucharist in 'Diet America.'" *Horizons* 25/1 (1998): 43–57.

McFague, Sallie. *Life Abundant: Rethinking Theology and Economy for a Planet in Peril*. Minneapolis: Fortress Press, 2001.

McFee, Marcia. "Primal Patterns: Ritual Dynamics, Ritual Resonance, Polyrhythmic Strategies and the Formation of Christian Disciples." Dissertation, Graduate Theological Union, Berkeley, March 2005.

Merleau-Ponty, Maurice. "The Primacy of Perception and its Philosophical Consequences." In *The Primacy of Perception and other Essays on Phenomenological Psychology, the Philosophy of Art, History and Politics*. Edited and introduced by James M.
Edie. Evanston, IL: Northwestern Univ. Press, 1964.

Millais, John Everett. *The Parables of our Lord and Saviour Jesus Christ*. Introduction by
Mary Lutyens. New York: Dover, 1975.

Miller-Mutia, Sylvia Jean. "Action, Relationship, and Time: The Contribution of Bodies to
a Fuller Eucharistic Anamnesis." Thesis, Pacific School of Religion, Berkeley, 2002.

Mittmann-Richert, Ulrike. "Historische und legendarische Erzählungen." In *Supplementa: Einführung zu den Jüdischen Schriften aus hellenistisch-römischer Zeit*. Edited by
Hermann Lichtenberger, and Gerbern S. Oegema. Gütersloh: Gütersloher, 2000.

Moltmann, Jürgen. *The Coming of God: Christian Eschatology*. Translated by Margaret
Kohl. Minneapolis: Fortress Press, 1996.

Moody, Heather. "The Fear of Scarcity, the Power of Abundance, and the Challenge of
Sufficiency." Unpublished paper. Berkeley: Graduate Theological Union, 2004.

Moore, George F. *Judaism in the First Centuries of the Christian Era: The Age of the Tannaim*. Volume 2. Cambridge: Harvard Univ. Press, 1954.

Morley, Janet (ed.). *Bread of Tomorrow. Prayers for the Church Year*. Maryknoll, N.Y.:
Orbis, 1992.

Morrill, Bruce T. "Initial Consideration: Theory and Practice of the Body in Liturgy
Today." In *Bodies of Worship: Explorations in Theory and Practice*. Edited by Bruce T.
Morrill. Collegeville, Minn.: Liturgical, 1999.

——— (ed.). *Bodies of Worship. Explorations in Theory and Practice*. Collegeville, Minn.:
Liturgical, 1999.

———. *Anamnesis as Dangerous Memory: Political and Liturgical Theology in Dialogue*.
Collegeville, Minn.: Liturgical, 2000.

Morrison, Toni. *Beloved*. New York: Knopf, 1987.

Murphy, Debra Dean. "Bread, Wine, and the 'Pledge of Heaven': A (Wesleyan) Feminist Perspective on Eucharist and Eschatology." *QR* 14 (1994/1995): 401–412.

Osborne, Kenan B. *Christian Sacraments in a Postmodern World: A Theology for the Third
Millennium*. New York/Mahwah, N.J.: Paulist, 1999.

Pangritz, Andreas. "'Solches tut zu meinem Gedächtnis': Eine Kritik der Domestizierung von Erinnerung in der kirchlichen Abendmahlslehre." In *Erinnern: Erkundungen zu einer theologischen Basiskategorie*. Edited by Paul Petzel and Norbert Reck.
Darmstadt: Wissenschaftliche Buchgesellschaft, 2003.

Park, Eung Chun. *Either Jew or Gentile: Paul's Unfolding Theology of Inclusivity*. Louisville and London: Westminster John Knox, 2003.

Patterson, Orlando. *Slavery and Social Death*. Cambridge, Mass.: Harvard Univ. Press,
1982.

Plutarch. *Plutarch's Morals*. Edited by William W. Goodwin. Boston: Little Brown,
1870.

Power, David N. *Sacrament: The Language of God's Giving*. New York: Crossroad, 1999.

———. "Words That Crack: The Uses of Sacrifice in Eucharistic Discourse." In *Living
Bread, Saving Cup: Readings on the Eucharist*. Edited by R. Kevin Seasoltz. Collegeville, Minn.: Liturgical, 1987.

Priddat, Birger P. "Moral Based Rational Man." In *Homo oeconomicus: Der Mensch der
Zukunft?* Globale Solidarität: Schritte zu einer neuen Weltkultur 2. Edited by Norbert
Brieskorn, and Johannes Wallacher. Stuttgart/Berlin/Cologne: Kohlhammer, 1998.

Priest, J. "A Note on the Messianic Banquet." In *The Messiah: Developments in Earliest Judaism and Christianity.* Edited by James H. Charlesworth. Minneapolis: Fortress Press, 1992.

Procter-Smith, Marjorie. "Our Bodies, Our Blood: Christian Feminist Eucharistic Praying." In *Praying with Our Eyes Open: Engendering Feminist Liturgical Prayer.* Nashville: Abingdon, 1995.

Procter-Smith, Marjorie. "Something Missing: Memory and Imagination." In *In Her Own Rite: Constructing Feminist Liturgical Tradition.* Akron: OSL (1990), 2000.

Kwok, Pui-lan. *Postcolonial Imagination and Feminist Theology.* Louisville: Westminster John Knox, 2005.

Quesnell, Quentin. "The Women at Luke's Supper." In *Political Issues in Luke-Acts.* Edited by R. J. Cassidy and P.J. Scharper. Maryknoll, N.Y.: Orbis, 1983.

Radford Ruether, Rosemary. "Eschatology and Feminism." In *Lift Every Voice: Constructing Christian Theologies from the Underside.* Edited by Susan B. Thistlethwaite and Mary Potter Engels. Maryknoll, N.Y.: Orbis, 1998.

———. *Sexism and God Talk: Toward a Feminist Theology.* Boston: Beacon, 1983.

Ramadanovic, Petar. *Forgetting Futures: On Memory, Trauma, and Identity.* Lanhan/Bolder/ New York/Oxford: Lexington, 2001.

Ramshaw, Gail. *Liturgical Language: Keeping It Metaphoric, Making It Inclusive.* Collegeville, Minn.: Liturgical, 1996.

Reik, Theodore. *Listening with the Third Ear.* New York: Farrar, Straus, 1949.

Remembering Slavery, *African Americans Talk about Their Personal Experiences of Slavery and Emancipation.* Tapes of Smithsonian Productions' Radio Documentary, 1998.

Richter Reimer, Ivoni. *Frauen in der Apostelgeschichte des Lukas: Eine feministisch-theologische Exegese.* Gütersloh: Gütersloher, 1992. English translation, *Women in the Acts of the Apostles: A Feminist Liberation Perspective.* Translated by Linda M. Maloney. Minneapolis: Fortress Press, 1995.

Ricoeur, Paul. "The Metaphorical Process as Cognition, Imagination and Feeling." *Critical Inquiry* 5 (1978): 143–59.

Rockefeller, Steven C. "The Earth Charter: Building a Global Culture of Peace." *The Ecozoic Reader* 2/1 (Fall 2001): 13-11.

Rosaldo, Renato. *Culture and Truth: The Remaking of Social Analysis.* Boston: Beacon, 1993.

Rossing, Barbara R. *The Rapture Exposed: The Message of Hope in the Book of Revelation.* Boulder, Colo.: Westview, 2004.

Rost, Leonhard. *Einleitung in die alttestamentlichen Apokryphen und Pseudepigraphen einschließlich der großen Qumranschriften.* Heidelberg: Quelle und Meyer, 1971.

Runge, Ford C. et al. *Ending Hunger in our Lifetime: Food Security and Globalization.* Published for the International Ford Policy Research Institute. Baltimore and London: John Hopkins Univ. Press, 2003.

Saliers, Don E. *Worship as Theology: Foretaste of Glory Divine.* Nashville: Abingdon, 1994.

———. *The Soul in Paraphrase: Prayer and the Religious Affections.* New York: Seabury, 1980.

Sanders, E. P. *Paul and Palestinian Judaism: A Comparison of Patterns of Religion.* Philadelphia: Fortress Press, 1977. German translation: *Paulus und das palästinensische Judentum: Ein Vergleich zweier Religionsstrukturen.* Göttingen: Vandenhoeck & Ruprecht, 1997.

Saunkeah, Bruce. "So Over Coming Out." Reflection given in a chapel service at Pacific School of Religion in October, 2004.

Sauter, Gerhard. "The Concept and Task of Eschatology: Theological and Philosophical Reflections." *SJT* 41 (1988): 499–515.

Sawicki, Marianne. *Seeing the Lord. Resurrection and Early Christian Practices.* Minneapolis: Fortress Press, 1994.

Scarry, Elaine. *The Body in Pain: The Making and Unmaking of the World.* Oxford and New York: Oxford Univ. Press, 1985.

Schillebeeckx, Edward. "Transubstantiation, Transfinalization, Transignification." In *Living Bread, Saving Cup: Readings on the Eucharist.* Edited by R. Kevin Seasoltz. Collegeville Minn.: Liturgical, 1987.

Schottroff, Luise. "Celebrating God's Future: Feminist Reflections on the Eschatology of Jesus." *In Time—Utopia—Eschatology: Yearbook of the European Society of Theological Research of Women.* Leuven: Peeters, 1999.

———. "Der Hunger Jesu." In *Kontexte der Schrift. Volume 2: Festschrift für Wolfgang Stegemann.* Edited by Christian Strecker. Stuttgart: Kohlhammer, 2005.

———. "Die Befreiung vom Götzendienst der Habgier." In *Wer ist unser Gott? Beiträge zu einer Befreiungstheologie im Kontext der 'ersten' Welt.* Edited by Luise and Willy Schottroff. Munich: Chr. Kaiser, 1986.

———. "Die Lieder und das Geschrei der Glaubenden: Rechtfertigung bei Paulus," *EvTh* 60 (2000): 332–47.

———. "The Songs and the Cries of the Believers: Justification in Paul." Available from www.chora-strangers.org/pdf/Is_Songs_and_Believers.pdf. Internet; accessed 27 August 2006.

———. "Gesetzesfreies Heidenchristentum." In *Von der Wurzel getragen: Christlich-feministische Exegese in Auseinandersetzung mit Antijudaismus.* Edited by Luise Schottroff and Marie Theres Wacker. Leiden/New York/Köln: Brill, 1996.

———. *Befreiungserfahrungen: Studien zur Sozialgeschichte des Neuen Testaments.* Munich: Kaiser, 1990.

———. *Die Gleichnisse Jesu.* Gütersloh: Gütersloher, 2005.

———. *Lydias ungeduldige Schwestern: Feministische Sozialgeschichte des frühen Christentums.* Gütersloh: Gütersloher, 1994.

Schultz, Irmgard. *Der erregende Mythos vom Geld: Die neue Verbindung von Zeit, Geld und Geschlecht im Ökologiezeitalter.* Frankfurt: Campus, 1994.

Schwöbel, Christoph. "Last Things First? The Century of Eschatology in Retrospect." In *The Future as God's Gift: Explorations in Christian Eschatology.* Edited by David Fergusson and Marcel Sarot. Edinburgh: T&T Clark, 2000.

Sen, Amartya. *Mortality as an Indicator of Economic Success and Failure.* Florence, Italy: UNICEF, 1995.

Sheldrake, Philip. *Spaces for the Sacred: Place, Memory, and Identity.* Baltimore: John Hopkins Univ. Press, 2001.

Shell, Donald. "The Dancing Saints." In *God's Friends* 8/2 (August 1997); see also www.saintgregorys.org. Internet; accessed 28 April 2006.

Smith Jr., Archie, and Ursula Riedel-Pfaefflin. *Siblings by Choice: Race, Gender, and Violence.* St. Louis: Chalice, 2004.

Smith, Adam. *Der Wohlstand der Nationen.* Translated by Horst Claus Recktenwald. Munich: Deutscher Taschenbuch, 1978.

————. *The Nature and Causes of the Wealth of the Nations.* The Works of Adam Smith 2. Reprint of the edition of 1811–1812. Aalen: Zeller, 1963.

————. *The Theory of Moral Sentiments.* Edited by Knud Haakonssen. Cambridge: Cambridge Univ. Press, 2002.

Sölle, Dorothee. "Life without Suffering a Utopia?" In *The Strength of the Weak: Toward a Feminist Christian Identity.* Translated by Rita and Robert Kimber. Philadelphia: Westminster, 1984.

Sontag, Susan. *Regarding the Pain of Others.* New York: Farrar, Straus and Giroux, 2003.

Stäblein, Christian. *Predigten nach dem Holocaust: Das jüdische Gegenüber in der evangelischen Predigtlehre nach 1945.* Arbeiten zur Pastoraltheologie 44. Göttingen: Vandenhoeck & Ruprecht, 2004.

Stacey, Michelle. *Consumed: Why Americans Love, Hate, and Fear Food.* New York: Simon & Schuster, 1994.

Stendahl, Krister. *Der Jude Paulus und wir Heiden: Anfragen an das abendländische Christentum.* Munich: Kaiser, 1978.

————. *Paul among Jews and Christians and other Essays.* Philadelphia: Fortress Press, 1976.

Stern, David E. "Remembering and Redemption." In *Rediscovering the Eucharist: Ecumenical Conversations.* Edited by Roch A. Kereszty. New York and Malwah, N.J.: Paulist, 2003.

Strack, Hermann L. and Paul Billerbeck. *Kommentar zum Neuen Testament aus Talmud und Midrasch.* Volume 4/1. Munich: Beck (1928), 1961.

Strack, Hermann L. and Günter Stemberger. *Einleitung in Talmud und Midrasch.* Munich: Beck, 1982 (seventh edition).

Suchocki, Marjorie Hewitt. *In God's Presence: Theological Reflections on Prayer.* St. Louis: Chalice, 1996.

Sutter Rehmann, Luzia. *Vom Mut, genau hinzusehen: Feministisch-befreiungstheologische Reflexionen zur Apokalyptik.* Lucerne: Edition Exodus, 1998.

Taft, Robert F. *The Dyptichs.* Orientalia Christiana analecta 238. Rome: Pontificum Institutum Studiorum Orientalium, 1991.

Talley, Thomas J. "From *Berakah* to *Eucharistia*: A Reopening Question." In *Living Bread, Saving Cup: Readings on the Eucharist.* Edited by R. Kevin Seasoltz. Collegeville, Minn.: Liturgical, 1987.

Tanner, Kathryn. *Economy of Grace.* Minneapolis: Fortress Press, 2005.

Taubenschlag, Raphael. "Das Sklavenrecht im Rechte der Papyri." *ZSSR* 50 (1930).

Terrell, JoAnne Marie. *Power in the Blood? The Cross in the African American Experience.* Maryknoll, N.Y.: Orbis, 1998.

"The Anaphora of the Twelve Apostles." In *Prayers of the Eucharist: Early and Reformed.* Third edition, revised. Edited by R. C. D. Jasper and G. J. Cumming. Collegeville, Minn.: Liturgical, 1990.

"The Great Thanksgiving." In *The United Methodist Book of Worship.* Nashville: United Methodist Publishing House, 1992.

The United Methodist Hymnal: Book of United Methodist Worship. Nashville: United Methodist Publishing House, 1989.

Theißen, Gerd, and Annette Merz. *Der historische Jesus: Ein Lehrbuch.* Göttingen: Vandenhoeck & Ruprecht 1996 (second edition, 1997). English translation: *The*

historical Jesus: A Comprehensive Guide. Translated by John Bowden. Minneapolis: Fortress Press, 1998.

Townes, Emily. *In a Blaze of Glory: Womanist Spirituality as Social Witness.* Nashville:
Abingdon, 1995.

Wainwright, Geoffrey. *Eucharist and Eschatology.* Akron, Ohio: OSL, 2002.

Waldenfels, Bernhard. "Das Un-ding der Gabe." In *Einsätze des Denkens: Zur Philosophie von Jacques Derrida.* Edited by Hans Dieter Gondek and Bernhard Waldenfels.
Frankfurt a.M.: Suhrkamp, 1997.

Wandel, Lee Palmer. *The Eucharist in the Reformation. Incarnation and Liturgy.* Cambridge: Cambridge Univ. Press, 2006.

Weaver, Denny. *The Nonviolent Atonement.* Grand Rapids: Eerdmans, 2001.

Wendebourg, Nicola. *Der Tag des Herrn: Zur Gerichtserwartung im Neuen Testament auf
ihrem alttestamentlichen und frühjüdischen Hintergrund.* Neukirchen: Neukirchener,
2003.

Wendorff, Rudolf. *Zeit und Kultur. Geschichte des Zeitbewusstseins in Europa.* Wiesbaden:
Westdeutscher, 1985 (third edition).

Wengst, Klaus. *Didache (Apostellehre), Barnabasbrief, zweiter Klemensbrief, Schrift an
Diognet.* Darmstadt: Wissenschaftliche Buchgesellschaft, 1984.

Weth, Rudolf (ed.). *Das Kreuz Jesu: Gewalt, Opfer, Sühne.* Neukirchen: Neukirchener,
2001.

White, James F. *The Sacraments in Protestant Practice and Faith.* Nashville: Abingdon,
1999.

Williams, Delores S. *Sisters in the Wilderness: The Challenge of Womanist God-Talk.* Maryknoll, N.Y.: Orbis, 1993.

Wilson, D. Mark. "Little Is Never Enough: Sermon on Deuteronomy 26, 1-11." Pacific
School of Religion, November 2004.

Wire, Antoinette C. *Holy Lives, Holy Deaths: A Close Hearing of Early Jewish Storytellers.*
Leiden/Boston/Cologne: Brill, 2002.

Young, Allan. *The Harmony of Illusions: Inventing Post-Traumatic Stress Disorder.* Princeton: Princeton Univ. Press, 1995.

Young, Iris Marion. "The Scaling of Bodies and the Politics of Identity." In *Justice and
the Politics of Difference.* Princeton: Princeton Univ. Press, 1990.

Zerubavel, Eviatar. *Time Maps: Collective Memory and the Social Shape of the Past.* Chicago and London: Univ. of California Press, 2003.

Zimmerman, Joyce Ann. "Beauty and the Beast: Criteria for Artful Liturgy." In *Postmodern Worship and the Arts.* Edited by Doug Adams and Michael E. Moynahan.
San Jose: Resource, Inc., 2002.

Zizioulas, John. "The Eucharist and the Kingdom of God (Part 1)." *Sourozh* 58 (November 1994): 1–12.

INDEX OF BIBLICAL VERSES

INDEX OF NAMES AND SUBJECTS

NAMES

Isherwood, Lisa, 127, 216

Jackson, Colette, 128, 216
Janowski, Bernd, 220-21
Janssen, Claudia, 63, 207-8, 219
Jenkins, Jerry, 41, 203
Jesus, Jesus Christ, 1, 3, 6-13, 20, 26-28, 31-36,
    39-41, 49-59, 61-62, 64-66, 69, 72, 74-84,
    86, 96, 101, 105-6, 111, 114-15, 117-19,
    128-29, 131, 137, 139-48, 150-54, 157-64,
    167, 169-70, 172, 178, 185-89, 194, 198,
    200-203, 205-7, 209-10, 212-16, 218-19,
    221-22, 225
Johnson, Mark, 200
Josephus, Flavius, 35-36, 202, 209
Joswig, Benita, 219, 228
Jung, L. Shannon, 208-9
Jungmann, Joseph A., 116, 214-15
Justin Martyr, 106, 114, 154, 213

Kearney, Richard, 201
Kelleher, Margaret Mary, 200-201
Keller, Catherine, 22, 43, 46, 200, 203-4
Keshgegian, Flora A., 227-28
Kieckhefer, Richard, 115, 215
Kilmartin, Edward, 101, 114, 213-14
Kimbrough, S.T. Jr., 199
King Nebuchadnezzar, 60
King, Martin Luther, 164
Kirchhoff, Renate, 207
Klauck, Hans-Josef, 221
Klawans, Jonathan, 198
Klein, Stephen J., 203
Kodell, Jerome, 198
Koenig, John, 207
Krüger, René, 76, 209
Kwok, Pui-lan, 43, 199, 203

LaHaye, Tim, 41, 203
Lange, Dirk, 169, 225
Lathrop, Gordon W., 110, 136, 167, 214, 218,
    224
Lazarus, 31
Lelwica, Michelle, 72, 208-9
Lockward, Jorge A., 199
Lohse, Eduard, 221
Lorey, David E., 226-27
Lucian, 120-21, 216
Luther, Martin, 95, 132, 214, 217
Luz, Ulrich, 206

Manstetten, Reiner, 210
Marcia, James, 224
Martin, Dale, 218-19
Martin, Joan M., 20, 200, 219
Marx, Karl, 89-90, 211
Mather, Cotton, 43
Mauss, Marcel, 92-93, 211
McCormick, Patrick T., 208

McFague, Sallie, 98, 212
McFee, Marcia, 171, 225
Merleau-Ponty, Maurice, 218
Merz, Annette, 206
Midas, 85, 89
Millais, John Everett, 117-18, 215
Miller-Mutia, Sylvia Jean, 176, 226
Mittmann-Richert, Ulrike, 207
Mitulski, Jim, 134-36
Moltmann, Jürgen, 20, 200
Moody, Heather, 212
Moore, George F., 205
Morley, Janet, 163-64, 223
Morrill, Bruce T., 197-98, 201, 217, 228
Morrison, Toni, 185-86, 227
Moses, 31-32, 38, 42, 64, 82, 99, 150
Murphy, Debra Dean, 45, 46, 203-4

Osborne, Kenan B., 198
Ovid, 85, 209

Pangritz, Andreas, 222
Park, Eung Chun, 202
Patterson, Orlando, 227
Paul, 6, 8-9, 13, 32-33, 56-57, 59, 63-64, 118-19,
    121-22, 132, 137-41, 147, 150-52, 160-62,
    197, 202, 206-8, 218-19, 222-23
Pepin, Jacques, 70, 208
Peter, 80-82, 178, 199, 204, 226
Pinochet, Augusto, 143-45
Pliny the Elder, 85
Plutarch, 89, 211
Power, David N., 211, 213-14, 219
Priddat, Birger P., 86, 87, 210
Priest, J., 205
Procter-Smith, Marjorie, 163, 223
Puritans, 42

Quesnell, Quentin, 198, 205

Radford Ruether, Rosemary, 46, 203
Ramadanovic, Petar, 227
Ramshaw, Gail, 136, 218
Reik, Theodore, 168, 224
Richter Reimer, Ivoni, 216
Ricoeur, Paul, 24, 201
Rockefeller, Steven C., 96, 212
Romero, Oscar, 18
Rosaldo, Renato, 226
Rossing, Barbara R., 203
Rost, Leonhard, 206
Runge, Ford C., 209

Saliers, Don E., 125, 126, 197, 198, 216
Sanders, E.P., 206
Sapphira, 120-21
Saunkeah, Bruce, 182, 226
Sauter, Gerhard, 199
Sawicki, Marianne, 225

Scarry, Elaine, 169, 224, 225
Schillebeeckx, Edward, 217
Schottroff, Luise, 159, 200-3, 205, 207-9, 218, 222, 230
Schultz, Irmgard, 211
Schwöbel, Christoph, 199, 203-4
Sen, Amartya, 73, 209
Sheldrake, Philip, 188
Shell, Donald, 164, 191, 223, 224
Simon, Arthur, 209
Smith Jr., Archie, 225
Smith, Adam, 86-88, 210-11
Sölle, Dorothee, 123, 216
Sontag, Susan, 220
Sosa, Pablo, 145
Stäblein, Christian, 225
Stacey, Michelle, 208
Stemberger, Günter, 201
Stendahl, Krister, 62, 66, 207-8
Stern, David E., 157, 222, 225
Strack, Hermann L., 198, 201, 216
Strayer, Janet, 224
Stuart, Elizabeth, 127, 216
Suchocki, Marjorie Hewitt, 123, 216
Sutter Rehmann, Luzia, 200

Taft, Robert F., 216
Talley, Thomas J., 213
Tanner, Kathryn, 208

Taubenschlag, Raphael, 218
Terrell, JoAnne Marie, 219
Theißen, Gerd, 206
Townes, Emily, 21, 200
Trypho, 154, 221

Wainwright, Geoffrey, 197, 204-7
Waldenfels, Bernhard, 93, 95, 212
Wandel, Lee Palmer, 217
Weaver, Denny, 52, 204, 220
Welker, Michael, 220
Wendeboug, Nicola, 206
Wendorff, Rudolf, 211
Wengst, Klaus, 208, 222
Weth, Rudolf, 220, 221
White, James F., 217
Williams, Delores S., 142, 219
Williams, Stanley Tookie, 2, 4, 197, 219
Wilson, D. Mark, 108, 214
Winthrop, John, 42
Wire, Antoinette C., 221

Young, Allan, 226
Young, Iris Marion, 217

Zerubavel, Eviatar, 226
Zimmerman, Joyce Ann, 201
Zizioulas, John, 204

SUBJECTS

absence, temporal, spatial, 5, 23-24, 69, 82, 145, 189
accumulation, 84, 86-90, 94, 96, 99, 107, 109
Advent, 1-2, 4, 20
agape, agape meal, 10, 67, 198
anamnesis, 6, 13, 51, 145, 157-58, 162, 166-67, 170, 172-73, 175-76, 187, 194, 197, 201, 222, 226, 228
    christological anamnesis, 163
    eschatological anamnesis, 14, 157, 161-67, 170, 172-74, 189, 192, 195-96, 220
anaphora, 50, 106, 204, 213
    attributed to Hippolytus, 106
    of St. James, 50
    of the Twelve Apostles, 51, 204
anthropology, 10
anti-Jewish, anti-Jewish interpretation, anti-Jewish polemic, 30, 34, 76, 114, 154, 198, 206, 219
apocalypse, apocalyptic, apocalypticism, 11, 20-22, 27-28, 40-46, 52, 64, 106, 198-200, 203-4
    apocolyptic sensitivity, 21, 123
Apostolic Tradition, 54, 114-15, 154, 204

Basileia, basileia tou theou, God's just world, kingdom of God, 7, 19, 32-34, 39, 46, 53, 55, 67, 124, 170, 202, 204

Birkat Ha-Mazon, 103-4, 106, 198, 213
blessing over bread, *see* words over bread
blood, 12, 33, 51, 53, 57-61, 115, 127, 130-32, 138, 142, 146-50, 152, 177, 206, 215, 219, 221, 223
body, 3-4, 6, 8, 11, 13-14, 17-18, 21, 23, 29, 40, 43, 46, 51, 57, 62-65, 69, 71-73, 80, 82, 85-86, 88-89, 99, 107, 114-15, 118, 127, 129, 131-46, 148, 152, 160, 167, 169, 172-76, 178-79, 181-83, 187-88, 194, 196, 198, 200, 208, 210, 212-13, 215-19, 221, 224-25, 227
    embodiment, 3, 17, 25, 34, 41, 45, 71, 100, 162, 164, 172, 192, 195-96
    see also body memory
body of Christ, 6, 13-14, 18, 46, 62-65, 69, 101, 114, 118-19, 124, 131-40, 143, 153, 163-64, 174, 176, 183-83, 197, 215, 219
body politics, 4-5, 13, 127-29, 131, 133-35, 137, 139, 141-45, 147, 149, 151, 153, 155, 182, 200, 204, 217, 222, 225
bread, 3-10, 12, 17, 23, 26, 29, 33, 45, 50-52, 59, 62-64, 67, 69-70, 77-80, 82, 84-85, 89, 92, 96, 99, 101-6, 109-19, 122, 124, 126-27, 129-32, 134-35, 137, 142, 154, 165-66, 169-70, 181, 188, 197-98, 201, 203-4, 208, 212-15, 217, 219, 221, 223, 229

bread from heaven, manna, 77, 79, 82, 99, 100, 122
bread miracles, 77-80, 99
bread stories, 12, 27

chalice, 188, 216, 225
Christus Victor, 52, 106, 143, 204, 220
collection, 13, 34, 39, 69, 121-22, 167, 179, 214
colonial desire, colonization, 41-43
coming of God, 2-3, 12, 19, 22, 25, 30, 33, 38, 40-41, 51, 56-57, 76, 200
community at table, 10, 18, 54-55, 141
consecration, 92, 101, 140
covenant theology, 59, 61-62, 66, 146, 207
creation, 6-7, 16, 18-19, 24, 26-27, 55, 62-64, 67, 77, 79, 84, 88, 92, 95-96, 98, 106, 110-12, 114-15, 124-25, 141, 154, 165-67, 169, 173, 195, 206, 223-25
critical otherworldliness, 26, 28-30, 201
cup, 9, 33, 55, 58-59, 61, 99, 105, 119, 129, 132, 137, 148, 154, 205, 213, 217, 219, 221
cup ritual, 59

death, 2-3, 6-9, 11-12, 19-20, 22, 26, 28, 33, 39, 49-52, 55-59, 61-65, 70-71, 73, 76-77, 79-80, 82, 94-96, 106, 111, 118-21, 123, 129-31, 133, 135, 141, 143, 146-55, 157-58, 160-63, 165, 169-70, 178, 182, 188, 190-91, 197, 204, 207-8, 211, 213, 219-23, 227
death penalty, 2-3, 197
Didache, 8, 12, 50, 65-67, 105-6, 154, 169, 170, 197, 208
diet, dieting, 5, 18, 70-73, 208
diptychs, 126, 216
disciples, 7-9, 27, 53-57, 64, 75, 78-79, 114, 123, 138, 162, 170, 174, 188, 205, 223, 225
disruption, 26-27, 175-76, 182, 196, 225
doxology, 105, 108
dualistic, dualistic thinking, 10, 30, 40, 45-46, 51, 119, 139-41, 199, 200, 219

early childhood, 4, 71
eating, 3, 5, 10, 13, 23, 25, 36, 49, 54-55, 59, 65, 67, 69-72, 105-6, 128, 131, 133-34, 142, 166, 170, 208, 223
eating disorders, 5, 12, 18, 25, 69, 71-73, 127
economy of grace, 12, 30, 69, 77, 84, 91-92, 94, 96, 98, 100-101, 109-110, 127
embodiment, see body
empathy, 7, 13-14, 86, 125, 131, 145, 162, 166-70, 172, 176, 182, 219, 224
epiclesis, 51, 126
eschatology, 6-7, 18-22, 26, 28, 30, 32-33, 35-36, 38-40, 44, 46, 49, 64, 197-207
eschatological anamnesis, 13-14, 157, 162-66, 172-74, 189, 192, 194-96, 220
eschatological imagination, 4, 6-7, 11-12, 15, 18, 20, 22, 25-30, 41-42, 44-45, 47, 49-50, 69, 74, 84, 87-88, 90-91, 95, 111, 114, 118,

123, 126-27, 145-46, 165-67, 170, 172, 174, 176, 182, 199, 201
eschatological meal, 49, 53, 65, 69
eschaton, eschatos, eschata, 19, 20, 199
eternity, 30, 35, 95, 208
Eucharistic prayers, 23, 26-27, 51-53, 65, 67, 106, 154, 158, 163-64, 172, 176, 204, 213-16, 224
eucharistein, eucharistia, 10, 103, 197, 213
Eucharistic celebration, 4, 17, 44, 47, 95-96, 98, 102, 107, 110, 112, 131, 133, 142, 153, 170, 187-88
Eucharistic community, 61, 65, 101, 153
Eucharistic life, 5, 47, 69, 84, 87-88, 111, 125-27, 134, 145, 158, 162, 171-72, 174, 176, 183, 189, 195
Eucharistic liturgy, 3, 13, 24, 41, 47, 50-51, 91, 102, 104-5, 128, 143, 152, 155, 163, 165, 168, 171, 176, 181-82, 223
Eucharistic meal, 57
Eucharistic memory, 172
Eucharistic practice/praxis, 5, 8, 12, 56, 59, 74, 80, 144, 152, 157
Eucharistic sacrifice, 101-2
Eucharistic space, 188, 190
Eucharistic theology, 3, 5-6, 45, 50, 146, 158, 166, 197
Eucharistic traditions, 91, 159, 220, 222
Eucharistic words over the bread, 63, 67, 146, 149, 152, 161
Exodus, 9, 33, 42, 77, 82, 99, 159, 173, 200, 203

First Apology (Justin), 106, 213
flesh, 59, 104, 131-32, 135, 167, 206, 215, 225
food, 3-5, 9, 11-13, 16-18, 23, 25, 33, 55, 67, 69-75, 78, 84, 88, 98-99, 101, 103-4, 106-7, 109-11, 119, 121-22, 127-28, 133, 135, 208-10, 213

gift, 3, 5, 8-9, 12-13, 15-16, 51, 62, 67, 69, 91-96, 99, 101-2, 105-12, 114-16, 118, 122, 126-27, 147, 149-50, 155, 165-67, 169, 199-201, 208, 211-15, 224
gift exchange, 12, 91-96, 98, 101-2, 106, 108-10, 127

HIV, HIV-positive, AIDS, 133-35, 176-77
Holy Communion, 5, 195
Holy Spirit, 6, 51, 126, 131, 133, 135, 163, 189
Homo oeconomicus, 6, 12, 69, 84-91, 97, 102, 107-8, 123
hope, see resurrection hope
hunger, 3-5, 10, 12, 18, 25, 27, 31-32, 69, 71, 73-78, 80, 82, 84-85, 110, 127, 133, 208-9, 219

imagination, 3, 4, 6-7, 11-12, 15, 17-31, 33, 35, 37, 39, 41-45, 47-50, 69, 71, 74, 84-88, 90-91, 95, 97, 102, 111, 114, 118, 123-24, 126-27, 136-37, 142, 145-46, 165-67, 169, 172, 174, 176, 182, 194, 199-201, 203-4, 210, 223